Language-in-education Policies

D1810354

MULTILINGUAL MATTERS

Series Editor: John Edwards, *St. Francis Xavier University, Canada*

Multilingual Matters series publishes books on bilingualism, bilingual education, immersion education, second language learning, language policy, multiculturalism. The editor is particularly interested in 'macro' level studies of language policies, language maintenance, language shift, language revival and language planning. Books in the series discuss the relationship between language in a broad sense and larger cultural issues, particularly identity related ones.

Full details of all the books in this series and of all our other publications can be found on http://www.multilingual-matters.com, or by writing to Multilingual Matters, St Nicholas House, 31-34 High Street, Bristol BS1 2AW, UK.

Language-in-education Policies

The Discursive Construction of Intercultural Relations

Anthony J. Liddicoat

MULTILINGUAL MATTERS
Bristol • Buffalo • Toronto

Library of Congress Cataloging in Publication Data
A catalog record for this book is available from the Library of Congress.
Liddicoat, Anthony
Language-in-Education Policies: The Discursive Construction of Intercultural Relations /
Anthony J. Liddicoat.
Multilingual Matters: 153
Includes bibliographical references.
1. Language and languages – Study and teaching. 2. Language policy . 3. Multicultural
education. 4. Education, Bilingual. 5. Language planning. I. Title.
P119.3.L63 2013
306.44'9–dc23 2012044140

British Library Cataloguing in Publication Data
A catalogue entry for this book is available from the British Library.

ISBN-13: 978-1-84769-914-5 (hbk)
ISBN-13: 978-1-84769-913-8 (pbk)

Multilingual Matters
UK: St Nicholas House, 31–34 High Street, Bristol BS1 2AW, UK.
USA: UTP, 2250 Military Road, Tonawanda, NY 14150, USA.
Canada: UTP, 5201 Dufferin Street, North York, Ontario M3H 5T8, Canada.

The policy of Multilingual Matters/Channel View Publications is to use papers that are
natural, renewable and recyclable products, made from wood grown in sustainable forests. In
the manufacturing process of our books, and to further support our policy, preference is given
to printers that have FSC and PEFC Chain of Custody certification. The FSC and/or PEFC logos
will appear on those books where full certification has been granted to the printer concerned.

Typeset by R. J. Footring Ltd, Derby
Printed and bound in Great Britain by Short Run Press Ltd

Contents

Acknowledgements

I would like to thank a number of people without whom this book would not have been possible: Jo Winter and Anne Pauwels for their support and hospitality during the preparation of this book; Adriana Díaz and Timothy Jowan Curnow for their collaboration on earlier versions of the Italian study in Chapter 3 and the Colombian study in Chapter 4; and Reiko Yoshida, Enza Tudini and Giancarlo Chiro for advice on translation.

1 Introduction: Language-in-education Policy, Discourse and the Intercultural

Ricento (2006) argues that language policies exist in some form in all societal domains. It is in the domain of education, however, that such policies often have the most impact on the members of a society. Language policies for education play an important role in the ways in which a society articulates and plans for the futures of its members. These policies are sometimes explicitly articulated in official documents but may often exist in more covert forms underlying the assumptions and practices of language use and language learning in educational contexts. Policies deal with what is valued in a society and so language policies represent articulations of the beliefs and attitudes of a society about the value of languages and their use. This book examines the ways in which such beliefs and attitudes are articulated in policy. In order to do so, it focuses on a subset of language policies – those concerned with the teaching and learning of non-official additional languages. These educational policies are aimed at expanding the linguistic repertoires of the members of a society, for some specific valued future end use. They therefore articulate beliefs and attitudes about the nature of interactions between diverse linguistic and cultural groups. That is, they are concerned with issues of intercultural communication and construct these issues through the ideologies present in the societies involved.

Language Planning and Language Policy

Language policy exists in relation to language planning and each constitutes a different sphere of activity in the decision-making process around language. Kaplan and Baldauf (2003) note that although 'language planning' and 'language policy' are often used as synonyms, they represent different forms of activity, with language planning being the preparatory work which leads to the formulation of language policy. The implementation of a language policy also includes language planning work to organise activities and approaches. Thus, planning and policy are in interrelationship at various points.

Language planning is a deliberate effort to influence the function, structure or acquisition of languages or language varieties within a speech community (Kaplan & Baldauf, 1997). It involves intervening in the linguistic ecologies of a society, with the aim of influencing its future linguistic practices. It has become conventional to identify four core areas of activity in language planning (Kaplan & Baldauf, 1997):

- *Status planning* – language planning activities that relate to the selection of languages to perform particular functions in a society and the varieties of languages which will be used. It is concerned with questions external to the language itself. The most commonly investigated dimension of status planning is the selection of official languages, but status planning also involves decisions about other aspects of language use, such as languages for school learning (van Els, 2005), languages as media of instruction (Tollefson & Tsui, 2004) and languages for religious purposes (Liddicoat, 2012).
- *Corpus planning* – language planning activities relating to the form of a language. Corpus planning relates to decision-making regarding the standardisation and codification of a language, including its orthography, syntax and lexicon – termed *graphisation, grammatication* and *lexication* by Haugen (1983) – and the development of new linguistic resources to enable the language to be used in new domains or to achieve other social goals (linguistic purism, gender-neutral language, etc.) (Liddicoat, 2005a).
- *Prestige or image planning* – language planning activities relating to the ways in which particular language or language varieties are perceived and valued by a community, including promotional activities and language spread programmes (Ager, 2005a, 2005b; Haarmann, 1990).
- *Language-in-education or acquisition planning* – language planning activities relating to the teaching and learning of languages, especially at school. These activities include the development of literacy, the acquisition of additional languages and language maintenance programmes (Baldauf & Kaplan, 2005). Language-in-education planning often overlaps with other areas of planning as it can involve activities relating to other forms of language planning.

Language policy, as the outcome of language planning, typically involves the work of governments, or of other authorities, and consists of the choices made about languages and their relationship to social life (e.g. Djité, 1994).

It is the formalisation of decision-making about language in the form of laws, regulations, statements of process and procedure through which a language plan will be implemented. Djité (1994) argues that language policy consists of processes both at the level of society and at the level of language. At the societal level, he allocates to language policy the identification of relevant problems, the formulation of alternatives to address these problems and choosing from among these alternatives. He argues that the language level involves the processes of articulating linguistic norms which a community will use.

Language policies operate in societies not simply as political collectivities but as speech communities – groups of people sharing common expectations and norms about language (Spolsky, 2004). It is a speech community that provides a context in which language policy operates. Spolsky (2004) identifies three components of language policy in any speech community:

- language practices – the languages that a speech community selects as parts of its linguistic repertoire and the ways in which these are used;
- language beliefs or ideology – the beliefs the speech community has about languages and their use;
- specific efforts made to modify or influence the practices of the speech community.

The model presented here is one in which language policy is seen as something far broader than policy as policy document: it is a series of behavioural and attitudinal responses to language, which may be articulated explicitly or implicitly (Kaplan, 1991; Sayers, 1996). Language policy is therefore conceived as a pervasive feature of societies rather than simply as an action of government, in that it is predicated on society as a whole, not just those who have authority in society. Language policies are relevant in any group context in which some form of norm about language use exists and language policy contexts can range from the macro-level of government through a meso-level of authorities and institutions to a micro-level of community organisations and even individuals (Baldauf, 2005b, 2006, 2008; Liddicoat & Baldauf, 2008).

The most obvious manifestation of policy is in the form of governmental, or other institutional, documents which record aims, objectives and procedures for achieving some future directed outcome. However, Spolsky (2004) makes the point that language policy does not exist simply in the form of official documents such as language laws, legal records or regulations. Official policy documents are simply the most obvious manifestation of language policy. Language policy also exists in less tangible and less codified forms. Such documents form only part of the policy process, which involves the production of texts, the texts themselves, their ongoing revision and the processes of implementation (Taylor *et al.*, 1997). Lo Bianco (2005) also argues that the discourses which surround the development and articulation of policy are also a central part of the policy process. Language policies can exist in strong forms even without being articulated in documentary form. Language policy documents are therefore only a part of the overall language policy of a society. Nonetheless, language policy texts are useful examples of a particular class of ideological production. This is because they function within their ideological and discursive ecologies in particular ways to shape the ways languages are used and understood. In particular, they are interventions into the language ecology that seek to shape that ecology to particular ends by mobilising the resources of the state for language objectives. That is, they constitute part of the ideological state apparatus (Althusser, 1976). Further, they are explicit, tangible and authoritative statements of policy positions.

Spolsky's (2004) model suggests that language policy has both behavioural and ideational dimensions. The behavioural dimension comprises two different types of activity – practices and attempts to modify practices – while the ideational dimension consists of beliefs, that is, of ideology. In reality, the behavioural and the ideational are interrelated, as a community's language practices are influenced by beliefs and ideologies about languages, and in turn practices influence and reproduce these ideologies and beliefs. Schiffman (1996) brings the ideational and the behavioural together as the context from which language policy grows and argues that language policy is ultimately grounded in linguistic culture, which he defines as 'the set of behaviours, assumptions, cultural forms, prejudices, folk belief systems, attitudes, stereotypes, ways of thinking about language, and religio-historical circumstances associated with a particular language' (p. 5). Language policy is therefore inherently contextualised in language ideologies.

Schiffman (1996) makes the point that the beliefs a speech community has about languages in general and its own language in particular are shaped at least in part by the beliefs the speech community has about specific other languages – that is, a speech community has ideologies about language, about its own language and about other languages, which are interrelated through language policy. Language ideologies are systems of beliefs about the nature of language, how language works and how it should work, and are consequential for linguistic practices and judgements about them (Cameron, 2006). Language ideologies are not simply beliefs about language itself but, as Verscheuren (2008) argues, are beliefs about the nature of linguistic communication. Such ideologies construct the ways in which the language of a speech community is understood and used and also how it is positioned in relation to other languages, including those spoken in the same society.

Speech communities are located within language ecologies (Haugen, 1972; Mühlhäusler, 2000), in which the various languages present are in mutually influencing relationships. Moreover, these ecologies are not ecologies of equal members but rather are subject to hierarchies of prestige. That is, some languages are more successful in their ecologies than others. Bourdieu (1982) has argued that languages are used in a market setting in which all languages present are attributed value and different languages are valued differently. The more desirable a linguistic practice is in its marketplace, the greater the value assigned to it and the greater the accrued symbolic capital which comes from mastery of that practice. Bourdieu maintained that different ways of speaking are ultimately measured against the practices of the dominant group in the social space which constitutes the linguistic marketplace. This means that in any society, the language variety of the dominant group will have more value and prestige than other varieties. These hierarchical differences between languages are not trivial, as they are bound up with ideological and cultural constructions, which attribute greater value to large, successful, dominant languages and lesser value to smaller, minority languages. These differences of value influence what gets planned in the language ecology, what needs to be planned and the reactions accorded to particular interventions in language.

Shohamy (2007) also notes that language ideologies are not separate from the political ideologies which exist within society and that beliefs about language may be influenced by other ideological constructs. That is, languages are integrated into a broad framework of beliefs about the world because language is not easily separable from other aspects of the social and political world. In particular, language plays a central role in the construction of nations as imagined communities (Anderson, 1991) by providing an important reference point for and index of national identity. The ways in which national identities are understood and the ways in which languages are implicated in this understanding therefore have the capacity to shape both societal attitudes and beliefs about language varieties and how a polity deals with the languages within its territory.

Language Policies and Education

Language is one of the fundamental dimensions of education and government policies for education often include reference to language issues. The relationship between language policy and planning and education is complex, as education is both something that is the object of work in language planning and policy and also a mechanism through which language planning and policy goals are achieved. For example, policies resulting from status planning or corpus planning may be implemented through teaching – the language(s) designated as the official language(s) of a society may be used as the medium of instruction or the linguistic forms developed through corpus planning may be disseminated through schooling. Such activities can be considered as the educational dimension of other forms of language planning and policy – what Haugen (1983) refers to as the implementation aspect. These activities are primarily related not to the planning of education but to the use of education for other language goals. Language policy will also specifically apply to the scope of education, shaping the teaching and learning of languages within the educational sector, especially in school education – that is, language-in-education policies. Such policies frame the language issues that will be addressed through education and the linguistic resources that education is designed to develop.

Language-in-education policies, as Kaplan and Baldauf (1997) note, are a form of human resource development planning. They operate to develop language capabilities that the society identifies as important for social, economic and other objectives. Such policies articulate which languages will be developed through education as part of the linguistic repertoire of the society and the purposes for which those languages will be developed. In this way, policies project an imagined future linguistic situation and make provisions to bring this into existence. They may also serve a nation-building function, not only in terms of developing human resources, but also as symbolic reinforcements of the existing imagined community (Anderson, 1991) embodied in the polity.

Models of language-in-education policy have tended to focus on those dimensions of education which the policies address. For example, Kaplan and Baldauf (1997, 2003) have described six such dimensions:

- *access* – policies regarding which languages are to be studied and the levels of education at which they will be studied;
- *personnel* – policies regarding teacher recruitment, professional learning and standards;
- *curriculum and community* – policies regarding what will be taught and how the teaching will be organised, including the specification of outcomes and assessment instruments;
- *methods and materials* – policies regarding prescriptions of methodology and set texts for language study;
- *resourcing* – policies regarding the level of funding for languages in the education system;

- *evaluation* – policies regarding how the impact of language-in-education policy will be measured and how the effectiveness of policy implementation will be gauged.

These dimensions are all within the education system itself and what can be called the mechanics of providing languages in schooling. They comprise a series of areas of activity which language-in-education policies may address and which may apply in a broad range of language planning contexts.

Language-in-education policies cover many language teaching and learning practices. The primary focus, however, is the teaching and learning of the official language(s). Beyond that, such policies vary in their scope and emphasis and can be typologised as follows:

- official language education policies;
- foreign language education policies;
- minority language education policies;
- external language spread policies.

Official language education policies

In polities where there is an official language and this language is the majority language, language-in-education policy typically deals with the acquisition of literacy in the official language by those who already speak it (Liddicoat, 2007b). This may be accompanied by educational work to effect 'dialect levelling' where there is social or geographical variation in language use (Williamson & Hardman, 1997). Policies relating to the teaching and learning of official languages may also address the acquisition of the official language as an additional language where there is a perception that a significant population (indigenous minorities or immigrants) do not speak it. In officially multilingual societies, language-in-education policies typically envisage the teaching of literacy in at least one of the languages as a first language, together with (additionally) the acquisition of one or more official languages. For example, education policies in predominantly English-speaking Canada often require students to study French for some period of their schooling (Early, 2008).

Foreign language education policies

Most societies have policies about the teaching and learning of additional languages in the education system. These typically concern the learning of languages not normally spoken by members of the society and for which the normal mode of acquisition is through the education system. In many cases, these are the official languages of other polities.

There is a common distinction made in the educational literature between foreign language learning and second language learning, on the basis of a sociolinguistic distinction between the two. Littlewood (1984) frames this distinction in the following terms: second language learning involves the learning of a language which has social functions in the community where it is learnt, whereas a foreign language has no established functions in the learners' community and is learnt primarily for communication outside one's own community. Littlewood's definition therefore emphasises the communicative goal of language learning in the two contexts – community internal and community external (see also Saville-Troike, 2006).

Where the second language is the official language of the learners' community, for example, in the case of an immigrant learning the language of the host country, the linguistic and sociolinguistic contexts for learning that language can be considerably different from the learning of a foreign language. With the learning of a minority language, the situation is different again. For example, Chinese is the largest minority language spoken in Australia, and therefore if non-Chinese children learn it they are still learning a language which has social functions within the Australian community.[1] Nonetheless, many Australian learners of Chinese have no contact with that language outside school and their learning context therefore resembles a typical foreign language context. The issue here is what constitutes the learner's community. If 'the community' equates with the nation-state as a whole, learning Chinese is learning a second language; if, however, the community equates with only that part of Australia in which the learner lives and functions, learning Chinese may be either learning a second language or learning a foreign language. For the policy-focused purposes of this book, the distinction between second language and foreign language is not particularly significant, as policies in the contexts examined either do not make the distinction or are framed as foreign-language learning, and for this reason the term 'foreign language learning' will be used.[2] Where policy documents do refer to second language learning, they invariably refer to the teaching and learning of official languages rather than to other additional languages that may be used in the society, and so can be considered as forms of official language education policies.

Minority language education policies

In countries with linguistic diversity, language-in-education policies may articulate ways in which non-official languages are included in education.

Minority language education policies cover two distinct contexts: indigenous languages and immigrant languages. For example, the European Charter for Regional or Minority Languages (Council of Europe, 1992) explicitly excludes immigrant languages from its provisions (Liddicoat, 2002). Even though these policies may be separated, their main concerns are frequently similar. For instance, minority language education policies may cover issues such as the development of literacy in non-official languages used by either indigenous people or immigrants. Such policies are, though, invariably connected with policies for disseminating the official language(s) of the state to members of linguistic minority groups, and it is important to consider whether such policies are designed for the teaching and learning of the minority language in its own right (i.e. for the purposes of speakers of the language) or whether they are part of a strategy for enhancing the teaching and learning of the official language (Liddicoat, 2007b).

External language spread policies

Some governments have established policies for the teaching and learning of their own official languages beyond their borders. Policy work in this area is not as directly applied as in other language policy contexts, as governments cannot usually directly influence education in other polities. Policy activities in this domain tend to involve the establishment of opportunities for language learning outside formal education, various forms of support for language teachers, and educational programmes and promotional activities. External language spread policies may be closely linked with cultural policies, in which case they consider language as a form of cultural product for dissemination. In some instances, external language spread policy may also be integrated with aid policy, where acquisition of the language is something which will enhance economic or social development. One common feature of external language spread policies is that they usually involve the establishment of independent or quasi-independent bodies outside the usual governmental apparatus of the state, such as the Alliance Française, the British Council, the Goethe-Institut, the Cervantes Institute, the Japan Foundation or the Confucius Institutes.

Different polities have different types of language-in-education policies and not all of the above types of policy will be found in all polities, at least as explicitly articulated policy expressed in documents. What is presented in policy documents will depend on the ways in which the polity constructs issues around languages as needing to be addressed through education.

Language-in-education Policies as Discourse

Language-in-education policies typically exist in textual form as policy documents, laws and so on, and can be studied as evidence of official work in the area of language and education. It is possible to examine such texts in different ways. Ball (1993) distinguishes a fundamental difference between viewing policy as text and viewing policy as discourse. This distinction represents different but interrelated ways of working with and analysing policy documents. Language policies are texts in the sense that they are 'materially durable products of linguistic actions' (Wodak, 2006: 177) but also in the sense that they are available for – and require – interpretation in order to be implemented. That is, language policies are read as texts and are treated as texts in the ways they are used. Ball (1993) emphasises the written text as being contextualised in existing relationships of power and inequality, which shape both how the text is created and how it is used. A written policy represents a compromise between different forces within the social world – the text is a product of its environment. Moreover, the interpretation of the text is also contextualised by what the reader brings to the act of reading the document. A policy text will be read in a plurality of ways, with each reader developing a different understanding of what the text means. The meanings of the policy text cannot be controlled by writers, although the writers' intention is one element of the process of interpretation. Ball (1990, 1993) recognises that policies are developed and interpreted in complex ways and that policies themselves are unfinished texts subject to contestation, (re)interpretation and change (see also Bakhtin, 1981, 1994).

The diversity of interpretations is most significant in the implementation of policies. Ball (1990, 1993, 1997) notes that implementation is not a straightforward application of a text but rather is subject to the various interpretations made by actors in the policy process as the texts are enacted. Policy documents are taken up, adapted, resisted and contested in local contexts and local power relationships (Ball, 1990, 1997; Ramanathan, 2005). The process of implementation involves agency on the part of those implementing a policy, although this agency is constrained. Ball's (1990, 1993, 1997) work makes the point that policy enactment is not necessarily predictable and that policy implementation is inevitably *ad hoc* and messy because it involves social agents making, reshaping and contesting meanings in their historical, ideological and practical contexts.

Policies exist as discourses in two ways. They are instances of language-in-use, being communicative acts composed of words, phrases, sentences and utterances, what Gee (1990) terms ('little d') *discourse*. This can be thought of as their textual nature as linguistic productions. They also exist in combination with other social practices (beliefs, behaviour, values, ways of thinking, clothes, food, customs, perspectives, etc.), what Gee refers to as ('big d') *Discourse*. 'Little d' discourses derive their meaning not simply from their linguistic form but from the 'big d' Discourses in which they are produced and read. That is, it is the combination of the text and its context which produces the meaning. Discourse is therefore a form of linguistic and extra-linguistic meaning. Muetzelfeldt (1992: 4) argues that discourse understood as meaning includes more than language and sees language itself as articulating 'the complex of ... notions, categories, ways of thinking and ways of communicating that constitutes a power-infused system of knowledge'. Language policies are discourses in two senses: they are instances of language in use, which interact and combine with other social practices to define and thereby create the realities with which they deal (Gee, 1999).

In investigating language policies as discourse, the focus is placed on the ways in which language defines and sets limits on what is said and understood in the policy context by discursively organising the categories for thinking about and acting on language. As Althusser (1976) argues, it is through the organisation of categories that ideology frames limits on what can be said and thought about the social and political world. The language of policy works to define the field to which it is applied (Ball, 1990) because policies are linguistic acts which work upon the social world. Policies, as discourses, contain, (re)produce and transmit values and assumptions about the phenomena they seek to act on and thereby define what is valued by those engaged in policy-making (Considine, 1994). Through the language they use and the contexts in which they use it, texts present ways of understanding the phenomena they describe within a context of values and assumptions embedded in the linguistic culture (Schiffman, 1996: 59), that is, in the beliefs that a community has about language or its language ideologies.

Policy texts as linguistic acts are therefore not simply acts which communicate decisions, ideas and responses, but rather they also constitute and construct the objects they communicate and in so doing bring into play ideologies. As Foucault argues, discourses are:

des pratiques qui forment systématiquement les objets dont ils parlent. Certes, les discours sont faits de signes; mais ce qu'ils font, c'est plus que d'utiliser ces signes pour designer des choses.
practices that systematically form the object about which they speak. Certainly, discourses are made up of signs; but what they do is more than using language to designate things.[3]
(Foucault, 1969: 66–67)

This means that through the language they use and the contexts in which they use it, policies construct ways of seeing the world. If discourse is viewed as being something beyond communication, it follows that policies themselves can be studied as constitutive practices – not as things that governments do, but as ideological constructions of the world. As Schiffman notes (1996: 59), 'Language policy … is not just a text, a sentence or two in the legal code, it is a belief system, a collection of ideas and decisions and attitudes about language'.

The provisions of a language policy are responses to perceived current problems, and language policies are therefore designed to bring about social transformation (Gee, 1994a, 1994b; Gee & Lankshear, 1995). That is, they seek to change the nature of the social world they encapsulate. Language policies thus articulate a language issue as an existing problematic version of the social world, which will be transformed into a new, less problematic social world through action on language. The essence of policy, then, is to identify problems and to provide ways of acting to address them. However, language policies do not simply present a plan of action in response to a perceived need, but also construct the action and need in particular ways. In so doing, policy texts encode the world in certain ways and privilege some ways of understanding the world over others. Both problem and solution are discursive constructs. Language problems are not simply situations which exist in the world and require resolution: problems, as Watts (1993/94: 119) argues, 'only come to be that way when they have become part of a discourse'. This means that in constructing languages issues as being worthy of attention and action, policy discourses include or exclude various candidate versions of the problem. Matters that are included become the objects of action, while other matters are excluded not just from action but from the world represented by and constructed through the policy. Decisions about languages in education are therefore not simply linguistic decisions but reflect the political, social and cultural realities in which languages are used (Shohamy, 2007). Policies, through language, identify what things in the world will be constituted as problems, what the parameters of that constitution will be and what will be foregrounded or backgrounded in the construction of the problem.

By discursively constructing elements of language as problems, policies contain within them their own rationales for resolving those problems. The primary effect of policy is, then, discursive: it creates the ways in which the concepts it contains are understood and thought through and acted upon (Foucault, 1969). The discourses of language policies thus bring into being language-related problems and propose actions which are designed to resolve the discursively created problem. This means that policy texts are both projections – they articulate some future social world in which the problems of the present social world have been removed or ameliorated – and plans of enactment – they articulate the processes and actions through which problems will be addressed (Gee, 1994b). Projective texts are usually generated by and circulated among those responsible for decision-making. They look forward and describe future contexts, the realisation of which is dependent on the text being endorsed and acted upon. Policy documents help to bring about the activities of which their very writing forms a part. In so doing, they become enactive texts which guide future action. These concepts allow policy documents to be treated as socially transformative work: they are projective in that they form part of a process of education reform and offer a vision of what education can and/or should contribute, and they are enactive as they are formulated to guide actions in order to achieve the envisioned reform.

Policies as discourses thus represent enactments in language of certain ways of thinking about the world. They engage with issues of power and reproduction in ways which mean they are not simply prescriptions for action but also prescriptions for understanding. They produce and reproduce a society's ideological constructions of the social and political worlds. In particular, policies articulate subject positions for participants in relation to the knowledge and practices they encompass. A language user, seen as the product of a policy, is a particular type of individual participating in particular practices through the languages with which the educational system has endowed him/her.

Policy documents can be seen as both instantiations and re-presentations of cultural models of the concepts they enshrine (Shore, 1996). Shore argues that cultural models refer to 'an extensive and heterogeneous collection of "models" that exist both as public artefacts "in the world" and as cognitive constructs "in the minds" of members of a community' (Shore, 1996: 44). These models shape human behaviour in obvious ways and inform the stances that members of a society adopt towards the things in their world. Language-in-education policy documents represent an encapsulation of a cultural model that exists in the society about the nature and purpose of language and, specifically for this book, the nature of intercultural relationships as a dimension of communication and of intercultural interactions. That is, language-in-education policy documents represent a particular understanding of the nature of and value given to language. By being inscribed in official discourses, this particular understanding becomes the privileged understanding on which practices will be based, because it provides a contextual framing in which decision-making about language education is made, and this framework constructs the possibilities of compliance or resistance in the actual practice of language teaching.

Policy documents as discursive practices are themselves located within other discourses around the matters they treat and are not isolated from these (Lo Bianco, 1999). Ricento and Hornberger (1996) use the onion as a metaphor for the multiple layers through which language policy develops and each of these layers can be understood as a discursive field. That is, a policy document is one element of a complex of discursive fields which exist prior to, within and after the production of the document itself and is never independent of other discourses. For Muetzelfeldt (1992), policies as the projects of state institutions, party politics and social movements draw on the discourses which exist within the society in which they are created and at the same time they have an impact on the wider society from which they draw by shaping social categories and positioning people within those categories. Policies therefore both index the discourses which exist at the time of their creation and shape future discourses.

Within this complex discursive field, however, not all discourses are equal. Policy documents have a particular authority within the discourse context because they are vested with authority, in that they are constructed as the voice of government on behalf of a society, or, as Fox and Meyer (1995: 107) state, they are 'authoritative statements made by legitimate public institutions about the way in which they propose to deal with policy problems'. Similarly, Codd (1988) argues that policy documents can be said to constitute the official discourse of the state about the matter they treat. Thus, language-in-education policies produced by and for the state are instances in which language serves a political purpose and constructs officially sanctioned meanings. This means that, once a language education policy has been developed and released, it participates in the discourse around language in a particular way because of the authority it holds. That is, policies represent a form of authoritative discourse (Bakhtin, 1981).

Authoritative discourses are discourses which do not acquire their authority from their content – their persuasiveness – but rather come with authority already imbued in the text itself. As Bakhtin argues, the source of its authority is external to the text, 'located in a distanced zone' such as the 'past' or a 'hierarchically higher' order (Bakhtin, 1981: 342). In the case of policies, as texts voicing government's decisions, they draw authority from the hierarchical power of government and represent 'images of official-authoritative truth' (Bakhtin, 1981: 344). The authority of policy texts derives also from their location within *regimes of truth* (Foucault, 1994), in which only the dominant discourses about a phenomenon are heard as authoritative. In particular, policies can be understood as instances of *governmental truth* (Weir, 2008). Governmental truth resides in the theoretical knowledges and power apparatuses used by authorities to manage relations between persons and things. Policies therefore have legitimacy as statements of prospective futures because they are represented as the voice of authority and present this future as an uncontested, monologic worldview. Authoritative discourses do not necessarily enter into dialogue with other discourses or points of view available to the individual; indeed, authoritative discourse can be considered 'pre-dialogic', in that the relationship between ideological systems connected with the particular discourse are not immediately apparent and interactions between ideologies are not portrayed. As authoritative discourses, language-in-education policy documents can be read as official versions of ratified, but not always explicitly stated, ideologies about the role and functions of language in education. There is therefore a need to investigate such discourse in terms of its ideological framing.

Language-in-education Policies as Ideology

The term 'ideology' has a range of meanings and, before considering the ways in which language-in-education policies function as ideology, it is necessary to consider ways of understanding ideology itself. One possible interpretation of 'ideology' is that it refers to a committed political philosophy or doctrine. This conceptualisation appears, superficially at least, to be particularly relevant: language-in-education policies are the products of political organisations (governments) and can therefore be understood as statements of the political positions of those who make them. For example, Sonntag (2000) analyses how the political agendas of left-wing and right-wing political parties lead to different ways of understanding the role of English as an official language in India. However, this view of ideology as a committed political position often has a negative connotation: '"ideology" suggests something inflexible and propagandistic, something politically unfree' (Emerson, 1981: 23). Such a framing suggests that ideology is a special, and deviant, case of political thought, which is of limited application and not necessarily always present.

This view of ideology stems from early Marxist critiques of ideology and the associated idea of false consciousness. In the middle of the 19th century, Marx and Engels argued that ideologies were essentially political constructs and saw them not simply as systems of belief but as expressions of dominant material relationships. That is, they serve to legitimise and maintain power relationships within society. Ideologies for Marx and Engels were distorted beliefs about social realities that obscured reality for the purposes of political domination. Ideologies are therefore a delusion about the actual relationship between belief and reality – that is, a false consciousness of reality. Marx and Engels saw false consciousness as being inherently a feature of the dominating class and argued that dominated classes were free from ideology because they perceived their position in society directly, not through systems of beliefs (Marx & Engels, 2011).

Some later Marxist writers separated ideology from a basis in class and argued that ideologies are more general and pervasive. In the 1920s Lukács argued that false consciousness was not a feature of ideologies but rather a generalised problem of perception and knowledge. False consciousness is not a product of ideology but rather the result of the practices of social and political life that obscure the nature of social and political relationships for *all* members of society. This obscuring of reality benefits some groups and oppresses others. Domination is the result of a false consciousness that is shared by the rulers and the ruled. Because social realities are obscured by social practices, ideologies are needed as a response to false consciousness. Lukács argues that the irrational structure of capitalist society requires ideologies to explain apparent contradictions, either to support or to oppose a particular view of social reality. Ideology, for Lukács, was a committed political position that did not necessarily come from and support a dominating group, but rather served to intervene in society to construct the ways in which social issues are understood (Lukács, 1988).

The positions of both Marx and Engels and Lukács imply a separation between reality and ideology and an understanding that there is a true reality and a false understanding of it. Ideologies are accounts of reality with political purposes. Althusser (1965, 1976) has argued against such a separation and instead sees ideologies as the organisation of signifying practices (language, discourse, etc.) that constitute humans as social subjects. That is, ideologies are constituent parts of the realities they account for – they are systems of belief that constitute the world for those who hold them and that adapt individuals to 'their social functions by providing them with an imaginary model of the whole, suitably schematised and fictionalised for their purposes' (Eagleton, 2007: 151).

The idea of false consciousness in ideology has been critiqued because it implies an objectively true world that is falsified through discourse. If, however, ideologies are considered as representations that constitute and construct the realities to which they refer, then it is hard to maintain a true/false dichotomy of belief systems because there is no external objective reality against which to measure the truth of beliefs (Hawkes, 1996). Moreover, ideologies themselves are parts of everyday realities, not specifically political propaganda or entrenched doctrinal views, and restricting the domain of ideology to explicitly articulated political doctrines would obscure much of what is ideological within them. While language-in-education policies may reflect such overt doctrines, they are also imbued with more subtle ideological elements. It is therefore necessary in considering language-in-education policies as ideological to consider the nature of ideology more broadly.

This broader conception of ideology, as suggested above, involves seeing ideas and beliefs as constituent parts of the natural and social world. This understanding derives in part from the work of Bakhtin and his associates writing in the first half of the 20th century. This body of work develops an understanding of the Russian term *идеология* (*ideologiya*), which has a broader and less political sense than the English term:

> The Russian *'ideologiya'* is less politically coloured than the English word 'ideology'. In other words, it is not necessarily a consciously held political belief system; rather it can refer in a more general sense to the way in which members of a given social group view the world. (Roberts, 1994: 249)

Taking such a perspective on ideology means that it becomes possible to see language, text and discourse as ideological, as they embody systems of belief which may not be consciously held or articulated but which pervade the ways in which ideas are constructed and communicated. This is a view of ideology that removes it from the idea of a special form of political commitment and instead locates it as a form of shared meaning in interpreting the world. Using such a perspective, Verscheuren (2012) defines ideology as a pattern of meaning or frame of interpretation used for understanding social reality. That is, ideology provides a framework within which the social world is understood as having a meaningful shape and form. Moreover, in contrast to the view that ideologies are special, committed political positions, Verscheuren argues that they are typically accepted as common-sense formulations about the world, which are shared by members of a group and are typically unquestioned. Further, ideologies can be either explicitly articulated or implicit, and it is not the manner of articulation that constitutes something as an ideology.

Ideologies are an element of the ways in which human beings see the phenomena of their world as having a meaningful form. Voloshinov (1929) sees ideology as a process through which the natural and social worlds are given meaning or value, and language as the ultimate vehicle for the creation and communication of ideology:

> Все идеологическое обладает значением: оно представляет, замещает нечто вне его находящееся, т.е. является знаком. Где нет языка — там нет и идеологии.

Everything ideological possesses meaning: it represents, stands for something that is located outside itself, i.e., it is a sign. Where there is no language – there is no ideology.
(Voloshinov, 1929: 13)

For Voloshinov, ideology is a system of meanings in which signs, such as those which compose language, create meanings which go beyond referential meaning and create relationships between what is being referred to and the world beyond it. He states that ideology requires language for its existence – it is language which creates and communicates ideologies – but also acknowledges that any sign system, of which language is only one, is inherently ideological: 'Где знак — там и идеология' ('Where there are signs there is also ideology') (Voloshinov, 1929: 14). Ideology is therefore a form of discourse in which the linguistic and non-linguistic are brought into a meaningful relationship: ideology is not an epiphenomenon which exists alongside language but rather a constituent part of language. This means that any act of language use contains ideology, that ideology is not a product of certain types of language or text and that any communicative act can be investigated as an ideological production. Ideologies are created and transmitted through discursive practices and are inherent in those practices (van Dijk, 2000).

Ideologies exist within acts of social communication. In fact, for Voloshinov, ideology can be expressed only through acts of social communication: 'Ведь бытие знака является не чем иным, как материализацией этого общения. Таковы все идеологические знаки' ('Indeed, the existence of the sign is nothing but the materialisation of this contact. All ideological signs are such') (Voloshinov, 1929: 18). This means that language use is the primary site in which ideology exists. The production of language as communication both draws from and contributes to the ideologies which inform that production. This is because acts of communication create, transmit and reproduce as meaningful the world about which they communicate.

Language-in-education policies as discursive interventions in the social world therefore are ideological interventions which, through the language they use, create meaningful formulations of the social world with which they engage. They are ideological at many levels because they encapsulate cultural ideas, presumptions and presuppositions about language and about language use (Gal, 2009). They contain, (re)produce and transmit values and assumptions about the phenomena they seek to act on and thereby define what is valued by those engaged in policy-making (Considine, 1994). They are not ideological simply in the sense that they represent the views of political organisations such as governments, but also in the sense that they represent articulations which construct the world they discuss by conveying a pattern of meaning or frame of interpretation which is brought to bear on that world.

Ideologies can be seen not simply as communicated systems of belief but also as purposeful interventions in the social world. As Eagleton (2007: 9) argues, ideology 'concerns the actual uses of language between particular human subjects for the production of specific effects'. Such a view of ideologies was recognised by Lukács (1988), who saw ideologies as tools for either reinforcing or opposing false consciousness. Similarly, Althusser (1965) argues that, while on the surface ideologies are referential in that they account for perceived realities, below the surface they can be emotive (expressing lived realities) or conative (achieving effects). Thus, an account of ideology involves not only understanding the belief system itself but also the function of the belief system in its social and political context. Ideologies are deployable political resources that can be used to gain particular ends and represent points of possible or actual contestation about the nature of the social world (Eagleton, 2007). It is in this way that ideologies relate to dominance and resistance.

Ideologies gain power in the social and political world when they come to be accepted not as political constructions of that world but as descriptions of it, that is, when they become normalised as common-sense ways of thinking about the world (cf. the notion of habitus as posited by Bourdieu, 1972, 1980). This occurs when the belief systems of a particular group become a dominant ideology in a society. As van Dijk argues:

> when a group accepts a dominant ideology as a reflection of their own goals, desires or interests, or as a representation of a natural or otherwise legitimate social order, their ideologies may turn into beliefs that are taken for granted or simply common sense. (van Dijk, 2000: 102)

As normalised ways of thinking about the world, ideologies have a fundamental relationship with questions of power because ideologies can work to legitimise the power of a dominant social group or class (Eagleton, 2007).

Ideologies are therefore hegemonic – they afford the possibility for a group to organise society as a whole in accordance with its interests and consciousness. Gramsci (1975) understands hegemony as the ways in which the governing power wins consent to its rule from those whom it subjugates. Hegemony, for Gramsci, is a non-coercive relationship of dominance in which dominated groups consent to the belief systems and power relations that exist in the society:

consenso *spontaneo* dato dalle grandi masse della popolazione all'indirizzo impresso alla vita sociale dal gruppo fondamentale dominante, consenso che nasce «storicamente» dal prestigio (e quindi dalla fiducia) derivante al gruppo dominante dalla sua posizione e dalla sua funzione nel mondo della produzione.

spontaneous consent given by the great masses of the population to the direction imposed on social life by the fundamental dominant group, a consensus that is born 'historically' from the prestige (and thus from the confidence) that the dominant group enjoys from its position and from its function in the world of production.

(Gramsci, 1975: 9, emphasis in original)

This means that hegemony results from the powers of the ideologies of the dominant group to shape not only society but also perceptions of society by both dominant and subordinated groups.

Hegemony involves 'a wide range of practical strategies by which a dominant power elicits consent to its rule from those it subjugates' (Eagleton, 2007: 115–116) and these strategies, according to Gramsci, include ideologies. For Gramsci, to win hegemony means to establish moral political and intellectual leadership by diffusing one's own worldview throughout the fabric of society in such a way that one's own interests become equated with those of society at large. Dominant groups legitimise their domination of others through the privileging of particular systems of belief. They may promote beliefs and values that are congenial to the dominant group and denigrate or exclude ideas which challenge their dominance. Ideologies thus become organising forces, which are psychologically valid and which fashion the terrain on which people act. The ideologies found in language policies can be understood as one of the hegemonic strategies through which relationships of power between language groups are reproduced and the dominance of particular languages are discursively naturalised.

The impact of ideology on the enactment of language-in-education policies as hegemonic practices has been critiqued extensively. For example, Tollefson (1991) has argued that language-in-education policies create inequalities between learners by marginalising some students and privileging others. Such inequalities result from factors such as which languages or language varieties are included in educational provision and the access that learners have to particular types of language learning. Similarly, Pennycook (2000) has shown that the ideologies of Anglicism and Orientalism in colonial language policies in Asia functioned to maintain social inequalities. Studies such as these see the ideological impact of language-in-education policies on questions of inclusion and exclusion in the educational system.

Tollefson (2002) identifies six key critical issues relating to language-in-education policies:

(1) the forces affecting such policies and the constraints they impose on alternatives;
(2) the ways states use policies to manage access to education and language rights and the consequences of this for minority groups;
(3) the ways states use these policies for political and cultural governance;
(4) how policies create, sustain or reduce conflict among groups;
(5) how global processes influence local policy contexts;
(6) how minorities develop educational policies that serve their needs in the face of pressure from more dominant groups.

These issues largely concern the impact of decision-making about language in the education system on local contexts of linguistic and cultural diversity and focus on the consequences of such decisions for education, particularly the education of members of linguistic minorities. Issues 3 and 4 on this list also point to a wider impact of language-in-education policies in society. What is missing as an explicit focus in such a framing of language-in-education policy is what could be called the *educative value* (Liddicoat, 2005b) that is allocated to language in the policies themselves and the location of those languages in the projected life worlds in which the languages learnt will be used. It is this dimension that is the focus of the present book. In language-in-education policies that plan the acquisition of additional languages, the specific educative value of language learning may be framed in terms of the development of relationships between different linguistic and cultural groups. The educative value of language learning relates to the purpose for which languages are learnt and such purposes are typically, although not always, expressed in terms of communication between the learner and a speaker of the target language – that is, of an intercultural relationship. The construction of the nature of that intercultural relationship is an ideological position relating to values and assumptions about the nature of the relationship and the ways in which languages play a role in this relationship.

Language-in-education Policies and the Construction of Intercultural Relationships

It has been argued here that language-in-education policies, as projective texts, can be seen as formulations of an expected future pattern of language use. Language-in-education policies which are concerned with any form of multilingualism seek the development of such multilingualism for use in some imagined world. This means that such policies are not simply articulations of language learning but also articulations of a future in which those languages will be used. This future is understood and presented within an ideological perspective which concerns things such as the purposes and the practices of multilingualism and the value attributed to particular languages.

Policies for multilingualism bring people into a communicative and social relationship through knowledge of more than one language. This relationship is an ideological construct, in that it is a product of a value system in which certain patterns of language use and certain types of linguistic and social relationship are understood as meaningful and desirable. Such value systems are selective and exist in relationship with perceptions of power and prestige in the community for which a policy is developed. This means that language-in-education policies can be understood not only as formulations of provisions for learning a language but also as formulations of how the resulting multilingualism will be deployed in interactions with others. In the articulation of a policy, some types of relationships between speakers of different languages and members of different cultures will be highlighted while others will be omitted or backgrounded.

Viewing language-in-education policies as formulations of valued intercultural relationships means seeing the domain of such policies in a more elaborated way. Much work on language policy has focused on the content of policy documents in terms of what is provided and how, and the impact of such provision on society, but in purely educational terms. This way of understanding language-in-education policy does not emphasise how language learning is understood as having an impact on and a function in the world outside education. However, each of these foci does have a connection with the world beyond the classroom and the ways in which each is elaborated will be underpinned by the ideological positionings of those articulating the policy.

Language-in-education policies may deal with a range of different issues with different aims and objectives in language learning and each object has a potentially different relationship to multilingualism and hence to intercultural relationships. As has already been discussed, one focus of language-in-education policies is the teaching and learning of the official language(s) of a polity. In many cases, this involves the teaching of such languages as the first language of students and, in such cases, the orientation tends to be monolingual and monocultural. In other cases, policies may be concerned with teaching additional languages for members of indigenous or immigrant linguistic minorities. Such policies seek to change the linguistic repertoire of members of minorities and they do envisage a form of intercultural relationship, in that they bring members of such minorities into new relationships with speakers of the dominant language. Language-in-education policies may focus on expanding the linguistic repertoires of students in other ways, for example, by adding languages other than the official language – this may be a language spoken within the polity, for example, an indigenous or immigrant language – or it may be a language spoken outside the polity – a foreign language. Such policies focus on forms of intercultural relationship – they project a future in which students will interact in some way with speakers of those languages.

Language-in-education policies may also focus on the teaching of minority languages to speakers of those languages for the purpose of language maintenance. Where this is done, these languages are typically taught and learnt in combination with an official language. In such cases, the minority language is taught primarily for the purposes of intracultural relationship (i.e. within the indigenous or immigrant community), while the official language serves an intercultural purpose.

In that particular language-in-education policies are oriented to inter-cultural relationship by envisaging the use of languages between members of different cultures, they may project very different realities within the same policy context. 'Intercultural relationship' is not a unitary phenom-enon: very different sorts of relationships are possible between groups (Berry, 1997; Van Oudenhoven et al., 2006). The relationship between cultural groups may be unidirectional, where the onus for engagement rests with only one of the participant groups, the other remaining with its own cultural context. Alternatively, the relationship may be multidirectional, where the various participants involved take responsibility for and par-ticipate in processes of engagement and adjustment. There are also more extreme forms of intercultural relationship. One is the denial of cultural differences between groups – that is, a relationship of assimilation. In such relationships, actions are undertaken to remove dimensions of difference so that an originally intercultural relationship becomes an intracultural one. Alternatively, intercultural relationships may take the form of separation – an entrenchment of difference and avoidance of engagement beyond one's own cultural group. 'Intercultural relationship' is therefore a multivalent phenomenon in which diverse expectations and positionings are possible. Such positionings form part of the ideological apparatus of language-in-education policies, as they articulate value positions which frame how the learning of languages will be realised in projected future interactions.

The sorts of views of the intercultural discussed above do not problema-tise the idea of culture as a classification of groups. They tend to assume a homogenised, bordered world in which cultures are easily identified and people are easily allocated to cultures (and languages). It is perhaps un-surprising that this is the case in language-in-education policy, as there is increasing agreement that intercultural education more generally has been based on the concept of culture as a fixed static entity, especially in terms of national culture (e.g. Abdallah-Pretceille, 2003; Dervin, 2008, 2011; Finch & Nynäs, 2011; Repubblica italiana, 1986). Culture as national culture in par-ticular has predominated, and this understanding may fit well with policy documents as articulations of the linguistic and cultural work of national governments. According to Bayart (2002), the fixed, static understanding of culture – often called *culturalism* – is characterised by three problematic assumptions: it understands cultures as sets of stable, timeless representa-tions; it sees the boundaries between cultures as clear-cut; and it is founded on a view that culture is endorsed by coherent political orientations. When culture is understood in this way, what is represented as a cultural practice may misrepresent as coherent and stable activities that are in reality diverse and contested (Phillips, 2010: 5). This view of culture ignores the performed nature of culture as 'a practical activity shot through with wilful actions, power relations, struggle, contradiction and change' (Sewell, 1999: 44). In so doing, it privileges culture as a form of group identification over the individual's experience of and action in cultures.

Although the framing of culture in policy texts may be done in terms of groups, especially national groups, the individual is nonetheless present in the futures that are discursively projected in such texts. The conceptualisa-tion of relationships between linguistically and culturally diverse groups operates not only at the level of intergroup relations but also at the level of the individual group member as an actor in such relationships. Language-in-education policies therefore can be seen as projections not only of intergroup relationships but also of actors in these relationships. Discussions of literacy policy often mention the ways in which the policy document constructs the 'literate subject' – the individual who is the product of literacy education (Grant, 1997; Luke, 1992). Luke (1992) argues that educational policies and the resulting practices do not simply teach literacy but rather construct particular types of individuals with 'particular ways of speaking, acting, and being' (p. 123) who represent the 'morally regulated, literate subject' (p. 124). That is, educational policies create particular types of people. In the case of language-in-education policies for teaching additional languages, it is possible to identify similar constructions of individuals as the products of education, that is, 'intercultural subjects' – individuals who are equipped with certain capabilities and practices for communicating with others. While the intercultural subject is analogous to the literate subject, they have a quite different status in educational policy and practice. All literacy policy envisages a literate subject – that is, literacy is a feature of all educational provision and everyone who receives an education is expected to become literate (or will be considered to have failed in their education). Language-in-education policy for the teaching and learning of additional languages is not the same, as not all people who receive an education will acquire or be expected to acquire an additional language and only certain types of learners will be expected to become intercultural subjects. The identification of those people is an ideological determination.

There are in fact two issues for investigation of the intercultural subject. The first concerns the characteristics attributed to that subject. That is, what practices are the projected intercultural subjects expected to be able to use in interactions with members of other cultures through the language(s) they have acquired? The policies relate to the nature, purpose and extent of the practices to be developed. This issue then relates to the sorts of intercultural relationships the intercultural subject is expected to engage in. The second issue relates to who is projected to become the intercultural subject – that is, who will be expected to deploy intercultural practices to engage with diverse others. If intercultural relationships are understood as a form of accommodation, there is a question about who will be expected to accommodate to whom. In contexts where there is social and/or linguistic inequality, the answer to this question is telling in terms of how the policy addresses power relationships. For this reason, in examining language policies it is important not simply to examine the provisions of the policy documents – those things which will be enacted in Gee's (1994a, 1994b) terms – but also to examine what is projected as the end result of the policy. As in the case of the literate subject in literacy policy, the nature of the intercultural subject is not usually explicitly stated but rather is represented in the underlying ideology of the text.

The focus of this book is on language policies for teaching additional languages in a number of contexts, the ideological construction of inter-cultural relationships projected by the texts, and consequentially the construction of the intercultural subject. This will involve consideration of the provisions of the policy – the content – but the aim is not so much to document this content but to examine how the provisions of the policy construct worldviews about the use of languages in contexts of diversity, whether that diversity is internal or external to the polity itself.

About This Book

This book aims to examine the ideological underpinnings of language-in-education policies which explicitly focus on adding a new language to the learner's existing repertoire. It therefore considers a number of policy contexts in which language-in-education policy articulates the development of some form of multilingual capability. Such policies are found in different contexts with different audiences.

- Policies for foreign language learning usually presuppose that the dominant language of a polity has already been acquired, and focus instead on the addition of a language to the repertoire of students. In such contexts, the intercultural relationship of interest is usually between members of the polity and some external other.
- Language-in-education policies for educating immigrants focus on the teaching of the dominant language of a polity, which may be done in conjunction with the teaching of the immigrant language; these policies seek to establish intercultural relationships between the host community and the immigrant group.
- Language-in-education policies for indigenous groups also concern the teaching of the dominant language of the polity, possibly alongside an indigenous language, to establish a relationship between the indigenous group and the dominant group.
- External language spread policies focus on the teaching of a polity's own language to people from another society and envisage a form of intercultural relationship between the national group and some foreign other.

Each of these contexts provides for different relationships between the language learner and the group who speak the target language, and in different polities different understandings influence how policy is designed.

Each chapter in this book takes the form of a series of three case studies in which policies relating to a particular area of language-in-education policy are examined. The case studies are intended as explorations of issues and do not aim to provide a comprehensive overview of the ideological possibilities for language policy in each domain.

For Chapters 2–4, respectively discussing foreign language learning, immigrant languages and indigenous languages, case studies are drawn from language policy in Australia and Japan. These polities have been chosen because they represent very different contexts in which language policy is developed. Australia is a country which is characterised by a high level of linguistic and cultural diversity and has officially recognised its diversity at the policy level through policies of multiculturalism. Education policy in Australia is complex, as policies exist at national (Commonwealth) level and also at State and Territory level; the case studies, though, deal only with national policy documents. Japan, in contrast, is characterised by a self-image as a monoethnic nation and neglects or downplays its linguistic and cultural diversity. These views have implications for the ways in which policies for the teaching and learning of immigrant and indigenous languages are framed. In the discussion of policies for immigrant language education, the third case study comes from Italy, which is a country for which immigration has only recently become a significant policy issue, and for which membership of the European Union has also provided a context in which linguistic and cultural diversity have significant import. For the discussion of indigenous language policy, the case study comes from Colombia. Colombia has an explicit commitment to indigenous languages in its constitution, unlike either Australia or Japan, and so provides a point of contrast in terms of the starting point for its policy development.

In terms of the teaching and learning of foreign languages, Australia and Japan also contrast. Australia is a nation which has as its dominant language a widely spoken international language – English. Foreign language education is directed towards a diverse range of languages of other polities, many of which actually have a community presence in the country as the result of immigration. Japan's foreign language policy is much more focused, with an almost exclusive emphasis on the learning of English. In the discussion of foreign language education, the third case study is taken from the European Union, with an examination of Union-level policies. The European Union represents a unique language-in-education policy context, as it involves policy development relating to independent nation-states within a context of a developing federation, with commitments to multilingualism and to establishing a common European identity.

The discussion of language spread policies (Chapter 5) omits Australia, where such policy is a relatively minor focus and the case studies are drawn from Britain, France and Japan. Again, the contexts vary considerably. Britain is involved in language spread policies for a widely used and growing international language. In contrast, language spread policy in France is developed in a context in which the language functions as an international language but the impact and prestige of the French language have been felt for a considerable period of time to be under threat from other languages – first German and then English. Japan's language spread policy is designed to promote a language which has had a very limited international role.

The book is structured so that each chapter considers one language planning context. Chapter 2 focuses on second/foreign language education and examines policies relating to the teaching and learning of languages other than the official languages of the polity for the purposes of wider intercultural communication. In such contexts, intercultural relationships are constructed between members of the local/national community and other communities and are located within particular purposes for the development of intercultural capacity. The chapter features case studies of policies from Australia, Japan and Europe. Each of these cases shows a different, and in some cases changing, framing of the intercultural relationship envisaged and the nature and purpose of the intercultural communication envisaged.

In Chapter 3 the focus is on language education policies for immigrants and consideration is given to policies on the teaching and learning both of the official language of the host polity and of the languages of the immigrants themselves. The intercultural relationship constructed in such policies involves the social relationships projected between immigrants and mainstream populations. The case studies examine policies for Australia, Japan and Italy. One of the issues that emerge from the study of these policies is that the intercultural relationship being envisaged can involve either accommodation of the immigrant to the mainstream – that is, interculturality can be seen as a device for integration – or as a mutual accommodation of groups. The intercultural subject here is therefore either a person who accommodates to the culture of others or one who integrates into the mainstream while maintaining a personal, private cultural distinctiveness.

Chapter 4 examines language-in-education policies for indigenous people and includes consideration of policies relating to the teaching and learning both of the official language of the host country and of indigenous languages. The intercultural relationship constructed in such policies involves the social relationships projected between indigenous and mainstream (colonising) populations. The case studies in this chapter examine Australia, Japan and Colombia. They demonstrate that such policies tend to construct interculturality as involving a process of subordination to the language and culture of the dominant group, which maintains the hierarchy of languages in the polity. One feature of such policies is that interculturality is expressed as a way of integrating indigenous people into the mainstream without adjustment of the mainstream's values and practices. The framings of interculturality in such policies have much in common with policies for immigrant languages, as interculturality is again constructed as a consequence of maintaining diversity. The intercultural subject here is therefore a person who integrates into the mainstream while maintaining a personal, private cultural distinctiveness and a culturally subordinated position.

Chapter 5 examines the external language spread policies through which one polity seeks to foster the teaching of its language in other countries. The case studies focus on language spread policies for English, French and Japanese. The chapter argues that interculturality in such policies reflects a desire to enhance the symbolic capital attached to a particular language.

The intercultural subject is constructed as an individual who recognises the value of engagement with the language and culture being taught.

Chapter 6 will draw together the common themes across each language planning context and examine the commonalities and differences in the ways in which intercultural relationships are constructed through policies. The chapter will draw together some common themes that span policy contexts in Japan and Australia to show the coherence between the different manifestations of language-in-education policy in these two polities. It will also return to the themes of ideology and power to examine how language-in-education policy texts construct the nature or purpose of language education in ways that project relationships that both produce and are influenced by ideologies about languages and their speakers.

Notes

1. According to the 2011 Australian census, Mandarin Chinese was the most widely spoken immigrant language in Australia, with 319,500 speakers, representing 1.7% of the Australian population (Australian Bureau of Statistics, 2012).
2. The usefulness of the dichotomy between second and foreign languages has also been questioned in the educational literature, for example, by Kramsch (2002) as the aims and objectives of each have considerable overlap.
3. All translations in this book are the author's own, except where otherwise indicated.

2 Policies for Foreign Language Learning

Introduction

The study of an additional language as part of formal education has been a common feature of national education systems and, after policies framed around learning official languages, is probably the most common subject of language-in-education policy. In the early development of such policies, the learning of an additional language was considered to be an academic exercise aimed primarily at intellectual development rather than at the development of a communicative capacity (Musumeci, 2009). Intellectual development was the main focus of the grammar-translation method developed in the mid-19th century and was influential at the time when many governmental education systems came into being. The focus of learning was on language analysis and declarative knowledge of grammatical rules (Stern, 1983). Such language policies cannot truly be said to concern the development of an intercultural capability, as no real communicative partner was envisaged for the learner. In fact, much of this teaching focused on the acquisition of classical languages, for which no real human interlocutor from the target language speech community was even possible. Although a view of language learning as intellectual training has persisted it has been paralleled by a view of language learning that has emphasised the need for the capacity to use the language for communication (Widdowson, 1972). This view constructs language learning as a preparation for the development of a communicative relationship with members of another culture and this envisages some form of intercultural relationship.

The history of language education, and hence of language-in-education policy, in many polities shows movement between academically focused, intellectual training views of language learning and practically oriented, communication-focused views.[1] This movement can be in either direction.

For example, Cryle *et al.* (1994) report that the early teaching of French in the Australian state of New South Wales involved a focus on teaching for practical, professional purposes, which later was replaced by a more intellectual emphasis, while Butler (2007) reports that language education in Japan has oscillated between an academic and a practical focus. These possible rationales – intellectual training versus practical communication – mean that language policies for foreign language education have not always envisaged an intercultural objective and that languages can be taught and learnt for policy purposes other than engagement with others. The intercultural subject is therefore not a stable entity in such policy and documents may be silent on what such an individual may be. Its realisation is embedded in ideologies about the nature and purpose of language use and also about the nature and purpose of education more generally.

In policy contexts in which some intercultural relationship is envisaged, that is, in policies that focus on communication as a learning objective, such relationships are constructed between members of the local national community and other communities and are located within particular purposes for the development of intercultural capacity. The intercultural subject is a member of the polity for which policy has been developed, who is to interact with some linguistically and culturally different other. The identity of the other varies. Most commonly, it is envisaged as someone from another polity in which the target language is an official language, but there are other possibilities. Most significantly, the development of English as an international language means that it is possible for policy documents to envisage interactions not only with, or not even primarily with, native speakers of English, but with a diversity of people, who may not be specifically identified, with English used as a lingua franca. In addition, 'foreign' languages may be represented in policy as a means of promoting interactions with linguistic and cultural minorities within a polity (and so may be taught as second languages): for example, the teaching of Spanish to speakers of English in the United States.

The case studies here span three polities with diverse intercultural subjects and relationships. Moreover, in each of the polities considered – Australia, Japan and the European Union – the representations of the forms of intercultural relationship and the understanding of the intercultural subject have evolved over time in the policy-making for foreign language education.

Language-in-education Policy in Australia

Language-in-education policy has been a fertile field in Australia and since 1987, when the first national policy was developed, there have been many policy documents produced at different levels. In a survey of language policy history from 1970, Lo Bianco and Gvozdenko (2006) identified at least 67 policy-related reports, investigations or substantial enquiries into language education. There have been more since that survey was undertaken. The large number of policy documents results in part from the way in which education is structured in Australia. Education is an area shared by the Commonwealth and State and Territory governments – a total of nine jurisdictions, each with its own policy documents. In addition, there has been a rather short-term perspective on language-in-education policy in Australia and policies tend to be frequently replaced.

The involvement of the Commonwealth government in language-in-education policy for the teaching of foreign languages is a relatively recent development as, prior to 1987, such policies were articulated only by State and Territory governments. The Commonwealth intervention came as a response to a perceived problem in the provision of language education, with a movement away from compulsory language education as a part of the secondary school curriculum, which followed the release of the Wyndham report on education commissioned by the New South Wales government (Wyndham, 1957).[2] That report argued that foreign language teaching was a part of an elitist education and was less suitable for comprehensive education (Croft & Macpherson, 1991a). This reaction against language teaching was the result of a shift in the ideological construction of education whereby it no longer focused on the development of elites but rather on the development of the capabilities of the general population (Fiala & Lanford, 1987). The ideas from New South Wales' Wyndham report spread through other jurisdictions, with the result that Australian education nationally moved from a situation in which a large proportion of students studied a small number of classical and modern languages (Wykes, 1958; Wykes & King, 1968) to one in which relatively few students studied a relatively large number of languages (DEET, 1989b). From the late 1970s, the declining numbers of students studying languages and the increasing emphasis in Commonwealth policy on multiculturalism created a situation in which the Commonwealth government came to reconsider its role in language-in-education policy (for an overview see Foster & Stockley, 1988; Ozolins, 1993). The result was that, from the 1980s, the Commonwealth became the main driver of language-in-education policies for the learning of additional languages in schools, with States and Territories developing policies largely to implement Commonwealth directions, although often with limited success (Liddicoat & Curnow, 2009).

In Australia, many different forms of language learning are integrated within the same policy provisions. There is in particular a broad overlap between the teaching of foreign languages and the teaching of immigrant languages. This overlap is not only at the level of education policy but it is also the case that some languages studied in Australia as foreign languages are also present as languages of immigration. Australia's policy for teaching these languages is included in this chapter on foreign language education because there is little distinction made in the policy between immigrant, indigenous and other learners of these languages, and the policy provisions for language study generally reflect processes of foreign language learning rather than learning by first language speakers or heritage language speakers. It is therefore not really possible to focus on foreign language education to the exclusion of second language education or even first language education. However, it must be acknowledged that there is tension between these foci of policy and the tension itself reflects dimensions of the ideology of language-in-education policy in Australia. This issue is returned to in the discussion of immigrant language policy in Chapter 3.

The focus of this case study is on national (Commonwealth) policy documents and two different types of policy: policies of the Commonwealth government, which seek to shape language education across the whole country, largely by influencing the way the Commonwealth funds education at State and Territory level; and nationally agreed policies, which are produced through collaboration between Commonwealth and State and Territory governments. The discussion covers the following policies:

- the National Policy on Languages (NPL) (1987–91) (Lo Bianco, 1987);
- the Australian Language and Literacy Policy (ALLP) (1991–2005) (DEET, 1991a, 1991b);
- the National Asian Languages and Studies in Australian Schools (NALSAS) strategy (1994–2002) (COAG, 1994);
- the National Statement and Plan for Languages Education in Australian Schools (2005–08) (henceforth Statement and Plan) (MCEETYA, 2005);
- the National Asian Languages and Studies in Schools Program (NALSSP) (2009–12) (DEEWR, 2009b).

Of the policy documents, all except that for the Statement and Plan were produced by the Commonwealth government. The Statement and Plan is different from the other policies discussed here in that it is not a policy of the Commonwealth government but rather a policy ratified by all ministers of education – State and Territory as well as Commonwealth. Further, although the NALSAS strategy was based on a national report (COAG, 1994) and was an activity of the Commonwealth government, carried out with Commonwealth funding, the programme comprised State/Territory initiatives.

The NPL was Australia's first comprehensive language policy and was presented in a substantial document, running to over 300 pages. In responding to the perception that Australia's collective language knowledge was seriously inadequate, the NPL stressed that Australia was linguistically diverse and that Australia needed to support a large range of languages. The development of intercultural communication skills and the overall enhancement of cultural capital were put forward as two of the core reasons for promoting language learning in Australian education. In addition, language learning was represented as an activity which would foster cultural insights and lead to the maintenance and promotion of diversity (Lo Bianco, 1987: 48). These goals for language and culture learning were consistent with the more general goals the NPL put forward for a language policy: equity, economic development, external relations and educational enrichment.

The NPL expressed its language learning objective as 'a language other than English for all' and this formulation effectively encapsulates a number of very different linguistic realities, ranging from the new learning of what for the learners are essentially foreign languages through to the maintenance of first languages that happen not to be English. This blurring of boundaries represents a problem within the construction of multiculturalism in the Australian context, in that multicultural policies are directed towards immigrant groups, often with a focus on establishing equity, but at the same time are supposed to be all-inclusive. There has been in Australia an ideological construction of cultural diversity as a particularist or specialist agenda which compromises the position and identity of the Australian mainstream (Ang & Stratton, 1998; Betts, 1988). Concern for ethnic particularism, the idea that the maintenance of linguistic and cultural distinctiveness constitutes a form of special treatment for minorities, has a long history in Australia. It was specifically rejected at the time of the introduction of the mass immigration programme following the Second World War through an explicit government policy of assimilation of all immigrants to the dominant language and culture and a promise made to the Australian people that immigrants would in a short time become indistinguishable for other Australians (Jupp, 1995). Ethnic particularism is especially associated with the idea that diversity destabilises society, by creating groups whose interests do not coincide with national interests, that is, those of the dominant group. It is therefore an ideological construction of diversity that frames multicultural society as being fragmented by attachments to ethnic groups that are separate from a perceived core national identity (Béteille, 1998) – that is, it is an ideology of difference as division. It is essentially therefore an ideology of fear for the integrity of national identity. Multiculturalism as a social positive – the government position from 1978 – therefore represented an ideological break with the past in official discourses on immigration and the maintenance of immigrant languages and cultures. This new positive ideology of diversity did not, however, replace the previous ideology of ethnic particularism but rather existed alongside it in complex ways. This coexistence of different ideological constructions of diversity reflects the fact that ideologies are internally complex, with conflicts between their various elements that need to be renegotiated and resolved (Eagleton, 2007). This conflict is explored further in Chapter 3.

Language, as a highly salient marker of difference, therefore needed to be treated in a way which addressed the real language needs of minorities but without evidencing particularism. In the NPL, this tension was expressed through statements that language learning is for all, which masked the internal variation that such a policy entailed. This in turn influenced how the policy constructed understandings of intercultural relationships, because such relationships necessarily involve a construction of an inter-cultural subject, the agent of such relationships. If the language learner is understood as a speaker of English learning another language as essentially a foreign language, then the intercultural relationship envisaged is one between the learner and some projected other who uses that language. This other may be internal to Australian society, if the language is a community language, or external to Australian society, if the language is not used, or at least not widely used, in Australia, or possibly both.

There are many references in the NPL to language maintenance and it is usually represented as one of two pathways to language competence. For example:

> For a large number of Australians, this bilingualism would occur if they maintain their first language as they learn the national language. This policy advocates therefore, extension and improvements so that progressively it will be easier for non-English-speaking Australians to develop and maintain a bilingualism which is beneficial to them and to the society. For the majority of Australians, however, becoming bilingual will involve learning, as a second language, a language other than English. (Lo Bianco, 1987: 44)

This quote presents language maintenance and other modes of language learning as being essentially the same activity. This presentation is designed to counter an ideological construction of multiculturalism as ethnic particularism. The text quoted responds to the ideology of multi-culturalism as particularism in two main ways. First, it locates language maintenance together with the development of capabilities in English; that is, it accompanies integration into the Australian mainstream. Secondly, it states that the benefit of language maintenance is not only personal but also national ('beneficial to them and to the society'). In this way, the NPL constructed the intercultural subject as essentially the same – a person interacting across cultures – regardless of the ways the capability to do so is acquired. The first language speaker and the second language learner are therefore depicted as being engaged in the same process for essentially the same ends.

The policy also envisages an intercultural subject who is a member of a group which does not function in English but who does not have the linguistic resources to participate in that group:

> Learning second languages can also enable individuals to activate cultural, familial, social and economic networks which are otherwise closed off by language, but which are a part of their society. (Lo Bianco, 1987: 47)

This statement is focused on internal relationships within Australia ('their society') but the construction here seems to project a different sort of inter-cultural subject. In this case, the language learner is not someone who is separated from cultural others socially but rather linguistically. The language learner here appears to have a heritage connection with the language and its community which is weakened by the lack of language. The intercultural relationship envisaged is therefore one for the language learner within a cultural or familial group but which cannot at present be fully realised, for want of language skills. That is, language education does not seek to provide new forms of intercultural connection but rather permits existing connec-tions to be further developed.

Such a focus on language education for internal, and especially for maintenance, purposes runs the risk that language education begins to be seen as relating primarily to the agenda of immigrant minorities (ethnic particularism) rather than being relevant to the whole population. The policy therefore seeks to justify language learning as a necessity not only for those who speak minority languages but also for those who speak English:

> These [English-speaking] children speak, learn in and use the dominant language of Australia. For them, acquiring proficiency in a second language does not assume the immediate importance which learning English does for children of non-English-speaking background. But language education is very important for children of English-speaking background too. Their society is multilingual and their world is multi-lingual. (Lo Bianco, 1987: 127)

This statement characterises relationships within ethnic communities as demonstrating immediate importance, but that importance also exists for English speakers in engaging with the languages of others, both at home and overseas. These orientations are reflected in some of the purposes stated for language learning in the policy. The text quoted above attempts to construct a parallelism between linguistic minorities and the dominant group and to present language learning as an analogous activity for both, rather than as a special activity for minorities.

> At a social level, language education can potentially contribute to improving intergroup and intercultural education, enhancing thereby, the quality of relations between the component groups of Australian society. (Lo Bianco, 1987: 47)

In this quote, language learning is projected as being a mechanism for improving intergroup relationships within Australia. This statement constructs the existing situation in Australia as being characterised by relationships which are somehow impoverished by a lack of intergroup understanding, itself related to lack of access to the languages of others within Australia. In this statement, the language learner (archetypically the English monolingual) is constructed as a person who does not speak a language of some minority group and the intercultural relationship envisaged is an accommodation by the mainstream to a minority. The intercultural subject here is a person who is both socially and linguistically separated from others and for whom language provides a tool that overcomes this separation. This is effectively a mutual accommodation of social groups to each other, if read in relation to statements about the unifying role of English.

> English is a cohesive and unifying element in Australian society. It contributes to national and cultural identification and allegiance and serves as the common language of communication for Australians of different language backgrounds. (Lo Bianco, 1987: 71)

Thus, English provides a common language for the society and therefore provides a vehicle for intercultural relationships between the various ethnic groups. The learning of additional languages improves this communication, not because communication has not been established, but because communication is monodirectional – from minority to majority. English is therefore represented as the shared language of all Australians and as playing an inherently positive role in national social life by providing the common ground for all social groups.

The NPL also constructed intercultural relationships external to Australia (the multilingual world):

> Australia's geography necessitates a policy of language teaching choices which gives prominence to important languages of our region as second languages. (Lo Bianco, 1987: 15)

In this case, the context in which the intercultural subject will act is constructed as 'our region', that is, the Asia-Pacific, and the interactions envisaged are between Australians and those of other nations. It is thus an externally oriented intercultural relationship. The NPL recognised that, for some learners, the languages of their own ethnic group may also be a language which will be used for such interactions; however, these interactions were represented as different types of the same intercultural interaction. In particular, these interactions were understood within a context of economic advantage:

> Australian economic activities ... would benefit from the skilled use of the host countries' languages and active knowledge and appreciation of cultural values or behaviours. (Lo Bianco, 1987: 49)

In addition, language learning was promoted as a way to ensure the articulation of a specifically Australian worldview to others:

> It is in Australia's interests – and it is intrinsically worthwhile – that we promote accurate knowledge of Australia's national character, its values and culture, and that we reciprocate by promoting perspectives in Australian education which treat seriously and analytically the issues of importance and the cultural and historical characteristics of Asian/Pacific countries. This is an imperative of national security. (Lo Bianco, 1987: 49)

In this case, there is reciprocal framing of intercultural relations which involves expressing Australian realities and at the same time developing understanding of the realities of others. This exchange of understanding is in turn subordinated to questions of national self-interest. Language learning is therefore made into a component part of ideologies of nation and the need to preserve and protect the nation, and it is this ideological framing that is used to validate language learning as part of the country's educational agenda. That is, it is not so much the intrinsic worth of language learning that provides justification but national need. The framing of languages in terms of need incorporates all languages, including immigrant languages, into this agenda and in so doing subordinates aspirations of specific groups to broader national aspirations. Underlying this construction of the value of language learning is a deeper ideology of the value of education being found in its utility to the nation and that the purpose of education is to prepare citizens to achieve national interests.

The NPL is therefore a site of ideological conflicts which are played out in the discourses presented. By bringing language to the forefront, the NPL explicitly raises and acknowledges ideologies of diversity as divisive and particularist and argues against these by mobilising other ideologies of the nation and its needs. It simultaneously promotes language knowledge as a personal good and subordinates that personal good to the national good. By backgrounding personal benefit to group benefit, the discourses of the text work to diminish the relevance of particularist fears about diversity and to provide a new discursive field in which the role of languages can be understood. The emphasis on languages 'for all' likewise works to create significations around languages as common property for all Australians rather than being associated solely with linguistic minorities.

Given the discursive complexities that shape the policy, it is unsurprising that the construction of the intercultural subject in the NPL is multivalent and the relationships envisaged are variously represented. These relationships may be between the majority linguistic group and local linguistic minorities or they may be between Australians and external others. That is, the intercultural subject communicates to achieve the national interest, either as an actor in social cohesion or as an actor in external economic relations. Alternatively, the purpose of language learning may be understood in terms of strengthening existing intracultural relationships – that is, in terms of personal needs and wants. Intercultural relationships between linguistic and cultural minorities will presumably be accomplished through English, re-emphasising the place of English as not only the national language but also the language of national identity.

The complexity of the construction of the intercultural subject results from the blurring of boundaries between international and intra-national languages and this is achieved in part through a focus on the learning of particular languages rather than on the learning of language by particular groups. The NPL proposed a set of 'languages of wider teaching' – Arabic, Chinese, French, German, Indonesian, Italian, Japanese, modern Greek, Spanish (Lo Bianco, 1987) – which it saw as being of particular significance for Australian schooling. While proposing that these languages required a specific level of support, it also took great pains that this list was not designed to restrict the scope of language education (Lo Bianco, 1987: 125). That is, the discursive focus of the policy was ultimately placed on the languages to be learnt rather than on the learners. The list is ambiguous in terms of focus, as all the languages are official languages of other countries, allowing for an externally oriented construction of the goal of learning; however, some of the languages are also those of large immigrant groups, allowing for an internally oriented construction. The NPL did not specify which construction applied.

This ambiguity provided a way of uniting language learning as a common focus for all social groups, as languages can provide identifiable and unitary constructs which obscure internal social differences. What was proposed in the NPL was an undifferentiated provision of languages for different learning groups – that is, 'foreign' languages could be studied as first languages by students who spoke them at home, or as heritage languages by students who heard them spoken in their social groups but who could speak them well themselves, or as additional languages by students who had little or no connection with that language. There was in the NPL, therefore, a blurring of the identities, needs and values of different types of learners in order to construct language education as a unitary phenomenon, although there was recognition that programmes might need to vary. The focus, then, was on the *what* of learning – languages which address national needs – rather than on *who* is learning and in so doing the policy avoided the problems of particularism and special needs.

The next iteration of policy development, the ALLP, has been characterised by many as an attempt to limit the scope of the NPL (for example, Clyne, 1991; Liddicoat, 1996, 2009; Moore, 1991). The clear difference between the NPL and its successor lies in the paring down of the contexts in which language learning is presented as being of value. In the ALLP, language learning is represented as serving a role for internal national cohesion by promoting understanding and tolerance of diversity and as serving a role internationally by promoting and facilitating trade. These emphases can be seen as a movement away from the emphasis on social equality and personal development which were articulated in the NPL and a solidification of the utilitarian ideology of education. In particular, the focus on language as an individual good, which in the NPL is treated alongside discourses of national interest, is much reduced in the ALLP. Instead, where the individual is discussed, the focus is on the individual's contribution to the social and economic wellbeing of society. What can be seen here, though, is a continuation of the tension relating to ideologies of diversity as divisive ethnic particularism and the desire to counter this through an articulation of language learning as being relevant to all.

The ALLP maintains many of the ideas present in the NPL and arguments for language learning in the ALLP are based on multiculturalism:

'the development of cultural and linguistic diversity' (DEET, 1991b: 13) and interculturality 'to develop cross-cultural understanding' (p. 12), both of which can be subsumed into a single goal – 'to promote tolerance' (p. 62). These statements in the policy are relatively decontextualised. Cultural and linguistic diversity will be developed, but there is little projection of how what is developed will be deployed. For intercultural relationships within the country, the main construction used is 'tolerance', that is, the acceptance of the difference of others, rather than engagement in that diversity. The main focus on intercultural relationships is on those outside the country and these relationships are constructed almost entirely in economic terms. The ALLP adds a human capital dimension to the rationale for language learning and promotes language learning as a way of developing a resource which can be deployed for economic gain: 'maintain a pool of cultural resources to benefit business and industry' (DEET, 1991b: 16) and 'develop a knowledge of the culture and customs of other countries to strengthen trade' (p. 23). This additional utilitarian argument for language learning is in keeping with the stronger economic motivation of the ALLP and the reconceptualisation of education as the development of economically and vocationally useful skills inherent in the policy (Clyne, 1991; Liddicoat, 1996; Moore, 1991).

In the ALLP, it is the economic discourse that predominates and the discourses about the role of interculturality are constructed in terms of economic relations:

[The ALLP] must be firmly anchored in policies addressing the nature of Australia as a multilingual and pluralistic society in an increasingly internationalist world, and policies addressing the needs for both micro-economic and macro-economic reform. (DEET, 1991b: 12)

The policy is therefore explicitly focused on multilingualism in relation to the world beyond Australia, the 'increasingly internationalist world', and in relation to economic objectives. The possible internal cleavages over language and ethnic particularism which represented a tension in the NPL are therefore deflected by a focus on national (economic) interest and the role that the existing internal linguistic ecology can play in achieving it. The languages of immigrants in the ALLP document represent a part of the human capital which education seeks to develop:

Australian residents of non-English-speaking background constitute a benefit to government, business and industry through the pool of language and cultural resources, and other skills, which they represent. (DEET, 1991b: 16)

These people are therefore placed outside the scope of educational need – they are a pool of expertise.

Further, the focus of language-in-education policy in the ALLP had moved to the development of new learning of languages – the inclusion of language maintenance featured in the NPL was downplayed (Clyne, 1991). The reason for this shift appears to relate to an ideological framing of the purpose of education more widely as the development of new resources and capabilities. Existing resources therefore do not require a place in education as they already exist and do not appear to need further development.

In the policy, language education in formal schooling is equated with the learning of languages as foreign languages and educational provision for first language or heritage language speakers is not addressed as a policy goal. In this way, the potential differential between the English-speaking main-stream and ethnolinguistic minorities is removed and the focus is placed on the mainstream as the normal context for language education. That is, language learning is constructed primarily as a process of providing possibili-ties for the monocultural majority to develop the capacity for intercultural relationships with (external) others, primarily for economic purposes.

The ALLP designated a set of 'priority languages'. It proposed a focus on eight such languages, to be chosen by each State and Territory from a list of 14: Aboriginal languages (counting as one), Arabic, Chinese, French, German, Indonesian, Italian, Japanese, Korean, modern Greek, Russian, Spanish, Thai and Vietnamese. These are the only languages mentioned in the policy and, as in the case of the NPL, there is an ambiguity in the goal of language learning. The list is primarily made up of official languages of other countries, which are also in some cases languages of significant immigrant communities, but it also contains languages which are not official in other countries and which are inherently internally focused – Australian indigenous languages.[3] The list and the need to choose eight languages were actually a response to a difficulty which emerged in the discussion paper which led to the ALLP (DEET, 1990). The discussion paper attempted to reduce the NPL's nine languages of 'wider teaching' to eight 'priority languages' by omitting modern Greek from the list. The omission led to significant political reaction and this was resolved in the text through an indirectly imposed restriction in the form of an expanded list and language selection (see also Sussex, 1991). The attempt to omit Greek can be under-stood as part of the de-emphasising of languages relevant to internal cultural relationships in favour of those relevant to external economic relationships. Greek is a major community language in Australia, but is not a language which has been identified as being economically significant for Australia (see, for example, Stanley et al., 1990). Its inclusion in the final document reflects the political power of the Greek community and the community's ability to mobilise to ensure the symbolic recognition of its language in policy. The final list adds further languages to the NPL's list, most of which are Asian languages (Korean, Thai, Vietnamese), of which only Vietnamese represented a significant community language at the time. In this context there is an explicit focus on Asian languages and a lesser focus on European languages traditionally associated with Australian immigration.

The next policy text, the NALSAS strategy, fundamentally tied language learning to the development of human capital. This direction was clearly articulated in the title of the policy report which introduced the policy – *Asian Languages and Australia's Economic Future* (COAG, 1994). NALSAS, however, moved further in this direction than either of the earlier policies and the multicultural dimension found in those earlier documents is entirely absent. NALSAS therefore represents the final working through of an agenda that focuses language education on the interests of the nation as a whole rather than on the needs of particular communities within the country, thus further strengthening one ideological focus of the earlier texts.

NALSAS focused on the acquisition of four languages of Asia: Chinese, Japanese, Indonesian and Korean. Learning the particular constellation of Asian languages indicated by the NALSAS strategy was tied explicitly to developing 'cultural literacy for securing … [Australia's] economic future' (COAG, 1994: ii). Within this broad human capital focus, the core reason for studying Asian languages (and Asian cultures) was to develop communication skills, which are described either as 'culturally appropriate communication skills' (p. vi) or as 'intercultural communication skills' (p. 2), and to develop 'cultural sensitivity' (p. ii). Again, the rationale here is for learning cultural information which will facilitate interaction with Asia, specifically in the context of business and trade (Brock, 2001). The intercultural subject is therefore represented as an individual with knowledge of the Asian other (including knowledge of language) who is able to deploy this knowledge in economic activities to support international trade in the Asian region.

The particular languages designated for NALSAS were primarily languages with small communities in Australia, except for Chinese, which at the time represented a significant and growing ethnic community. Given this, the omission of any reference to Chinese language maintenance in the document is significant. In fact, the role of existing speakers of Asian languages in developing intercultural relationships for Australia is explicitly downplayed:

Another argument against proposals to expand Asian languages/cultures programs in Australia is that adequate expertise already exists in these areas in Australia through Australians of various non-English speaking backgrounds (NEBs). Once again this argument is flawed on a number of counts. (COAG, 1994: 61)

The quotation here focuses on those with existing (adult) expertise in the language, not on children whose language capabilities can be developed through education. The language capabilities of these adults are critiqued and doubt is cast on the actual language competency of these individuals in Asian languages, the lack of language maintenance in Asian language speaking communities and their proficiency in English (p. 62). There is an ideological construction of knowledge of an Asian first language here – that it entails a deficit in knowledge of English – that problematises the ability of speakers of Asian languages to function adequately in addressing national interests. Although the report identifies problems in the linguistic capabilities of individuals of Asian background, there is no discussion of ways in which education could address this. Instead, the focus switches to the learning of Asian languages by those who have no existing knowledge of them. Existing language abilities have now been completely excluded from the focus of language-in-education policy and the monolingual, monocultural, English speaker has become the default focus of educational provision.

The NALSAS strategy sees educative value solely in terms of the economic return generated by the resulting skills set. The learner partaking of languages and cultures education is seen as becoming economically useful and his/her contribution to broader dimensions of society external to the economy is no longer a salient dimension of educative effort. The inter-cultural needs of the learner are therefore defined by economic goals and objectives external to the learner, and learner- and society-based needs in-dependent of economic utility have at best a peripheral role in the educative vision (Scarino & Papademetre, 2001). Intercultural relationships therefore are constructed more as nation-to-nation relationships in the field of trade and other economic activities. Moreover, they are constructed in terms of a normalised English-speaking learner interacting with external others.

The next iteration of language-in-education policy, the 2005–08 Statement and Plan (MCEETYA, 2005), was a collaboration between all Australian ministers of education. One consequence of the collaborative nature of the policy document is that it is very general, as all statements had to be agreed by all ministers, in spite of different party affiliations and political positions. The Statement and Plan argued for language learning to be interculturally focused and in so doing emphasised the idea of intercul-tural relationships in a way which the preceding policies had not.

Inter-cultural language learning contributes to the overall education of learners, developing in them the capabilities to:

- communicate, interact and negotiate within and across languages and cultures
- understand their own and others' languages, thus extending their range of literacy skills, including skills in English literacy
- understand themselves and others, and to understand and use diverse ways of knowing, being and doing
- further develop their cognitive skills through thinking critically and analytically, solving problems, and making connections in their learning.

Such capabilities assist learners to live and work successfully as linguistically and culturally aware citizens of the world. (MCEETYA, 2005: 3)

The policy constructs a broad understanding of intercultural relationship which includes both contact with linguistically and culturally diverse others and also a process of self-reflection in relation to these others. At the same time, the learning of languages is at least partially subordinated to the educational development of the dominant language, in that it contributes to English literacy. This means that language learning is valued not simply for the possibilities of intercultural relationship that it affords but also as an adjunct for supporting the dominant language. The study of an additional language is therefore linked to a concern for the acquisition of literacy in the dominant language of the society and the value of language learning is understood, at least in part, in terms of its contribution to education in the dominant language. The learning of additional languages is therefore subordinated to the needs of the dominant language. This construction of additional languages as vehicles for developing English literacy is not presented in the policy document in relation to immigrant or indigenous children, but as a feature of mainstream education for members of the dominant language group. This construction of language learning as an element of English literacy became an important focus of the educational rationale for language learning following the release of a narrowly focused English literacy policy in 1998 which emphasised the economic importance of improved English literacy (DEETYA, 1998). The most developed versions of this discourse can be seen not in Commonwealth government policy but in State government policies. For example, the Victorian government produced a booklet for teachers to develop practices in language learning that would facilitate English literacy (DEETV, 2000), while the Tasmanian curriculum includes a subject area called 'English literacy (including Languages other Than English)' (Liddicoat & Curnow, 2009).

In spite of the articulation of many agendas for language learning, the focus in the Statement and Plan is on intercultural understanding. The intercultural relationships envisaged are both externally and internally oriented. There is considerable discussion of the implications of globalisation for intercultural communication:

> Twenty-first century education needs to engage with, and be responsive to, this changing world. It needs to develop in learners the knowledge, understanding and attributes necessary for successful participation and engagement within and across local, regional and global communities, and in all spheres of activity. (MCEETYA, 2005: 2)

Globalisation, represented here as 'this changing world', engenders a communicative need which spans all areas of activity and both local and international intercultural relationships. That is, language learning allows participation and engagement with diverse others, who may be within Australia or outside. The local relationships seem to be constructed as those between the majority and minorities:

> Language learning contributes to social cohesiveness through better communication and understanding. (MCEETYA, 2005: 2)

If social cohesion is to be assured through the learning of additional languages, the focus of learning is on those who do not already speak these languages, in order for them to be able to communicate with those who do. This is an implicit claim that communication through the dominant language alone is not adequate for developing social cohesion.

Although in the Statement and Plan socially oriented purposes predominate, languages are still represented in utilitarian terms. In particular, language learning is represented in terms of an investment:

> Developing in them language skills and inter-cultural understanding is an investment in our national capability and a valuable resource. (MCEETYA, 2005: 2)

This investment is economically useful and this benefit is emphasised at both the national and the individual level. The underlying educational ideology is that the purpose of education is a utilitarian one of developing resources to be deployed in the national interest:

Language learning …
- contributes to our strategic, economic and international development …
- enhances employment and career prospects for the individual.

(MCEETYA, 2005: 2)

In this way, the economically focused forms of intercultural relationship which predominated in the NALSAS strategy persist in the Statement and Plan, although they play a smaller role in the discourse than previously. The domain of application is also extended beyond the economic, and includes strategic needs, reflecting a post-9/11 discourse of security (see Lo Bianco, 2008) and an ideology of threat. The strategic needs which language learning will address are not clearly articulated in the policy document, but they coincide with the oblique introduction of a security rationale for language learning in the form of a quotation from the then head of Australia's armed forces: 'Language skills and cultural sensitivity will be the new currency of this world order' (MCEETYA, 2005: 2). The introduction of a heteroglossic military voice in the policy document links language-in-education policy with discourses relating to diversity in a wider context, most significantly those relating to the 'War on Terror'. This means that intercultural relationships, which are framed broadly in terms of positive engagement with diverse others, contain also the possibility of engagement with the suspicions, threatening other and invoke discourses relating to the need to secure safety from such others, articulated in the context of the ideologies of threat surrounding terrorism (Crichton, 2007).

The intercultural subject in the Statement and Plan is constructed in a complex way, in that the intercultural subject is variously an internally oriented communicator who uses language capabilities to achieve social cohesiveness or an externally oriented communicator who uses language capabilities for economic or security purposes. These purposes are not distinguished in terms of the learner population or the language being studied; rather, they are represented as generic, all-purpose outcomes of language study.

In 2009, the release of the National Asian Languages and Studies in Schools Program (NALSSP) (DEEWR, 2009b) represented a reintroduction of the NALSAS strategy in a revised form following a change of government in 2007.[4] The focus of the programme was on the four Asian languages of the NALSAS strategy and the aims and objectives remained very similar. The wider framing of the contribution of language learning to national interest of the Statement and Plan was replaced by a narrower economic framing. In part, the removal of security as a feature of the significance of language learning relates to the choice of languages involved (Chinese, Indonesian, Japanese and Korean), as these languages, with the possible exception of Indonesian, were not consistent with the ideology of threat that justified the inclusion of a security dimension.

The documents relating to this programme are brief and articulate only an economic understanding of the intercultural relationships which will result from language learning:

Asian languages and studies will equip the students of today with the skills to excel in the careers of tomorrow in our increasingly globalised economy. A greater cultural understanding and the ability to engage with our regional neighbours in their own language will help to build a more productive and competitive nation. This is beneficial for our economy, community and individuals, creating more jobs and higher wages and overall better opportunities for all Australians. (DEEWR, 2009a)

The relationships are again articulated in terms of their impact on economics, on the nation and on the individual. The intercultural subject is reduced to an economic actor and the relationships of value developed through languages are economic relationships.

As indicated at the start of this case study, Australian language-in-education policy for foreign language learning is ambiguous in that the foreign language dimension is never clearly differentiated from other language learning contexts. Instead, it seems to attempt to blend a range of different purposes and to present them as being facets of a common policy objective. Language study covers a broad gamut of possibilities which are not well acknowledged at the policy level and several different realities are conflated. There is an attempt in language-in-education policy to minimise discursively the possibility that language education could contribute to ethnic particularism; this is achieved by focusing language learning primarily on new learning of languages and then embedding other possibilities within the overall framing as if they were an alternative pathway to the same goal. Thus, in these policy texts, except perhaps for the NPL, the teaching and learning of immigrant languages, and to a lesser extent indigenous languages, are acknowledged as part of the scope of language education, while downplaying the learning of these languages by members of groups which have some identification with them. This stance seems to reflect a continuing concern in policy to respond to the mainstream's ambivalence about multiculturalism and the negative ideologies of the consequences of diversity (Dandy & Pe-Pua, 2010). The preoccupation with the place of language education in developing English would seem to be a manifestation of similar concerns, in which the predominance of the mainstream language is acknowledged in articulating the need for learning additional languages, and the purpose of learning is in part subordinated to the purposes of the dominant language.

These ambiguities influence how the intercultural relationships which language learning is intended to develop and the nature of the intercultural subject are understood. Both constructs appear to be conflations in which internally oriented relationships and practices stand alongside externally oriented ones as an often undifferentiated whole. Early articulations, such as those in the NPL, provide for intercultural relationships both within and outside Australia, which exist to achieve relatively similar goals: the social goals of understanding and tolerance, as well as economic goals, although social goals predominate in the learning of immigrant languages. The move to economically focused goals in later policies overlays the conflation of goals and purposes. This means that later policies come to marginalise the place of immigrant and indigenous languages, for which economic relationships are less important, while at the same time maintaining a policy focus on all forms of language learning.

The intercultural subject is similarly ambiguous as policies have implied an individual who is both a social actor involved in a range of relationships with diverse others and an economic actor whose knowledge constitutes a readily available form of human capital. As the focus on the economic actor increases, the nature of the social actor changes. Initially, the social actor is one who engages with diverse others through their languages to achieve communication with and understanding of the other. Later, this tends to be reduced, especially in the NALSAS strategy, to the development of knowledge of the other as an object of study which is deployed as understanding – the social dimension of the economic actor is not so much engagement to promote understanding, but the use of understanding for the accomplishment of economic activity. The intercultural subject is projected as achieving particular purposes in the national interest that are defined through ideological constructions of national needs.

Language-in-education Policy in Japan

Foreign language education, especially English language education, has been a focus of Japanese language-in-education policy since the period following the Meiji restoration in 1868. In the 1890s, foreign language education was formally established for middle and higher secondary schools, with English as the main foreign language, while French and German were offered in high schools as second foreign languages (Kitao & Kitao, 1995).

During this period, language study was closely associated with modernisation, which was in turn closely associated with ideas of westernisation (Nakamura, 2002). During the latter part of the 19th century, the focus of foreign language learning was on increasing communication between Japan and the west in order to appropriate practices and knowledge for the development of Japan. Foreign language education at the time was therefore practically focused (Butler, 2007; Butler & Iino, 2005) and envisaged active engagement with western culture and ideas. During this period, there was a fetishisation of the west, in which everything from the west was thought to be advanced, while traditional Japanese practices were looked at in a more negative light. It entailed the whole country embarking on a process of westernisation, referred to as *bunmei kaika* (civilisation and enlightenment) (Buruma & Margalit, 2004), in which the west was conceptualised as the source of knowledge and civilisation. Foreign languages were therefore prized as vehicles for accessing valued domains of knowledge. English-medium classes were delivered at tertiary institutions to encourage students to develop their knowledge of western theories and practices by reading foreign language documents (Amano, 1990).

Much of the post-Meiji enthusiasm for westernisation resulted from a sense of threat experienced after the realisation of Japan's technological inferiority compared with the west following the end to Japan's isolation under the Tokugawa Shogunate (1603–1868).[5] However, after the Japanese victories in the First Sino-Japanese War (1894–95) and the Russo-Japanese War (1905–06), the impulse to westernise slowed and a stronger nationalistic discourse emerged. In particular, the place of foreign languages as languages of instruction in tertiary education was questioned and a greater emphasis was placed on the role of Japanese in education, including its use as a language of instruction at tertiary level (Amano, 1990). Nonetheless, English remained important in elite education and *juken eigo* (受験英語, English for the entrance examination) was a dominant concern for those aspiring to university study (Fujimoto-Adamson, 2006). *Juken eigo* focused primarily on the acquisition of language rules and backgrounded communication. This focus downplayed the role of intercultural relationships through language and emphasised language learning as an intellectual activity. Japan increasingly distanced itself from foreign language education in the period leading up to the Second World War, as the dominant language taught, English, was increasingly perceived as an enemy language and therefore as a threat (Fujimoto-Adamson, 2006; Kitao & Kitao, 1995). During the pre-war period, the west was increasingly positioned in Japanese ideologies as a constraint on the position and possibilities of Japan on the world stage. Thus, rather than constructing the west as the source of development, as had been the case during the Meiji period, the west had become an obstacle to development (Buruma & Margalit, 2004).

Following the war, foreign language learning was re-established as a central part of education, again with the main focus on English, which was listed as a school subject in the educational reforms of 1947. In 1956, English was adopted as a subject in the entrance examinations for all high schools in Japan. The result was that, although English was not an officially mandated subject, it became, in the form of *juken eigo*, a de facto requirement for students to enter high schools (Butler, 2007). The post-war period opened with a period of domination of Japan by the occupation forces of the United States and its allies, during which Japan was reconstructed largely on western models and oriented towards English-speaking powers. When the direct domination of occupation ended, US influence continued to be exercised in less direct ways, but continuing the English-speaking hegemony (Ikenberry, 2004).

More recently, language planning for foreign language education in Japan has taken place within a broader educational policy of internationalisation (国際化教育, *kokusaikakyouiku*, 'international education'). The principal policy documents relating to language-in-education planning relating to *kokusaikakyouiku* are:

- 学習指導要領、外国語 (*The Course of Study for Lower Secondary School: Foreign Languages*) (Monbusho, 2002a, 2002b);
- 「英語が使える日本人」の育成のための戦略構想、英語力・国語力増進プラン (*Developing a Strategic Plan to Cultivate 'Japanese With English Abilities' to Improve English and Japanese Abilities*) (Monbusho, 2002c);
- 小学校学習指導要領解説: 外国語活動編 (*Explanation of the Elementary School Course of Study: Foreign Language Activities Book*) (MEXT, 2008).

The purpose of international education is to foster the development of *kokusairikai*[6] (国際理解, 'international understanding'). The Japanese word *kokusai* is made up of the components *koku* and *sai*, which together imply a meeting between countries, and so language education is framed as a form of intercultural relationship. In policy discourses *kokusairikai* is primarily conceived as an encounter between Japan and the English-speaking world and the emphasis within policy has been on the development of western styles of communication, specifically communication in English (Kubota, 2002; Morita, 1988). An alternative formulation of *kokusairikai* is *ibunkarikai* (異文化理解, 'intercultural understanding'), and these two terms are often treated as synonymous in policy texts. This means that intercultural understanding is international understanding and the sphere of the intercultural is unambiguously located in the context of external communication rather than internal communication within a culturally diverse Japan. The term *ibunka* itself, which is composed of the elements 異, *i*, 'different' and 文化, *bunka*, 'culture', is not semantically neutral. The *i* morpheme has connotations which suggest that the other culture is something that is *ayashii* (怪しい, 'dubious, doubtful'), *myou na* (妙な, 'curious, strange, funny, odd') and *wazawai* (災い, 'disastrous, calamitous'). *Ibunkarikai* involves, therefore, understanding of the dubious and strangely different culture of others.

Foreign language teaching in the Japanese educational context unambiguously means English language teaching. This is explicitly stated in the 2002 course of study for languages (Monbusho, 2002b): '必修教科としての「外国語」においては，英語を履修させることを原則とする' ('For compulsory foreign language instruction, English should be selected in principle') and in the primary school curriculum documents for 'foreign language activities' (MEXT, 2008: 8) '教育課程における外国語活動の位置付けは，次のようにした … 英語を取り扱うことを原則とした.' ('Foreign language activities are positioned in the curriculum as follows…. It is designated as a principle that English will be studied'). The policy is therefore one in which the languages of study are specified as external to Japan (外国語, *gaikokugo*, 'foreign language') in which the foreign world has become largely isomorphic with the English-speaking world.

The focus on English is justified by a discourse which locates English at the centre of international communication as a hegemonic language which has taken on the role of an international lingua franca:

> このような状況の中、英語は、母語の異なる人々の間をつなぐ国際的共通語として最も中心的な役割を果たしており、子どもたちが２１世紀を生き抜くためには、国際的共通語としての英語のコミュニケーション能力を身に付けることが不可欠です。
>
> In such a situation, English has played a central role as the common international language in linking people who have different mother tongues. For children living in the 21st century, it is essential for them to acquire communication abilities in English as a common international language.
> (Toyama, 2002)

English is asserted as the unquestioned international language and the sole desirable mode for international communication. The emphasis is on 'first circle' English varieties (Kachru, 1985), especially that of the United States (Kubota, 2002), in part because of American economic and cultural hegemony but also in part because it was reinforced by the post-Second

World War subordination of Japan to the United States; it was also a continuation of the ideological construction of the west from the Meiji period. The focus of internationalisation is clearly directed at communication with the economically and politically dominant English-speaking nations, rather than at communication across a broad geographic and linguistic spectrum. The locus of engagement for intercultural relationships is therefore a constrained one, even though the global nature of English is acknowledged and used to justify the policy.

Language-in-education policies envisage a form of intercultural engagement primarily with the English-speaking world, but this in itself says little about the nature of this relationship. This relationship is constructed in very specific ways in Japanese policy texts. The nature of this construction can be seen in the revised course of study for English in the discussion of the selection of teaching materials (Monbusho, 2002b). The following quote is from the course of study for junior secondary school and senior secondary school foreign language study (Monbusho, 2002a):

(2) … その際，英語を使用している人々を中心とする世界の人々及び日本人の日常生活，風俗習慣，物語，地理，歴史などに関するもののうちから，生徒の心身の発達段階及び興味・関心に即して適切な題材を変化をもたせて取り上げるものとし，次の観点に配慮する必要がある。…

イ 世界や我が国の生活や文化についての理解を深めるとともに，言語や文化に対する関心を高め，これらを尊重する態度を育てるのに役立つこと。

ウ 広い視野から国際理解を深め，国際社会に生きる日本人としての自覚を高めるとともに，国際協調の精神を養うのに役立つこと。

(2) … Teachers should take up a variety of suitable topics in accordance with the level of students' mental and physical development, as well as their interests and concerns, covering topics that relate to the daily lives, manners and customs, stories, geography, history, etc. of Japanese people and the peoples of the world, focusing on countries that use English. Special consideration should be given to the following…

b) Materials that are useful in deepening the understanding of the ways of life and cultures of the rest of the world and of Japan, raising interest in language and culture, and developing respectful attitudes to these elements.

c) Materials that are useful in deepening international understanding from a broad perspective, heightening students' awareness of being Japanese citizens living in a global community, and cultivating a spirit of international cooperation.

In this quote, the emphases on teaching Japanese identity through the vehicle of English can be seen quite clearly. Topics to be covered include aspects of Japanese life, history and so on, as well as those of other parts of the (English-speaking world), promoting a deeper understanding of Japanese identity and its place in the world. That is, one focus of English language learning is the development of understandings of Japan and the Japanese. The same focus on Japan is found in statements about language learning at primary school level:

> 外国語を用いて積極的にコミュニケーションを図るための内容と，日本と外国の言語や文化について，体験的に理解を深めるための内容との二つとした。
>
> There are two types of content: content for active communication by using foreign languages and content for deeper experiential understanding of the languages and cultures of Japan and foreign countries.
> (MEXT, 2008: 9)

In this case, content for foreign language learning is specified as being about both Japanese language and culture and that of the target language country. This means that the study of a foreign language and the study of Japan are not dissociated at any level of study.

In the texts above, therefore, Japaneseness is fundamental to accessing English and the purpose of English teaching is to foster Japanese identity. This framing of English education is closely tied to the Japanese ideology of *Nihonjinron* (日本人論, 'the question of the Japanese people'). *Nihonjinron* is an attempt to construct the parameters of a distinctive Japanese cultural and national identity (Befu, 1993, 2001; Dale, 1986; Kosaku, 1992; Miller, 1982). A core element in *Nihonjinron* is that Japan is linguistically and culturally homogeneous; that is, the Japanese are a homogeneous people (単一民族, *tan'itsu minzoku*) who constitute a racially unified nation (単一民族国家, *tan'itsu minzoku kokka*) (Sugimoto, 1999: 82). The perceived homogeneity is an ideologically constructed worldview rather than an accurate reflection of the nature of Japan, as it ignores the presence of both indigenous minorities, such as the Ainu, the Burakumin and the Ryukyu Islanders, and also immigrant populations (Maher & Yashiro, 1995; Murphy-Shigematsu, 1993, 2000). Nonetheless, in spite of the underlying diversity within Japan, *Nihonjinron* makes a fundamental equation between nationality, ethnicity and culture, which privileges the Yamato Japanese as the sole Japanese group. From the starting point of an ethnically homogeneous people, *Nihonjinron* attempts to frame Japanese identity in terms of the distinctive characteristics which constitute Japaneseness.[7] One dimension of this has been to emphasise the uniqueness of the Japanese people and society, which are constructed as not only unique, but also as being 'uniquely unique' (Gjerde & Onishi, 2000; Kosaku, 1992; Mouer & Sugimoto, 1986). This claim to singularity is manifested through comparative generalisation between 'westerners' and the 'Japanese', with special properties being attributed to the Japanese brain, social customs and language (Maher & Yashiro, 1995; Miller, 1982). The uniqueness of the Japanese constitutes a problem for others' understanding of Japan, its people, culture and worldview, and this lack of understanding needs to be resolved so that the Japanese are correctly understood by others.

This concern for the need to communicate distinctive Japaneseness to others leads to a policy for English teaching that is oriented to something intracultural rather than to something intercultural, and the purpose of engagement with others is to explore Japanese meanings and values. Japanese identity is represented as existing within an international context, and international understanding therefore involves an understanding of Japanese identity as part of globalisation, through exposure to aspects of English-speaking culture. It is a self-referential and culture-internal construction of the goals and purposes of foreign language learning. The focus on Japan in the framing of English language learning, and hence of international education, discursively frames intercultural relationships as those which are developed in order to communicate about Japan in the target language – it is a relationship which aims to disseminate Japanese ideas and values to others.

Kubota (2002) made a similar observation of the former course of study, which equally stipulated that English language study should enhance students' awareness of themselves as Japanese people in an international community. The first step in developing such an awareness is to develop an adherence to a particular conceptualisation of Japanese identity, which is unique, homogeneous and monolithic, rather than engaging with the complexities of identity as it is revealed in internationalised contexts (Parmenter & Tomita, 2000). That is, it constructs a nationalist, intracultural agenda rather than an internationalist, intercultural one as the impetus for engagement with others.

One important correlate of the need to articulate Japanese distinctiveness is that questions of self-expression in Japanese become closely integrated with policy about learning English. For example, in the press release from the education minister, Toyama, announcing the introduction of the new course of study, the intersection between using English and the expression of Japanese viewpoints is developed quite strongly:

また、同時に、英語の習得のためには、まず国語で自分の意思を明
確に表現する能力を涵養する必要もあります。

It is also necessary for Japanese people to develop their ability to clearly
express their own opinions in Japanese first in order to learn English.
(Toyama, 2002)

Here, and in other cases reported by Kubota (2002), language learning is
subordinated to a form of clear thinking with a concern for Japanese people
to be able to articulate Japanese viewpoints clearly in international contexts.
An important part of learning to express Japaneseness in a foreign language
is learning how to express it in Japanese, and the study of Japanese is to
form the basis on which Japan's international perspectives can be articulated. Internationalism is, therefore, part of the Japanese nationalising
discourse of *Nihonjinron*, which compares and contrasts 'self' with 'other'
with a view to establishing the distinctiveness of the Japanese (Ehara, 1992;
Masden, 1997; Yoshino, 1992). Within the *Nihonjinron* ideology, the study
of the language(s) of the other reinforces what it means to be Japanese,
in other words, distinguishing self from other, insider from outsider, 'we'
from 'they', and Japanese and non-Japanese (Masden, 1997: 57). As Johnson
(1983: 32) argues, *kokusaika* 'is merely the latest code word or jargon expression for a much longer standing tradition of intellectual discourse [that
is, *Nihonjinron*] about Japan' (see also Liddicoat, 2007a).

In the Japanese context, the development of communication in and
through English is important and desirable for international objectives,
but those objectives are envisaged in terms of the necessity for expressing
Japanese identity and Japanese points of view in an international context
(Hashimoto, 2000). That is, the purpose of intercultural relationships is to
disseminate a particular Japanese worldview to those who do not share that
view. This need for English language communication is constructed as a
requirement to represent Japanese thoughts and values in an international
area in which Japanese is not a language of international communication.
For example, in announcing the reformed course of study produced in 2002,
the Japanese Ministry for Education stated:

その一方、現状では、日本人の多くが、英語力が十分でないため
に、外国人との交流において制限を受けたり、適切な評価が得られ
ないといった事態も生じている。同時に、しっかりした国語力に基
づき、自らの意見を表現する能力も十分とは言えない。

At present, though, the English-speaking abilities of a large percent-
age of the population are inadequate, and this imposes restrictions on

exchanges with foreigners and creates occasions when the ideas and opinions of Japanese people are not appropriately evaluated. (Monbusho, 2002c)

Intercultural relationships are understood as being currently defective because of a lack of English language capabilities. Such relationships are therefore constructed within a framework of English dominance that normalises English as the language of intercultural engagement, reflecting the ideologies of English dominance that are seen in other aspects of policy. The lack of capability is in turn constructed as a lack of understanding of the Japanese by others. Intercultural relationships therefore are ones in which the Japanese express their perspectives through the medium of English. Thus, foreign language learning is seen as a vehicle for the expression of Japaneseness through other languages rather than as a way of mediating between Japanese and other perspectives. Hashimoto (2000) argues that the objective of Japan's foreign language education is to foster the 'Japanisation' of Japanese students of English: that is, to make them more Japanese. The relationship between the English language and Japanese identity is further encapsulated in the stated policy goal of the creation of 英語が使える日本人 (*Eigo ga tsukueru Nihonjin*); although this is officially translated as 'Japanese with English abilities', it is more literally translated as 'Japanese who are able to use English'. In this formulation, English is presented as a tool which adds to the communicative repertoire of the Japanese, but with no implied effect on their Japaneseness; if anything, the policy seeks to enhance this.

The impact of Japanese internationalisation is monodirectional – it allows Japanese self-expression in the world rather than articulating a mutually informing encounter between cultures. The emphasis, then, is on nationalistic values relating to particular conceptions of Japanese identity rather than engagement with international perspectives and interculturality (Kubota, 2002). The focus of *kokusaika* reflects the Japanese concept of *wakonyoosai* (和魂洋才), a slogan-like four-character expression signifying a close association between Japanese spirit (和魂, *wakon*) and western learning (洋才, *yoosai*). The emphasis in this concept is on acquiring western knowledge while maintaining a fundamentally Japanese worldview, in which Japanese attitudes and values remain unaffected by the integration of western systems (Nakamura, 2002). In this instance, there is a purposeful intercultural relationship which aims to discover that which is instrumentally advantageous to Japan, but which will not influence Japan in other ways. In this way, the educational goals and objectives of *kokusaika* throw into highlight a tension between nationalism and westernisation and the representation of Japan in an international context rather than an engagement with diversity, either in Japan or outside.

Even though the focus of *kokusaika* is on intercultural relationships with the wider world, the word itself is not identical in meaning with the English word 'internationalisation', especially insofar as internationalisation implies an opening up to the world (Suzuki, 1995). According to Suzuki (1995), *kokusaika* is concerned with spreading Japanese culture, values and history internationally, and moving the other to see the world from a Japanese perspective, in order to preserve Japan's interests and promote the 'correct understanding of Japan' (Suzuki, 1995). This means that *kokusaika* is less about transcending cultural boundaries and more about protecting them. As Ivy argues, rather than being a liberal opening to the world, *kokusaika*

> is a conservative policy that reflects the other side of a renewed sense of Japanese national pride, if not nationalism ... instead of opening up Japan to the struggle of different nationalities and ethnicities, the policy of internationalization implies the opposite: the thorough domestication of the foreign and the dissemination of Japanese culture throughout the world. (Ivy, 1995: 3)

In *kokusaika*, therefore, the development of international understanding is presented as resulting from the learning of English, and a knowledge of English is constructed as the vehicle through which the rest of the world can be understood. That is, a narrow equation is made between language learning and interculturality. Moreover, when culture is presented explicitly, it is inevitably an essentialised image of the relevant cultural contexts, whether of the English-speaking world or of Japan. In such representations, the intercultural is usually presented as a dichotomous opposition between Japan and the English-speaking world in which each is stereotypically depicted as being in opposition to the other (e.g. Wada, 1999). Moreover, while Japanese arguments for interculturality often emphasise the development of unbiased attitudes to other cultures and of intercultural communication skills, the approach to the cultural curriculum in Japan is very much one in which cultural information is presented as a set of static facts which are to be memorised in order to be reproduced in an examination format (e.g. Kotoo, 1992). The outcome of learning in this construct is neither a form of broadly focused understanding of other cultures nor a critically oriented intercultural perspective; instead, it is concerned with inventories of differences which reify the cultural boundaries between Japan and the English-speaking world.

The theme of using English to establish a relationship with others is one which exists from the beginnings of educational policy in the Meiji period, but the context has changed. In the Meiji period, English speakers were perceived as the dominant power but the purpose of the intercultural relationships established through English was to acquire knowledge which was lacking in Japan – that is, it was represented as a client relationship in which English allowed Japan to import modernisation. Contemporary policies are oriented to the same group but the focus is on the outward projection of Japan. Neither policy context has conceived the relationship between Japan and others to be bidirectional but the direction of transmission has been reversed. The intercultural subject proposed by contemporary policies is correspondingly an essentially, and essentialised, Japanese individual who is capable of expressing an approved version of Japanese reality to others.

Language-in-education Policy in the European Union

The policy for foreign language learning in the European Union grew out of the project for European integration and the official multilingualism of the Union. It has a particular concern for the official languages of member states. European language-in-education policy is articulated in a number of different ways:

- documents relating to language education –
  - *Teaching and Learning: Towards the Learning Society* (European Commission, 1995)
  - Council Resolution of 31 March 1995 on improving and diversifying language learning and teaching within the education systems of the European Union (European Council, 1995)
  - *Promoting Language Learning and Linguistic Diversity: An Action Plan 2004–2006* (Commission of the European Communities, 2003)

- documents relating to multilingualism –
  - *A New Framework Strategy for Multilingualism* (Commission of the European Communities, 2005)
  - Council Conclusions of 22 May 2008 on multilingualism (European Council, 2008a)
  - Council Resolution of 21 November 2008 on a European strategy for multilingualism (European Council, 2008b)

- documents relating to the European Year of Languages (2001) –
  - Decision No. 1934/2000/EC of the European Parliament and of the Council of 17 July 2000 on the European Year of Languages 2001 (European Council, 2000)

- Council Resolution of 14 February 2002 on the promotion of linguistic diversity and language learning in the framework of the implementation of the objectives of the European Year of Languages 2001 (European Council, 2002).

These documents provide an outline of European Union policy development in the area of the teaching and learning of foreign languages, and are frequently cited in other European Union texts relating to language policy issues.

The early language-in-education policy focus of the European Union is expressed most fully in the 1995 White Paper *Teaching and Learning: Towards the Learning Society* (European Commission, 1995), which sets as a goal for European education the acquisition of three European languages: an official language of the home nation of the learner and two other languages of the European Community. The policy therefore targets the development of language capabilities in the languages of member states and the emphasis is therefore on languages for internal communication within a united Europe. The text explains the need for such a policy:

> Proficiency in several Community languages has become a precondition if citizens of the European Union are to benefit from the occupational and personal opportunities open to them in the border-free Single Market. This language proficiency must be backed up by the ability to adapt to working and living environments characterised by different cultures.
>
> Languages are also the key to knowing other people. Proficiency in languages helps to build up the feeling of being European with all its cultural wealth and diversity and of understanding between the citizens of Europe. (European Commission, 1995: 47)

The first rationale for the policy is an economic one associated with notions of mobility within Europe. Languages are seen as prerequisites for engagement in the single market created by European unification. Language alone is represented as inadequate, needing to be accompanied by the ability to adapt to others. The economic dimension to language knowledge is one which is developed at a number of points in the document: it is included as a part of the project to develop employability and capacity for economic life. The second rationale is that languages are important for developing intercultural abilities, framed as 'knowing other people'. This intercultural dimension is linked to ideas of developing European identity as an element of European citizenship. This means that the intercultural engagement is represented here as part of a search for commonality – it is an engagement which will enable the language learner to participate more fully in a common Europeanness that extends beyond national distinctiveness. Europe is therefore ideologically constructed as being characterised by similarity rather than by difference, and diversity is to be understood within the parameters of overarching European commonality. The text actually represents linguistic and cultural diversity in two different ways: it is something to which the individual must be able to adapt, a construction which represents diversity as difference needing to be managed at the individual level; and it is something which is common to all. Language-in-education policy therefore projects a version of intercultural relationship which is both an economic relationship and a form of integration into a common European identity.

Similar ideas are developed in the other documents. The Council Resolution of 31 March 1995 on language teaching and learning locates language education in a broad context of the construction of a unified Europe:

> this resolution aims to provide a basis for reflection on how the educational systems themselves can continue the construction of a Europe without internal frontiers, and strengthen understanding between the peoples of the Union. (European Council, 1995)

Language education is therefore co-opted into the building of the European polity in a way which appears to conflate the idea of national and linguistic boundaries, with language education working to remove the internal linguistic boundaries of Europe. This polity-building agenda is also accompanied by an agenda for the development of intercultural understanding – and this seems to be a common conjunction in the construction of the role and value of personal plurilingualism in European language-in-education policy. These two motivations – polity-building and intercultural understanding – are related to the idea of languages as a means of access to European culture, as language education has the ability to enable 'every citizen to have access to the cultural wealth rooted in the linguistic diversity of the Union' (European Council, 1995). The focus of language use for the language learner is located within Europe in this policy, as the policy aims to 'promote, by appropriate measures, qualitative improvement in knowledge of the languages of the European Union within the Union's education systems, with the aim of developing communication skills within the Union'. The intercultural relationship envisaged here is therefore primarily an internal one, in the sense that it is focused on communication within Europe, which is characterised by commonality, although communication is external in the sense it is between inhabitants of different member states. The focus of the document is primarily on the role of languages in the construction of a united Europe; however, the resolution also briefly connects with the strong economic rationale found in the 1995 White Paper, noting that: 'A growing number of enterprises, including small and medium-sized enterprises, need colleagues who can master several of the languages of the Union'. Thus, recognition of linguistic and cultural diversity becomes relevant as a component of an economic understanding of intra-European relationships.

In the text establishing 2001 as the European Year of Languages (European Council, 2000), the ideas found in earlier policy documents were continued and developed. The diffusion of the underlying ideas of early texts is presented as a part of the activities of the European Year of Languages.

(c) to bring to the notice of the widest possible public the advantages of competencies in several languages, as a key element in the personal and professional development of individuals (including in finding one's first job), in intercultural understanding, in making full use of the rights conferred by citizenship of the Union and in enhancing the economic and social potential of enterprises and society as a whole. (European Council, 2000: 3)

This text gives one of the roles of the European Year of Languages as the dissemination of European Union ideologies about languages. Thus, the activities developed by the European Union for the European Year of Languages adopted a specifically ideological agenda which sought to inculcate widely the authoritative discourse of the Union about language. This means the policy took a role in disseminating its own ideological constructions as a policy objective. The constructs to be disseminated included the economic rationale for language learning both for the individual and for society, the development of intercultural understanding and a focus on rights. The rights discourse in this part of the text appears to replace the polity-building discourse of earlier texts but is actually closely linked to it. In the contextual sections of the text, the relationship between rights and language is articulated in terms of mobility:

Article 18 of the Treaty establishes the right of every citizen of the European Union 'to move and reside freely within the territory of the Member States'. The ability to use foreign languages is essential in order in practice fully to exercise that right. (European Council, 2000: 1)

The text therefore equates the right to move freely within Europe – an aspect of the polity-building of a united Europe – with the acquisition of languages. That is, language learning enables the full exercise of the rights of citizenship within the polity. This is a recasting of the concern for developing Europe as a united polity – a focus which is essentially at the level of governance – with a formulation of union in terms of citizens' rights – a focus at the level of the individual. Nonetheless, the governance discourse is maintained to some extent when the text notes that 'The languages question is a challenge that must be tackled as part of the European integration process' (European Council, 2000: 1).

The other elements of the ideology to be disseminated during the European Year of Languages are also developed in the contextual sections of the document. The economic element is the least strongly articulated in the text, which simply notes that 'In addition to the human, cultural and political advantages, learning languages is also of considerable potential economic benefit' (European Council, 2000: 1). This text seems to privilege non-economic arguments above economic arguments for language learning, although it is the economic dimension which is most specifically framed ('finding one's first job') in the projected activities of the European Year of Languages discussed above. There is an emphasis on the role of languages in developing intercultural understanding, phrased as cultural awareness: 'It is important to learn languages as it enhances awareness of cultural diversity and helps eradicate xenophobia, racism, anti-Semitism and intolerance' (European Council, 2000: 1). The focus here has moved beyond issues of understanding and adaptation mentioned in earlier texts, to claims about the eradication of specific social phenomena related to intolerance. This is a shift in the framing of intercultural understanding, which earlier is constructed in a way which appears to imply understanding of those who speak another language, to an expectation that language learning will deal with a greater range of intercultural relationships, including those in which language itself may not play a significant role in framing the diverse other. The discourse around intercultural understanding in previous texts was linked to the ideology of a common European cultural heritage, and this remains present in the Council's 2000 text:

> Access to the vast literary heritage in the languages in which it was originally produced would contribute to developing mutual understanding and giving a tangible content to the concept of European citizenship. (European Council, 2000: 1)

The text here uses literature as the point of entry into understanding of others – a more limited framing than in other texts – but, like other texts, it links mutual understanding to an ideology of common European identity in the form of common citizenship. The emphasis on mutuality in this document constructs the projected intercultural relationship as one between equals, in which all citizens will respond to the issues posed by Europe's diversity.

In a resolution following up the European Year of Languages (European Council, 2002), the European Council returned to these ideas and developed them with different constructions. This text has a long contextual section, which begins with a series of references to other policy documents and then moves to sets of statements divided into two groups: statements that the policy 'emphasises' and those that it 'reaffirms'. In listing the emphases of the policy, the text refers to the role of languages in facilitating mobility, although without constructing this in terms of rights: 'knowledge of languages plays an important role in facilitating mobility, both in an educational context as well as for professional purposes and for cultural and personal reasons' (European Council, 2002: 2). It also re-emphasises the place of languages in common European culture, although it does not tie this specifically to literature: 'all European languages are equal in value and dignity from the cultural point of view and form an integral part of European culture and civilisation' (p. 2). Intercultural understanding is less emphasised. It is not listed as one of the 'emphases' of the policy, but it is found in a list of things the policy 'reaffirms':

> to ensure that study programmes and educational objectives promote a positive attitude to other languages and cultures and stimulate inter-cultural communication skills from an early age. (European Council, 2002: 2)

That is, language programmes are expected to develop intercultural under-standing, but it is not represented as something that is a result of language education *per se*. In the place of intercultural understanding, the focus of the policy is more on integration and cohesion. These are taken up in two of the four paragraphs which state what the policy emphasises. The first statement is the most developed:

> the knowledge of languages is one of the basic skills which each citizen needs to acquire in order to take part effectively in the European knowledge society and therefore facilitates both integration into society and social cohesion. (European Council, 2002: 2)

Language knowledge becomes a basic skill for participation, although here it is not framed as participation in Europe generally but rather in the European knowledge society. This emphasis on the knowledge society frames participation not so much in terms of social and cultural Europe but of economic Europe. The social dimension is framed not as participation but as integration and social cohesion. These ideas of integration and cohesion are a new theme in the polity-building discourse of Europe's language-in-education policy. Previous discourses referred to the role of language learning in the removal of internal boundaries in Europe through processes of mutual understanding. The emphasis on integration and cohesion moves from a concern with the removal of barriers to a concern for stability within the diversity of Europe (see Parton, 2011). The introduction of discourses of social cohesion shifts the discursive emphasis on diversity away from one which constructs diversity as cultural wealth to one which constructs it in terms of a problem to be managed – the implied opposite of cohesion being conflict. This changed emphasis is located as a response to the increasing diversity of Europe resulting from the increased number of member states:

> knowledge of languages is also beneficial for European cohesion, in the light of EU enlargement. (European Council, 2002: 2)

The focus on cohesion returns in a number of documents without significant development (notably European Council, 2008a, 2008b).

In 2003, the Commission of the European Communities released an Action Plan for language education. The Action Plan has a strong polity-building focus in the way it described the nature and benefits of language education. One of its themes was the role of languages in creating a 'common home':

> Building a common home in which to live, work and trade together means acquiring the skills to communicate with one another effectively and to understand one another better. (Commission of the European Communities, 2003: 3)

The common home is a reframing of the ideology of commonality, not only a cultural commonality but also a commonality of space. The common home depicted is a united Europe with a core economic focus and the role of languages is to ensure intercultural relationships between those who live in the common home. The same trope of the common home is also included in the Commission's 2005 *Framework Strategy for Multilingualism*:

> It is this diversity that makes the European Union what it is: not a 'melting pot' in which differences are rendered down, but a common

home in which diversity is celebrated, and where our many mother tongues are a source of wealth and a bridge to greater solidarity and mutual understanding. (Commission of the European Communities, 2005: 2)

In this case, an opposition is established between the idea of the common home and a melting pot. The common home is one where diversity is both inherent and valued and assimilation to a common norm is eschewed. In the common home, it is the first languages which are accorded direct value, which is both economic (a source of wealth) and social. The social value of first languages is attributed to their role in the development of both solidarity, reflecting claims for the value of languages in social cohesion, and intercultural understanding. This latter association is interesting in this context, as European Union policies usually emphasise the role of *additional* languages in developing understanding rather than first languages, which are often discussed more in terms of the linguistic boundaries between Europeans. The document does not, however, detail what the role of first languages is in developing mutual understanding.

In the Action Plan, the idea of the common home is coupled with the idea of mobility, which is itself associated with the polity-building work of the European Union:

The European Union is built around the free movement of its citizens, capital and services. The citizen with good language skills is better able to take advantage of the freedom to work or study in another Member State. (Commission of the European Communities, 2003: 3)

Language capabilities are therefore operationalised for the individual in terms of the possibilities for participating in Europe; people can exploit the commonality of Europe by personally participating in its diversity. The ideological value of languages and mobility is therefore strategic in the operationalisation of Europe's commonality in the context of economic activity. The economic focus of the domain of engagement with others draws on the idea of the knowledge-based economy, and language is seen as the tool to realise such an economy:

The European Union is developing a society based upon knowledge as a key element in moving towards its objective of becoming the most competitive knowledge-based economy in the world by the end of the decade. Learning other languages contributes to this goal by improving cognitive skills and strengthening learners' mother tongue skills, including reading and writing. (Commission of the European Communities, 2003: 3)

Language learning is represented here as a form of human capital but, in this case, not in terms of intercultural engagement. Rather, the learning of additional languages is constructed in terms of its contribution to the general development of the learner and to enhanced development of the learner's first language, representing a utilitarian framing of language learning from the perspective of member states, rather than a united Europe. Language learning is also represented as the mechanism by which tolerance and understanding of others can be achieved: 'Learning and speaking other languages encourages us to become more open to others, their cultures and outlooks' (Commission of the European Communities, 2003: 3). Language learning is therefore depicted in terms in which intercultural engagement is only one potential facet of application and is coupled with individual development. Individual development is represented as necessary for the development of the knowledge economy, which is discursively linked with literacy and the first language, while intercultural abilities are linked with entrepreneurship and globalisation:

> Also in this context, the Commission is working to develop the entrepreneurial spirit and skills of EU citizens (for example through the European Charter for Small Enterprises as well as the Green Paper on Entrepreneurship). Such goals will be easier to achieve if language learning is effectively promoted in the European Union, making sure that European citizens, and companies, have the intercultural and language skills necessary to be effective in the global market-place. (Commission of the European Communities, 2003: 3)

Languages, in the Action Plan document, do not seem to be reserved only for internal communication in Europe, as in much of the earlier policy discourse. Instead, they are seen as applying to intercultural relationships in a more internationalised context. This widening of focus is seen also in the way the document characterises the languages to be learnt:

> Promoting linguistic diversity means actively encouraging the teaching and learning of the widest possible range of languages in our schools, universities, adult education centres and enterprises. Taken as a whole, the range on offer should include the smaller European languages as well as all the larger ones, regional, minority and migrant languages as well as those with 'national' status, and the languages of our major trading

partners throughout the world. (Commission of the European Communities, 2003: 9)

The range of languages here is no longer restricted to 'Community' languages but now includes those of international trading partners. The economic focus therefore appears as a driver of a greater diversification in languages than is present in the discourses on polity-building. This external focus is even more strongly articulated in a 2008 Council conclusion which states:

> with a view to promoting economic growth and competitiveness, it is important for Europe also to maintain a sufficient knowledge base in non-European languages with a global reach. At the same time, efforts should be made to uphold the position of European languages on the international stage. (European Council, 2008a: 10)

This document introduces a clear perception of the need for the teaching of certain non-European languages in the context of globalisation, but equally recognises a possible threat to the international status of European languages. The stance is therefore both outward looking and defensive, and implies that the importance of non-European languages, which need to be part of the knowledge base of Europe, is a potential threat to the symbolic capital of European languages. This perceived threat is also signalled in a companion Council Resolution (European Council, 2008b), which not only rearticulates the threat but proposes significant language spread activities to offset the threat.

The language-in-education policy documents of the European Union place the idea of intercultural relationship at the heart of its policy discourse. Intercultural engagement of various forms is seen as indispensable in a polity in which multiple languages are spoken as official languages of member states, which may or may not be officially multilingual themselves. The intercultural relationships envisaged are tied closely to a small number of contexts – personal mobility within Europe and the economic sphere, in which knowledge of languages and intercultural understanding are represented as indispensable. They are framed ideologically through the commonality of Europe, which is characterised by internal diversity that cannot privilege specific languages given the realities of the constituent parts of the European Union as independent nation-states with their own dominant languages and language groups. The intercultural relationships constructed by these documents are internally focused, as the emphasis is generally on relationships between citizens of the European Union, although later documents begin to make room for a wider field of engagement in the face of a perceived threat to the status and use of European languages.

This internal focus is enmeshed within a polity-building agenda in which the European Union discursively constructs language as a key element of the development of a united Europe. Language learning is constructed as a mechanism which contributes to a Europe without frontiers, by enabling the development of communication and mutual understanding. Thus individual plurilingualism and pluriculturalism become the outward manifestations of a preparedness to engage, within an ideologically constructed common Europe. The intercultural relationships envisaged between individuals are therefore not understood in purely personal terms but also as enactments of the broader European project. The emphasis of the polity-building discourse does, however, change over time as issues of stability and social cohesion are introduced in the wake of European enlargement and increasing diversity. The promotion of language learning for intercultural relationships is presented both as a way of responding to the diversity within Europe and as a response that is presented as mutual – that is, all Europeans are to engage with diverse others. At the same time, intercultural understanding is also attached to the discovery of European communality, in the form of a shared European identity with access to shared culture and civilisation, articulated in the diverse languages of the polity.

Conclusion

Each of the three case studies shows a different, and in some cases changing, framing of the intercultural relationship envisaged and the nature and purpose of the intercultural communication envisaged. These framings are drawn from the ideological constructions of the place and purpose of languages in the education system. In Australia, ideologies of utilitarian education for developing human capital construct languages as necessary for economic purposes, but these ideologies are in tension with the ways in which internal linguistic and cultural diversity is understood. In Japan, the ideology of *Nihonjinron* frames the purpose of English language learning as being associated with the cultivation and communication of Japaneseness. In Europe, the prevailing ideology is of European commonality and the ways in which this relates to actual linguistic and cultural diversity. In each of the policies investigated here, the intercultural relationship envisaged is one which works to achieve the perceived interest of the polity concerned.

In the case of Australia, foreign language learning has come increasingly to focus on economics. The capabilities and practices of the intercultural subject are largely constructed as those which will bring economic advantage and the intercultural subject has come to be seen in terms of human capital that can be deployed in a globalised marketplace. While the intercultural subject as economic actor may predominate in Australian policy discourse, this representation coexists alongside a more socially oriented construction. As an actor in the social world, the intercultural subject is one who connects in some way with people from other cultures through language abilities. This social dimension tends to be less stable than the economic one. In policy texts, the form of engagement of the intercultural actor ranges from an expectation of active participation with others to a more distanced form of engagement constituted through knowledge about the other. In most of the texts, it is this more distant form of engagement which is projected as the social dimension. Engagement with the other as knowledge about the other especially seems to parallel discourses in which an economic relationship predominates. The social dimension of the intercultural relationship is most strongly articulated in reference to language learning as a response to internal diversity in Australia and is backgrounded in policies focusing on the external use of languages, in which case it seems to become part of the toolkit for economic action.

In Japanese policy, the relationship is constructed as an engagement with others which disseminates Japanese ideas and understandings. The intercultural subject is an individual who can use the capabilities and practices acquired through language study to interpret the Japanese worldview for others. The policies construct the national interest as involving a better understanding of Japan – and in so doing discursively construct a lack of understanding of Japan's perspectives as a central problem of Japan's engagement with the world. The Japanese worldview to be presented is not itself unproblematic, as time needs to be spent in language learning to develop the learners' understanding of what constitutes the Japanese worldview. The intercultural subject is not therefore someone who disseminates his or her own views about Japan to others in an additional language, but rather one who can reproduce a particular officially sanctioned understanding of Japan and what it means to be Japanese. This means that the intercultural subject becomes an ideological actor transmitting a preferred understanding of Japan.

The European Union's policy documents are centrally concerned with the project to create a more united Europe through the development of a stronger European identity. This project exists alongside a set of related discourses which deal with economic relationships between member states and individual mobility within the Union. In European discourses, the intercultural subject as a social actor predominates, as it is through the capabilities and practices acquired by language learning that the project for establishing a common European identity is to be accomplished. The intercultural subject is one who acts as a European rather than simply as a member of a particular member state and so embodies the European project. The policies project an active relationship between the intercultural subject and others, mediated through language.

The discourses which project how the intercultural subject will act in the world present a sense of the nature of the relationship between the self and the other that will be enacted by the language learner. In Japan, the relationship between self and other is relatively monodirectional – the Japanese intercultural subject projects a Japanese worldview to others and seeks to modify the understanding of others. The relationship that is valued in policy is therefore not reciprocal and there is little sense of intercultural relationships transforming Japan. In fact, there appears to be an implicit problematising of the influence of others on Japan in the attention given to developing understandings of the Japanese worldview. It appears that there is a perception that this worldview has been in some way eroded over time, potentially as the result of external influences (this was articulated more explicitly in texts prior to the Second World War). Australian policies are less monodirectional in the framing of the intercultural relationship because the use of language capabilities for economic purposes requires some adjustment to the other. This adjustment to the other is, however, often constrained in the discourse to one of knowledge about the other, which remains external to the individual language user. That is, language learning does not affect the identity and self-concept of the learner but adds knowledge as a dimension of human capital that can be deployed in the economic arena. The European discourses project a more multidirectional relationship, as the development of a common European identity is a mutually accomplished goal. The purpose of language learning and the resulting forms of intercultural relationships in which learners will eventually engage is to transform a Europe of nation-states into a more synthetic whole; this implies a transformation of existing separate identities into a new common one.

Both Australia and the European Union have a polity-internal dimension to the intercultural relationships they construct. In Australia, it is the use of additional languages for communication with local linguistic minorities – especially immigrant minorities. In Europe, the internal dimension is communication between member states. In Australia, the internal dimension tends to be a secondary and often incidental outcome of the learning of the languages of other polities, while in Europe it is almost the exclusive focus of policy discourses. In both cases, where there is an internal dimension to intercultural relationships, a lack of social cohesiveness is constructed as a potential problem resulting from diversity. That is, there is an ongoing discursive construction of unity as being unproblematic for social harmony and diversity being counter-productive, even in policies which appear to be promoting such diversity. Language learning is seen as having a place in resolving this diversity, although the place of widespread plurilingualism as a response to diversity is more strongly articulated in Europe. It would appear in Australia that the issue of social cohesion is actually more strongly tied to assuring a common single language than to ensuring plurilingualism (see Chapter 3). Significantly, there is a considerable difference between Australia and Europe in the power relations between the groups involved in internal intercultural relationships. In European policy texts, the participants in such relationships are equals – there is no readily identifiable dominant group and much attention is given in European policy to ensuring equality between citizens of different member states (Rees, 1998). In Australia, this is not the case, as engagement is between the dominant group and linguistic and cultural minorities. The former situation would seem to promote plurilingualism as the linguistic response to diversity, as no one language can be constructed as a language of social cohesion, while in the latter case the dominant language – English – can readily be mobilised for this purpose.

These three polities demonstrate that language-in-education policies dealing with the same area of language education (here, the learning of a foreign language) can construct quite different ways of understanding the world. In each case, they present a view of the world in which the development of intercultural capabilities will respond to different types of problems and enact different agendas. In each case, the policies present an official, authorised discourse of what it means to be the speaker of an additional language and project very different ways of using languages in relationships with others.

Notes

1. For an overview of the historical development of language teaching see Howatt (1984) and Musumeci (2009).
2. For an overview of the Wyndham report and its impact on education policy see Croft and Macpherson (1991a, 1991b).
3. Of the States and Territories, only one, the Northern Territory, chose to include indigenous Australian languages in the list of languages to be taught in school. In most cases the list of languages supported by the ALLP was identical to that supported by the NPL.
4. Kevin Rudd, the Prime Minister from 2007 to 2010, was also the head of the committee which drafted the 1994 report on which NALSAS was based.

5. The Tokugawa Shogunate (徳川幕府, *Tokugawa bakufu*) was a feudal regime established by Tokugawa Ieyasu and ruled by the Tokugawa family. It is also known as the Edo period (江戸幕府, *Edo bakufu*), as the country was ruled from Edo, now Tokyo.
6. There are a number of terms that occur in the policy documents based on the root 国際, *kokusai*: 国際化, *kokusaika*, 'internationalisation'; 国際理解, *kokusairikai*, 'international understanding'; 国際化教育, *kokusaikakyouiku*, 'international education'.
7. It should be noted that such approaches are not restricted to school-based English teaching. Kosaku argues that the 'English conversation industry' has become a primary site for discourses on Japanese national identity and argues that globalisation has necessitated and enabled cultural nationalism, which leads the Japanese to focus 'excessively' on 'their differences from others' (Kosaku, 2002: 145).

3 Languages in the Education of Immigrants

Introduction

This chapter focuses on language-in-education policies for immigrants. Immigration may bring into a polity new ethnolinguistic groups and the presence of such groups raises two key educational issues. From the perspective of immigrant groups, there are two possible language education needs in host societies. One of these is education for the acquisition of the dominant language of the society in which they live. The dominant language is recognised as being important for employment, for participation in the host society and ultimately for acceptance (Olsen, 2000). In particular, immigrant parents have strong expectations that their children will acquire the official language of the host society through schooling. The other is the maintenance and development of their home language for subsequent generations. Language maintenance is strongly related to a sense of identity, history and continuity. Much research suggests that the preferred practice of immigrants, and probably the most beneficial, is to accommodate to the host society while maintaining their own language and culture (Berry, 2005; Liu, 2007; Nesdale & Mak, 2003; Neto, 2002). From the host country's perspective, the prime language education need of immigrants is the acquisition of the dominant language. In contrast, maintenance of immigrant languages by future generations may be perceived as a threat to the cultural and social traditions and institutions of the host society (Liu, 2007; Rex, 1995; Stephan et al., 2005). The preferred strategy of the mainstream is that immigrants assimilate with the host society. There are therefore competing and often conflicting agendas involved in the language education of immigrants, in which there is a consensus across groups about education in the dominant language, but quite different perspectives on education in a minority language. Government language-in-education policies are typically formulated from within the dominant group and so their attitudes to immigrants and diversity are significant. Any discussion of language-in-education policies for immigrants requires consideration of these two dimensions – the teaching of the official language of the polity to immigrants and the teaching of languages of immigrant groups within educational settings.

The educational issue which is most usually prioritised in discourses around language education for immigrants is the need for immigrants to acquire the official language(s) of the host society. This may be a core policy objective for both formal school education and for informal and adult education. In addition, there is a potential policy concern for the teaching and learning of the languages of the immigrant groups, either for the purposes of language or culture maintenance or as an educational response to linguistic diversity within mainstream educational contexts. In the teaching and learning of immigrant languages, there are two different groups which may be envisaged as learners, especially in the context of policies for school education. The learners may be identified as members of the immigrant group and the purpose of learning will be understood in terms of language and culture maintenance. Policies favouring the inclusion of language maintenance in education are typically articulated when it comes to be perceived that assimilatory policies are not suitable or effective in achieving social or educational goals. Alternatively, the learners of immigrant languages may be identified as members of the dominant linguistic group, who then acquire an immigrant language as an additional language. Such policies are rare but, where they exist, they seem to respond to a perceived problem of social disharmony which is conceived in terms of lack of understanding or lack of communication between immigrant and mainstream communities.

Throughout history, most language-in-education policy has ignored immigrant languages and focused on the teaching of the dominant language of the society through schooling. One discursive construction of the legitimacy of not including immigrant languages in education involves an argument that immigrants give up their claim to their language when they decide to migrate. Patten (2001) states that such a view may be grounded in an argument about the voluntariness of migration – if migrants decide to move to a place where a different language is spoken, and they do this willingly, they are choosing not only a change in geography but a change in language. According to Patten (2001) another argument that may be made about the non-recognition of languages involves the idea that a society would not willingly adopt an open immigration policy if the consequence was a proliferation in claims for languages. Both of these discourses bring into question the responsibilities a particular society has to support languages spoken by immigrants. They position these languages as external to the society and effectively delegitimise them as elements of the local linguistic marketplace (Bourdieu, 1982). Any decision therefore to include immigrant languages in education in some way involves a decision to accept a change in the linguistic ecology of a society.

The ways in which language-in-education policies construct intercultural relationships and intercultural subjects inevitably involve a negotiation of power. In contexts of immigration there is a power differential between the mainstream and the immigrant group in which the latter is typically subordinated and non-dominant (Deaux & Bikmen, 2010). Moreover, the dynamic of change resulting from immigration may mean that the dominant group becomes concerned with maintaining power in the face of a perceived threat to its position or status. Language, as a valued form of social capital, becomes important in the reproduction of power relationships. The exertion of power by the dominant group relates to a desire to stop changes in the society which are perceived to threaten the dominant group, culture and language. Liu (2007) argues that the process of adjustment to the new social circumstances which result from immigration can be more difficult for the dominant host group than for the immigrants themselves because the host group often does not realise that it will need to adjust, while immigrants are aware very early that change will be required.

Relationships between the dominant group and the immigrant group can be mediated through three basic patterns of language. The first pattern can be constructed as symmetrical – both groups are allocated responsibility for the successful working of these relationships, which is mediated through a combination of the language of the dominant group and that of the immigrant group. Alternatively they can be asymmetrical, usually presupposing a responsibility for the immigrant to achieve a successful relationship with the dominant group, reflecting the power differential between the two groups, which requires greater effort from the subordinated group than from the dominant group. Relationships are then mediated through the language of the dominant group. Both possibilities entail members of the immigrant group acquiring the language of the dominant group. The difference lies in where responsibility is allocated. Where only the dominant language is used to mediate intercultural relationships, the minority has to accommodate to the dominant group in a way which is not reciprocated. Were the dominant group to acquire the immigrant language, this would imply greater reciprocity. There is also a possibility at least of these relationships being mediated through the immigrant language only, although this option seems to have been rarely exercised. These possibilities imply different positionings of the intercultural subject, of who will be projected to become an intercultural subject through education, and of what form the interculturality will take.

Relationships within the immigrant group itself, in particular between generations, can also be conducted in the dominant language or the immigrant language, or a combination of the two. The policy issue here is what responsibility a society assumes for enabling particular forms of intergenerational communication to occur, or whether the use of a minority language in such contexts is a private or a collective concern.

Immigrant Language-in-education Policy in Australia

Australia is an immigrant society with a long history of linguistic diversity since the arrival of European settlers in 1788, although this diversity has been treated in different ways at different periods in Australia's history. The early colonial period of immigration, which was primarily, but not exclusively, from Europe, and particularly from Britain and Ireland, was marked by indifference to the languages of the immigrants on the part of colonial governments – they neither supported nor discouraged language maintenance, but nonetheless firmly entrenched English dominance (Clyne, 1991; Liddicoat, 1996). From the period of the gold rushes of the mid-19th century, Australia's linguistic diversity increased as the sources of immigration expanded beyond the traditional British and Irish sources, with significant numbers of immigrants arriving from China. This expansion was accompanied by increasing hostility towards ethnic and linguistic diversity. This hostility manifested itself most strongly in the Immigration Restriction Act of 1901, known as the White Australia policy, which used a repressive dictation test to limit immigration primarily to those of British origin (see McNamara, 2005). This meant that language education for immigrants was not a problem.

Following the Second World War, Australia entered a new period of mass immigration and increasing linguistic diversity. This period saw the end of the White Australia policy and, subsequently, immigration from Asia and more recently Africa. When Australia began to accept immigrants from countries outside its traditional English-speaking sources, an ideology of ethnic particularism emerged as a response to a perceived threat to the nation's cohesiveness and identity. The policy emphasis was very strongly on assimilation, with the expectation that immigrants would abandon their original language and culture in favour of the English language and Australian norms. English played an important role in this assimilatory policy and language education for immigrants was seen only in terms of the development of English. The policy of assimilation was not successful and post-war immigration produced significant, and changing, internal linguistic diversity in Australia. The 2006 Australian census identified over 200 immigrant languages spoken at home in Australia (DIAC, 2008). Since the late 1970s, Australia has had a policy of multiculturalism that recognised this linguistic diversity as a feature of Australia's cultural and linguistic make-up. Multiculturalism has led to the inclusion of a larger range of languages in Australian education as programmes in immigrant languages have come to be included in the scope of governments' educational provisions.

As discussed in Chapter 2, the teaching of immigrant languages is largely overshadowed within the context of language-in-education policy by a broader agenda of language learning. Because the teaching of immigrant languages has been integrated into more general language provision, the documents relating to language-in-education policy for immigrant languages in Australia overlap considerably with those for foreign languages. These policy texts may contain references specifically to the learning of immigrant languages by immigrant groups, but often they are more broadly focused. Immigrant groups may benefit from these policies to maintain and develop their languages; however, the policies themselves are not adapted specifically to these ends. There are also other areas of policy in which language education issues are present in Australia which do not fall within the broader scope of language learning, most notably those referring to issues relating to immigration and multiculturalism: that is, documents and programmes concerning multicultural education, English as a second language and ethnic or community language schools. Language-in-education policy relating to immigrants is complex as it involves both texts which set out objectives and programmes which are established and developed through a series of documents (notably Acts of Parliament) but which are not encapsulated within particular policy documents. There are therefore three categories of relevant material for understanding Australia's language-in-education policies for immigrants:

- language policy –
  - the National Policy on Languages (NPL) (1987–91) (Lo Bianco, 1987)
  - the Australian Language and Literacy Policy (ALLP) (1991–2005) (DEET, 1991a, 1991b)
  - the National Statement and Plan for Languages Education in Australian Schools (2005–08) (Statement and Plan) (MCEETYA, 2005)

- multicultural policy–
  - the Multicultural Education Program (MEP) (1979–89) (Committee on Multicultural Education, 1979)

- the National Agenda for Multicultural Australia (Office for Multicultural Affairs & Australian Advisory Council on Multicultural Affairs, 1989) (1989–99)
- the New Agenda for Multicultural Australia (Commonwealth of Australia, 1999) (1999–2011)
- Australia's Multicultural Policy (DIAC, 2011)

- programmes for immigration and multiculturalism –
  - the Adult Migrant Education Program (AMEP) (1949–)
  - the Child Migrant Education Program (CMEP) (1971–76)
  - the Ethnic Schools Program (1981–92)

The Commonwealth government's first substantial intervention in language-in-education policy concerned the teaching of English to immigrants. It very early established policies for the provision to adults of English as a second language (ESL) and English teaching was a regular part of settlement practices from the beginning of post-war mass migration. The AMEP was established in 1949 and has provided English language instruction as part of settlement programmes since that time (for the history of the AMEP see Burns & De Silva Joyce, 2007; Martin, 1998). The Immigration (Education) Act of 1971 established a right to 510 hours of English language learning for adult immigrants who do not have functional English, although it does not define what is meant by functional English. This policy has largely continued to the present and is seen as a regular part of the settlement provisions for adult immigrants. The policy is located within the immigration portfolio, a Commonwealth responsibility, and has largely been separated out from other language-in-education policy documents, although it has been included for mention in both the NPL and the ALLP.

While adult education was established early in Commonwealth government, English language provision for immigrant children in schools was not developed until 1971, with the introduction of the CMEP through the Immigration (Education) Act. This programme, which was funded through the Department of Immigration, represents a very early entry of the Commonwealth government into language-in-education policy for schools, which hitherto had been treated typically at State and Territory level, if at all. The goals of the CMEP were threefold (Foster & Stockley, 1988: 53):

- to teach non-English-speaking migrant children to speak the language – to promote oracy;
- to teach non-English-speaking migrant children to read and write English with understanding – to promote literacy;

- to provide activities which assist with the integration of these children into the corporate life of the school and the community.

These provisions are not simply educational aims for providing English to immigrant children but also construct the non-English-speaking child in specific ways. In particular, they represent the immigrant child as being in deficit. Such children are implied to have neither oracy nor literacy – as if to have no English means to have no language. The provisions of the Immigration (Education) Act equate the development of spoken English with oracy, rather than oracy in English, and do the same for literacy. Such children are represented as a linguistic *tabula rasa* and English is normalised as the sole language of a monolingual reality in which immigrant children who do not speak English have no place and no capabilities. There was an ideological construction of English as the only relevant language for Australia and that knowledge of other languages constituted a problem for access to the English language. The hegemonic place of English in Australian society was therefore reinforced. The focus of the document is assimilatory (Foster & Stockley, 1988) and the objective of teaching English is for the immigrant child to develop the capacities of the mainstream. The CMEP was terminated in 1976, when funding for English language provision was passed from the Department of Immigration to the Department of Education. This change meant that English language support was no longer treated as part of the settlement process for immigrants but as a part of broader education. This change was, however, one of administration rather than a change in emphasis.

The focus on English education for migrants, initially as a tool for assimilating immigrants into the Australian mainstream, was developed relatively early in Australia's educational policies. A focus on the languages of immigrants themselves did not appear until the official adoption of multiculturalism in the context of immigration policy. The first Commonwealth programme to focus on the teaching of immigrant languages was the MEP (Committee on Multicultural Education, 1979). The MEP divided multicultural education into two equal components. The first was the teaching of the languages of immigrant groups, while the remainder was devoted primarily to a variety of cultural sensitisation and intercultural studies. The agenda of the MEP was multicultural education for social objectives: language learning and intercultural understanding would foster social cohesiveness and social tolerance and, thereby, overcome the potential problem of divisions and ethnic particularism within a culturally and linguistically diverse society. In this way, the MEP represents a discursive change to the pre-existing ideology of threat from ethnic particularism.

In the area of language education, the MEP designated immigrant languages as 'community languages' or 'community languages other than English' and developed courses around them.[1] The term recognises that the languages are present within the ethnic communities of Australia, but it is not associated specifically with the teaching of languages to immigrant children. Thus, languages such as Greek and Italian are considered community languages by virtue of their use in Australia and are taught as community languages, regardless of whether they are taught in language maintenance programmes or as foreign languages. This is a manifestation of the blurred distinction between teaching the languages of immigrants to speakers of those languages and the teaching of foreign languages.

The orientation of multicultural policy in the 1970s – and subsequently – to immigrant groups[2] comes from a sense that multiculturalism means participation in two cultures, one's own and the mainstream Australia culture. If multiculturalism is understood in terms of participation in one's own culture and the mainstream, then for members of the mainstream culture there is only one culture in which to participate. In such a conceptualisation, the relevance of multiculturalism for the monocultural mainstream is difficult to determine, as there is no natural cultural focus for the learning of this group. Instead of projecting participation in cultures, multicultural education for the mainstream becomes reduced to superficial knowledge of the cultural peculiarities of others. Participation in the interculturality of Australian multiculturalism was therefore unidirectional – immigrant groups were to participate in two cultures but the general Australian population did not participate in multicultural society in the same way and were not expected to adjust their cultural behaviours as a consequence of multiculturalism.

One outcome of this development of multicultural policy was the introduction of the Ethnic Schools Program in 1981, which became the Community Languages Element in 1992 (for an overview of the Ethnic Schools Program see Baldauf, 2005a). The programme was designed to give government support to schools run by ethnic communities as part of their language maintenance work. In this framing of language maintenance, the delivery of language programmes is the responsibility of community organisations representing the various ethnic groups present in Australia; the government's role is limited to funding. The offering of a language maintenance programme is therefore a task allocated to individual communities rather than being part of the educational role of schooling. This means that language maintenance has come to be seen largely as a private, community task rather than one of mainstream schooling. One result of this has been that many immigrant languages have not found a place within

Australian schools and are provided through complementary provision, within communities of speakers. The school is therefore normalised as the site for developing the mainstream language and culture.

Ethnic schools, although funded by the government, are outside the normal school provision and usually take the form of after-hours or weekend classes. This means that education in such languages is conceptualised as an external additional activity that is part of the private world of leisure time rather than as a core element of public action. There is thus an ideological construction of diversity and its maintenance as a private matter that does not challenge the public hegemony of English. The primary object of the Ethnic Schools Program was to maintain the languages and cultures of immigrant students; however, the policy documents also include provisions for other students as a purpose of the programme:

> The Community Languages Element provides assistance to States and Territories and non-governmental school authorities to operate classes in the languages and cultures of ethnic communities for the benefit of both non-English speaking background and other students. (Australian Education Council, 1992: 197)

This statement, reporting the introduction of the Community Languages Element, frames the purposes of the programme as being the provision of immigrant languages for all learners. It therefore implies that the learning of such languages is relevant for all potential groups of learners and pre-supposes some learning of those languages by students who do not have a background in them. Such learning would therefore establish engage-ment between students from outside an immigrant community with that community through the community's own language. This focus of the Community Languages Element was later weakened, to envisage learning of languages for immigrants only and the development only of 'awareness' of community languages for others.

> The Community Languages Element assists students of language backgrounds other than English to maintain their languages and culture. It is also used to increase awareness among all students of the different community languages and cultures within Australian society. (MCEETYA, 1998: 7)

This formulation positions the mainstream as engaging with the immigrant community from an external point of view, in which immigrant groups, their languages and cultures become the objects of study rather than equal partners in interaction.

The establishment of ethnic schools disentangled the modes of provision of community languages under the MEP by targeting language maintenance specifically. Ethnic schools worked towards language maintenance through a variety of projects, some of which were aimed at children who were speakers of the community language and others of which taught the language to students of the relevant ethnic background who were predominantly or exclusively speakers of English. The establishment of government-funded ethnic schools meant that the educational emphasis on language maintenance for immigrants was developed outside the scope of regular schooling, and school education was often seen as more specifically relating to new learning of languages than with language maintenance programmes. The Ethnic Schools Program has undergone a number of revisions over time, but it has continued to remain the primary site for language maintenance programmes, outside regular education provision.

The development of the NPL in 1987 brought the two emerging trends in language education for immigrants – English as a second language and immigrant languages – into the same policy framework. The NPL treated the language education of immigrants in two different parts of the policy text (Lo Bianco, 1987) – one dealing with the acquisition of ESL and the other with the teaching and learning of immigrant languages. These two dimensions of the language education of immigrants are, however, closely related in the text:

> The overall purpose of teaching ESL to children is, firstly, for them to obtain full access to English proficiency and, highly desirably, to aim for first language maintenance, where possible. (Lo Bianco, 1987: 85)

This statement can be read as an explicit rejection of the assimilatory discourses of the past and locates English teaching and learning within a multicultural/multilingual agenda that is informed by an ideological construction of diversity as enrichment. The purpose of teaching the national language is therefore not one of replacing the students' existing languages with English but one of developing individual plurilingualism. The articulation of language maintenance as a goal of English teaching is a conflation of the purposes of language education, in that it seems to presuppose that teaching of one language – English – will in some way contribute to the learning or use of another. The main reason for this conflation would appear to be an attempt to distance the NPL from assimilationist views of the role of English in the settlement of immigrants.

Although language-in-education policies for teaching English and immigrant languages to children are brought into close relationship in the

NPL, the discourses around English and other languages are more complex. This is in part because English is discussed in contexts of both adult education and school education, while immigrant languages are discussed only as an element of school education. This is particularly notable in the discussion of adult literacy, where literacy provision is constructed in terms of the provision of literacy in English and not in terms of provision of literacy in the first language of the adult learner. The NPL also conflates provision of immigrant languages in education with other forms of language education, as discussed in Chapter 2. In fact, the place of immigrant languages is ambivalent in the NPL. They are sometimes discussed explicitly and in detail as a set of languages relevant to the linguistic ecology of Australia and at other times they are merged with other languages. The policy boundaries around immigrant languages are thus blurred and cut across other areas of language education.

The policy blurs not only the boundaries between different types of provision of immigrant languages but also the boundaries between the educational provision of English and that of immigrant languages. There is a series of tensions within the policy when it comes to dealing with the relationship of English to the languages of immigrants that relates to the potential threat such languages could pose for the hegemony of English. The policy constructs the inability to speak English in terms of a deficit or disadvantage:

> ESL for adults and children becomes an issue of the utmost importance to enable the maximum achievement of social participation, and economic and educational opportunity. (Lo Bianco, 1987: 85)

English as the language of mainstream Australian society is therefore represented as the language of access and opportunity and an inability to speak English is a factor that limits the possibilities of engagement. Value is therefore allocated to the practices and processes of the mainstream and the teaching of English is located within an ideology of equity and development. English becomes problematised only to the extent that, for those who do not speak English, other languages have importance:

> Domestically there are limitations to the educational, social and economic opportunities of large numbers of Australians which derive exclusively, or substantially, from questions of language (invariably being lack of proficiency in English). In addition, many component groups of Australian society depend on a language (or language variety) with which they identify, to promote, even in some cases ensure, their cultural survival and distinct groups. (Lo Bianco, 1987: 18)

In this text, a dichotomy is established between English and other languages. In this dichotomy, access to English is presented as being the most significant factor for ensuring opportunities in Australia, and that lack of English is a barrier to participation. At the same time, other languages cannot be abandoned because of their significance to the individuals who speak them. English and other languages are therefore depicted as being in tension. The solution to lack of opportunity is to acquire English, but maintaining other languages is necessary for cultural survival. That is, English cannot simply replace other languages. This tension reveals a discursive move away from assimilation, in that it allows distinctiveness as a rationale for preventing the shift to English, but at the same time problematises the retention of other languages as relating to deficits in English. The policy resolves this tension through the promotion of 'the achievement of stable bilingualism' (Lo Bianco, 1987: 85). The framing of bilingualism as the explicit goal of English language learning is the predominant discourse in the NPL about the teaching and learning of English. In this discourse, the preservation of distinctiveness through the preservation of language is balanced against the need for access to the official and dominant language of Australian society. This is framed largely within a discourse about bilingualism in which language proficiency is the focus rather than in terms relating to identity or participation in communities.

Although the NPL does include deficit/disadvantage ideas when it deals with English for immigrants (most explicitly in discussions of the 'lack' of English), it also counters this discourse with alternative constructions. For example:

> This policy recognises that these Australians [i.e. those who speak a first language which is not English], who are both children and adults, are invariably proficient speakers of at least one language other than English. This is an important fact to acknowledge so that incapacity in English is not assumed to equate with incapacity with language. (Lo Bianco, 1987: 85)

Thus, while speakers may lack English, they have other languages which offset this lack. The deficit represented by English is therefore both acknowledged and discursively reduced as the policy tries to navigate between the themes of the need for English and the value of immigrant languages. There is therefore recognition that English is required for participation in society (this is one of the equity rationales of the policy) and a distancing from earlier understandings of English teaching as the assimilatory tool of immigration policy. English learning is therefore constructed as a process of expanding the linguistic repertoire of language learners: 'adding a language to the existing repertoire' (Lo Bianco, 1987: 85).

Language education for immigrant groups is understood not only in terms of the acquisition of English but also in terms of the teaching and learning of immigrant languages. In discussions of language education generally, the provision of immigrant languages tends to be presented in an undifferentiated way, which conflates the learning of these languages by members of immigrant communities and new learning of the same languages by those without a background in the language. Further, in discussions of language maintenance, immigrant languages tend to be conflated with indigenous languages as instantiations of the category non-English-speaking background (NESB),[3] constructing a unitary identity based solely on their lack of English as a home language. These divisions reflect in some ways the sociolinguistic conditions of children of immigrants in Australia. The NPL acknowledges at various points three different types of immigrant learner: those who have migrated to Australia as speakers of the language of their country of origin and who do not speak English; those born in Australia and raised speaking their parents' language, with greater or lesser knowledge of English; and those who speak English and have little or no knowledge of their ethnic group. Thus, the policy needs to deal with both language maintenance and new learning of immigrant languages.[4]

The NPL devotes considerable attention to the maintenance of immigrant languages, and sees the role of education as the development of bilingualism, as already mentioned. This involves articulating the need to acquire English while at the same time presenting a view of English learning that is not assimilatory:

> When the first language is maintained, the planned learning of English at school and the informal learning of English out of school will result in advanced levels of bilingualism. Thus, wherever possible, English and the mother tongue ought to be developed in a complementary way, making it possible for young ESL learners to attain benefits both for their individual intellectual functioning and for the wider Australian community from their bilingualism. (Lo Bianco, 1987: 87)

In the text, learning English and learning the immigrant language are usually referred to in parallel. In this way the NPL makes explicit a goal of developing individual plurilingualism through education in which both the first language of the learner and English are developed. Further, it argues for this in terms of the national interest, although the benefit it confers is unstated. This issue of the national benefit of language maintenance is constructed in terms of Australia's overall linguistic capability: 'it [bilingualism] also contributes to benefits to the society, by enriching its linguistic resources' (Lo Bianco, 1987: 129). Thus, the document seems to construct young learners of immigrant languages as mediators between nations – as individuals who are positioned between English-speaking society and another linguistic community. The national benefit is therefore seen as a form of human capital which can be used to address the linguistic needs of the country. This focus is consistent with the externally and economically oriented rationales the policy gives for language education (Clyne, 1991; Liddicoat, 1996; Ozolins, 1993).

The discourse of national benefit is presented alongside a discourse of individual benefit. The discourse of individual benefits is, however, more developed in the text than that of national benefits, with longer and more detailed descriptions. These benefits are usually articulated in educational terms. One theme in this discourse is the value of continuous learning through the first language of students:

> As far as the more general educational justifications for such 'language maintenance' are concerned, it needs to be recalled that children's initial preschool learning is both conceptual and linguistic, and that these are interrelated. Non-English-speaking children therefore have done general language learning prior to starting school. Continuing this learning in the mother tongue can be more efficient than interrupting it to allow children to acquire English first. Continuing this learning can provide a sounder cognitive and linguistic base from which English can then be acquired. (Lo Bianco, 1987: 123)

This is an argument about educational efficiency: a shift to English is disruptive of learning. The goals of language maintenance are therefore equated with more general goals of educational success and respond to a perception that children of immigrants are at an educational disadvantage (Kalantzis & Cope, 1988). This discourse is therefore located within an equity agenda which is specifically articulated as one of the language-learning rationales of the NPL.

The educational argument in the quote above then moves from general educational development to the learning of English, in that language maintenance will improve the acquisition of English. Language maintenance for children is therefore not constructed as being of value in itself but rather as being an educationally efficient way of developing the language capabilities that will allow students to engage in the mainstream. In this way, language maintenance is presented as a pathway towards the linguistic ideal of the mainstream monolingual English-speaking community, and this is used as a specific justification for plurilingualism. The immigrant language is therefore subordinated to the dominant language and its value is constructed in terms of its contribution to the acquisition of English. The same arguments are taken up elsewhere in the text:

> For some children of non-English-speaking background ... their general educational prospects for successful learning are dependent to some extent on their continuation of their learning in [the] strongest language as a cognitive and linguistic basis to acquire English. Hence, some continued learning of the mother tongue and its development have aspects of equal educational opportunity which transcend the general value of language learning for them. (Lo Bianco, 1987: 129)

In this case, language maintenance is more explicitly constructed in terms of its effects on educational success, with educational success itself being the basis for the acquisition of English. Education in general terms is a 'basis to acquire English', implying that the acquisition of English is a higher, more significant educational goal than general learning through the first language, reflecting the hegemony of English in Australian society.

The NPL also develops a discourse of utility about the first languages of immigrant children by arguing for language maintenance as an apprenticeship in language learning which will have subsequent benefits:

> such children are likely to be able to learn additional languages better, all other things being equal, than monolinguals or poor bilinguals. Their initial bilingualism can serve as an apprenticeship, advantaging them in their language learning. If their first language is a language of major external importance to this country, advantages will accrue to the children, the Australian community and the nation. If they maintain a language not of significant international or regional demand, there remain the domestic, cultural benefits of bilingualism, individual benefits, and their enhanced capacity to acquire additional languages. (Lo Bianco, 1987: 129)

In this quote, children who maintain a first language and also acquire English are presented as being educationally advantaged in language learning. This argument therefore inverts the understanding of immigrant children as being educationally disadvantaged by their lack of English and constructs it in new terms.[5] The discourse of disadvantage, which sees immigrant children as educationally deficient in comparison with monolingual English speakers, is replaced by a discourse which takes plurilingualism as its norm. In constructing this inverted discourse, the NPL casts the new dimensions of comparison in terms of national benefit, re-invoking its own economic and external agenda for language learning. This in turn brings about a division of languages on the basis of their utility. Languages are seen as either significant for Australia or not. The maintenance of those languages which are significant is presented as enabling Australia to engage interculturally with international significant others to establish relationships of perceived national value. Other languages do not have utility in themselves, except in domestic, cultural terms. Instead, their value lies in enabling learners to develop capacity in other languages that do confer perceived national advantage. There is therefore an ideological construction of categories of value to which languages are assigned on the basis of their contribution to the broader ideologies that define national interest.

In the NPL, therefore, the maintenance of immigrant languages is represented as being significant for the individual in educational and other ways, but the benefit of this learning is not presented in its own terms as significant for the individual but rather in terms of its ability to achieve the goals of the wider society – it facilitates the acquisition of the mainstream language and it enables language learners to participate in intercultural relationships of national significance, either directly or by providing possibilities of new successful learning.

Two years after the introduction of the NPL, multicultural policy was reframed in the National Agenda for Multicultural Australia (Office for Multicultural Affairs & Australian Advisory Council on Multicultural Affairs, 1989). The Agenda grew out of a dissatisfaction with an equity-oriented multiculturalism and a desire by proponents of multiculturalism to expand its focus to broader perspectives, especially those of national self-interest (Liddicoat, 2009; Lo Bianco, 1988). The Agenda is not primarily either a language policy or an education policy; however, it does make some statements about language-in-education policy, and especially on the role of multicultural education as a resource for social cohesiveness and for economic development. The main language education dimension is the removal of barriers to the effective use of citizens within the economy: English language skills will increase the participation of minority groups in education and employment:

> Cultural difference continues to be associated with the likelihood and duration of unemployment in Australia.... Overall, those born in non-English speaking countries have higher unemployment rates than other Australians.... Poor English language proficiency and inadequate

knowledge of the Australian labour market – problems which are particularly acute among recent arrivals – exacerbate the problem. (Office for Multicultural Affairs & Australian Advisory Council on Multicultural Affairs, 1989: 129)

The document constructs cultural difference as being problematic for employment and associates deficits in English with such difference. English is presented as the language which will allow members of all ethnic groups to enter into the economic relationships that are necessary for strengthening the Australian economy.

Multiculturalism is also linked to a set of educative goals which focus primarily on the place of social sciences education in fostering tolerance, in particular through developing 'cross-cultural awareness'. Cross-cultural awareness is the key way in which intercultural relationships between groups are conceived in the policy. Education for multiculturalism is seen as developing for each learner a body of knowledge about mainstream and non-mainstream Australian ethnic groups. This is not seen as having a necessary relationship with language and indeed is located outside the field of languages education. Intercultural relationships are therefore represented as relationships that are mediated through the national language – the section of the Agenda policy document devoted to language begins by stating that English is the national language of Australia – and diversity becomes an object of study. The document then moves on to discuss the importance of language maintenance for all languages spoken in Australia and the importance of language learning, including both ESL and foreign languages. It justifies language learning in the following terms:

> Language learning has many rationales – intellectual and economic included – but the promotion of cultural understanding is one of the most important. (Office for Multicultural Affairs & Australian Advisory Council on Multicultural Affairs, 1989)

The role of languages in the Agenda is, then, clearly located in the context of interculturality (framed as intercultural understanding) and languages education is one of the key dimensions through which interculturality is to be developed. The section on languages concludes:

> Multicultural policies therefore seek to ensure that all Australians have the opportunity to acquire and develop proficiency in English, to speak languages other than English, and to develop cross-cultural understanding. (Office for Multicultural Affairs & Australian Advisory Council on Multicultural Affairs, 1989)

There is therefore within the document a two-part approach to interculturalism in education: a linguistic dimension, which frames intercultural
relationships as being related to proficiency in another language; and a non-
linguistic dimension, which frames relationships in terms of knowledge of
other cultural groups, largely in social science terms. In this construction,
all Australians are projected as intercultural subjects and the intercultural
relationship that they will develop is one of understanding others – that is,
as an outside observer of diversity. In this text, language education continues
to maintain the blurred boundaries between languages for immigrant
groups and new learning which existed in the NPL. It conflates these further
through the association of language learning with economic goals, which are
largely external to Australia, and English learning for the internal economy.

The ALLP (DEET, 1991b) maintained some of the discourse of the NPL,
while discontinuing some elements. In particular, its discursive handling of
the acquisition of English is significantly different from that of the NPL. The
inability to speak English is represented in the ALLP in deficit/disadvantage
terms:

> Unemployment levels for recently arrived immigrants are about three
> times higher than for Australian-born workers. Immigrants who do not
> speak English well or at all are particularly disadvantaged. Poor pro-
> ficiency in English is also a major reason for the under-employment of
> many migrants with high professional and technical qualifications in
> their country of origin. (DEET, 1991a: 55)

The ALLP, unlike the NPL, does not balance discursively the idea that
the inability to speak English is a deficit with the idea that those who do
not speak English have a capacity in another language. This means that
the discursive attempts in the NPL to counter a normalised and potentially
assimilatory focus on English with a view of English learning as adding to
linguistic repertoires is largely absent in the ALLP. There is therefore an ideological construction of English as the only language relevant to Australian
society and the speaking of other languages detracts from the ability to use
English. English and the languages of immigrants are no longer discussed
together and, as the adult education provisions of the policy apply only to
the teaching of English, the focus on developing bilingualism is entirely lost.
The maintenance of immigrant languages is addressed only in the discussion
of foreign language learning, which is articulated as having two goals:

> the widespread promotion of the teaching and learning of key languages
> in the national interest … for all learners

the maintenance and development through quality provision in all sectors of languages spoken as first languages by members of the Australian community. (DEET, 1991a: 61)

Language maintenance here is contrasted as an educational goal with the teaching of 'key' languages, although some immigrant languages can be considered as being included in the languages taught in the national interest.

In subsequent language-in-education policy, the language education of immigrants has tended to become invisible. Language-in-education policies have focused exclusively on the learning of foreign second languages by students who are presumed to be speakers of English. This means that policy has not considered the place of English in the education of immigrant children. Instead, ESL has been constructed in terms of English literacy development, in which it is treated as a problematic category. In discussion of the learning of other languages, the focus on the maintenance of immigrant languages has been lost and the emphasis has been placed entirely on the new learning of languages. In the National Asian Languages and Studies in Australian Schools (NALSAS) strategy (COAG, 1994) and its rearticulation as the National Asian Languages and Studies in Schools Program (NALSSP) (DEEWR, 2009a) (see Chapter 2), for example, there is no mention of maintenance programmes in the designated Asian languages, although one of these, Chinese, is the language of a significant community in Australia. The Statement and Plan (MCEETYA, 2005) for languages acknowledges the existence of immigrant languages in Australia as part of its rationale for languages education but it makes no specific comments on the place of these languages in education. Language maintenance is mentioned only in the context of indigenous languages. Immigrant languages are therefore represented as a part of undifferentiated language learning in which the particular needs of immigrants are no longer specifically articulated. The removal of both ESL and immigrant language maintenance from the scope of language-in-education policy documents has meant the loss of any discursive treatment of the 'stable bilingualism' that had been framed as the goal of language learning for immigrants by the NPL. Although this was already missing in the ALLP, the inclusion of both types of language learning in the same policy context meant that associations could be drawn across areas of education. The removal of English from language education documents and the blurring of the boundaries between language learning for immigrants and other forms of language learning have meant that immigrant learners are now absent from policy discourses, except in very superficial ways. Immigrants are no longer understood in language policy as having a special involvement in, or set of needs for, constructing intercultural relationships.

This reflects the blurring of boundaries between types of language learning in Australian policy discussed in Chapter 2 and works to remove language education from the focus of ethnic particularism by downplaying the language maintenance possibilities of language learning.

The same occlusion of language education for immigrants has also occurred in more recent multicultural policy documents. The New Agenda for Multicultural Australia (Commonwealth of Australia, 1999) was developed in the late 1990s as the result of a review of multicultural policy. The New Agenda has no section devoted to languages *per se* but language references are scattered through the document. This marks a move in multicultural policy away from language learning that extends the silence on language maintenance of language-in-education policy. Immigrant languages are therefore constructed as being of limited relevance in the development of intercultural relationships in Australia. While mention of cultural diversity is frequent in the document, there is no mention of linguistic diversity and the general tenor of the document is very different from that of the original National Agenda (Office for Multicultural Affairs & Australian Advisory Council on Multicultural Affairs, 1989) in that multiculturalism appears to have been largely separated from multilingualism, and language diversity and language maintenance are present only if considered to be in some way subsumed by cultural diversity and cultural maintenance. At the same time, the place of English as a common language is reaffirmed. The document does, however, refer to languages in the context of their usefulness for trade – that is, for externally oriented relationships. This is taken up in the only recommendation primarily concerned with language learning:

> Recommendation 29 In a multicultural society such as ours, proficiency in a language other than English is more than desirable; it can be a business or social imperative. If we are to engage the global marketplace and derive maximum benefit from it, Australia must maintain expertise in languages other than English, particularly the major languages of our region and the world. It is therefore very important that teaching languages other than English continues to be a priority and that the value of a multilingual community be better appreciated.... (Commonwealth of Australia, 1999)

It is notable that the arguments in recommendation 29 are not based primarily on a social view of the role and value of language and there is no explicit emphasis given to language maintenance for immigrant communities themselves. Instead, the emphasis is on external uses of language, especially its use in trade. A multilingual community is of importance, but the community envisaged is different from the multilingual communities established in Australia as a result of the demographic trends across two centuries. Language has become a tool for production rather than a feature of social and cultural life. The economically based ideologies of multiculturalism present in the Agenda reached a greater elaboration and a more central importance in the New Agenda.

From the perspective of language policy, the New Agenda provides two key principles for the construction of intercultural relationships for Australia. The first is the separation of multiculturalism from multilingualism (Liddicoat, 1996; Ozolins, 1993). Multiculturalism is constructed as an economically deployable knowledge of others, which frames the ways in which relationships between internal (Australian) cultural groups are to be understood. Its educational manifestation is the development, primarily through the social sciences, of a body of factual knowledge about a range of groups, to promote awareness or understanding in the sense of knowing something about other cultures. The second is the emphasis in language learning on communication outside Australia for the purposes of external trade. The focus of multiculturalism is thus both internal and external. Multilingualism appears to be primarily, if not solely, externally oriented, in that it is presented as deployable for trade, but as English is the national language it appears to be assumed that communication internally is the domain of English. This means that the forms of intercultural relationship envisaged as multilingual cease to have a clear social role and come to have primarily an economic one.

Australia's Multicultural Policy continues this dissipation of emphasis on language education for immigrants. The policy document (DIAC, 2011) marks a departure from other documents in that language education is not explicitly mentioned in the text in the form of either ESL or language maintenance. There are few references to language in the text in any context, although the policy does adopt a rights-focused view of language:

> These rights and liberties include Australians of all backgrounds being entitled to celebrate, practise and maintain their cultural heritage, traditions and language within the law and free from discrimination. (DIAC, 2011: 6)

These rights seem oriented to private language use and there is an expectation that such private decisions will be respected by others. However, there is no policy commitment to bring this private use into the public sphere or to promote it through language education. Multicultural policy has therefore separated from language policy entirely, leaving immigrant languages without specific educational provision.

The policies on language education for immigrants privilege the teaching of English over the teaching of immigrant languages, except for the NPL, which attempts a discursive balancing of the two. There appear to be two ways in which English is privileged. The first is through the emphasis placed on English for internal purposes – economic success, social cohesiveness, participation in society and so on. This emphasis addresses issues of both equity and successful settlement, but also caters to the fear of the emergence of ethnic particularism as a disruptive influence in Australia in the wake of a move away from more directly assimilatory policies. This is least strongly articulated in early policies, which were developed as part of a broad ideology of rejection of assimilation as an inappropriate settlement policy and becomes more strongly articulated with the passage of time. English is also privileged by the ways in which language-in-education policies conflate all forms of language provision into the one policy framing. This means that immigrant languages, specifically as the languages of immigrants themselves, are backgrounded and the focus comes to be on new learning of languages of external importance. Where these are disambiguated in policy, the discourse assumes that immigrant languages serve primarily for intracultural relationships (that is, within ethnic communities) rather than having a role in developing relationships beyond the community. These languages are therefore ideologically constructed as belonging to private space and localised in-group interactions and as having relevance primarily in such contexts.

The emphasis on English constructs the intercultural subject in language-in-education policies for immigrants as being a person who mediates between a home culture and a public culture. This means that the intercultural subject is not constructed in the same way for all learners and responsibilities are placed more strongly on immigrants, as people who bring a new culture into contact with the mainstream, to develop capabilities and practices to allow their participation in both cultures. The maintenance of an immigrant language is represented as a cost to the immigrant of retaining differences. The cost involves the requirement to become an intercultural subject in order to accommodate to the mainstream while maintaining a different language and culture. The intercultural subject is increasingly one who is linguistically and culturally different in the private sphere, but integrated in the public sphere, thereby preserving the hegemony of English.

For the Australian mainstream, the focus of intercultural relationships is not internal to the society but rather orients to economic relationships with other polities. The language capacities developed can serve as ways of engaging with others who speak that language within Australia, and so such relationships are not precluded although they do appear to be incidental to the purpose of language learning. As intercultural subjects, policies after the 1980s project that individuals will relate to diverse others within Australia in relatively passive ways – by knowing/understanding aspects of difference between the mainstream and minorities and by tolerating diversity within society. Active engagement with others is seen as economic in form and economic engagement within Australia is constructed almost exclusively in terms of the use of English and integration into the mainstream culture. The increasing emphasis on economic ideologies over time means that the social aims of language learning in early documents, such as improving social cohesiveness, are weakened and eventually replaced as goals of the mainstream. Instead, cohesiveness becomes a problem that is solved through integration of immigrants into the mainstream, neutralising the public display of difference.

Immigrant Language-in-education Policy in Japan

In spite of the enduring myth that Japan is a monoethnic nation, Japan has a long tradition of immigration, particularly since the mid-19th century. The immigrant population of Japan is composed of two main groups: those who arrived prior to the end of the Second World War and immigrated as subjects of the Japanese Empire; and those who migrated more recently, particularly after 1980 (Mori, 1997). The earlier phase of immigration consists primarily of immigrants from Korea and China, while the more recent phase predominantly involves people of Japanese origin who have migrated back to Japan from Latin America or Asia.

Chinese immigration began with the settlement of Chinese traders in the foreign trading concession in Nagasaki during the Tokugawa Shogunate (1603–1868) and the number of resident Chinese increased after the opening up of Japan in the Meiji period with the arrival of Chinese workers employed by foreign companies and of independent Chinese merchants. Following the First Sino-Japanese War (1894–95) many of these residents returned home; however, Japan acquired Taiwan as a colony following the defeat of China and immigration from there became more significant. The most significant migration into modern Japan dates from the Japanese annexation of Korea as a colony in 1910. From 1910 until 1945, a considerable number of Koreans were brought to Japan and during the Second World War immigration from Korea reached a peak because of programmes of forced mobility. By the end of the war, approximately two million Koreans were resident in Japan, although more than half of these people returned to Korea after the end of the war (Chapman, 2006). The number of Chinese people remaining in Japan after the war was considerably smaller, with about 14,000 Taiwanese choosing to stay in Japan.

In 1947, 'oldcomers' resident in Japan were required to register as aliens, although their status as non-Japanese was not legally established and they technically remained Japanese subjects, as they had been prior to the war. When the San Francisco Peace Treaty of 1951 recognised the independence of former colonies, residents from those countries were considered to be foreigners instead of Japanese subjects (Chapman, 2006; Morris-Suzuki, 2002). Oldcomers are therefore former colonial subjects who lost Japanese nationality following the conclusion of the Second World War. Such people are referred to as 'settled foreigners' (定住外国人, *teijū gaikokujin*) or as 'foreigners resident in Japan' (在日外国人, *zainichi gokokujin*), as are their children born in Japan. This means that they are constructed as outsiders, with an identity and affiliation located outside Japan, regardless of their individual life trajectories and circumstances. While the number of old-comers is significant, there has been little recognition of such immigrants in Japanese language-in-education policies for much of this period, largely because they were represented as being outside the scope of the Japanese education system, which was designed for Japanese nationals.

The beginning of return migration of ethnic Japanese people from overseas, especially South America, has, however, led to the development of some policies relating to the education of children of such immigrant groups in recent years under the name 多文化共生 (*tabunka kyousei*, 'multicultural coexistence'). These policies are framed in general terms which effectively encompass any immigrants. The terminologies adopted construct the identities of immigrants in a number of ways. In many cases, they are labelled simply as 'foreigners' (外国人, *gaikokujin*) or as 'foreign residents' (外国人住民, *gakokujin juumin*). Both terms emphasise the non-Japanese origins of these people and their social, cultural and ethnic distance from Japan. They locate immigrants within the dominant ideology of a monoethnic Japan by retaining their otherness while acknowledging their presence within Japan. In policies designed to include immigrants within the social policy parameters of modern Japan, such terminologies at the same time maintain the distance between them and Japan itself.

The policies also refer to immigrants using the borrowed term ニューカマー (*nyuukamaa*, 'newcomer'). The term 'newcomer', by emphasising the recentness of arrival of immigrant groups, separates out these people from those who migrated to Japan in the past. Policies also refer to a particular subset of foreigners, 'foreign residents of Japanese descent' (日系定住外国人, *nikkei teijyuu gaikokujin*), who constitute a separate group who receive particular treatment in policies. The presence of foreign residents of Japanese descent is primarily the result of changes to the law introduced by the Immigration Act 1990, which granted special visas for descendants of Japanese emigrants and their descendants up to the third generation. These visas enabled people of Japanese descent to remain in Japan long term without restrictions on the type of employment they undertook and were primarily designed as a politically acceptable way to recruit immigrants in unskilled occupations (Sugino, 2008). While the Immigration Act allowed such people to enter Japan, there is no settlement policy at national level and settlement issues are largely left to local jurisdictions. In this terminology, although the foreignness of these people is maintained, their place within the Japanese monoethnic nation is acknowledged. These terms exclude immigrants as foreign and put them at the margins of social existence within Japan – present in but not a part of society. The terms indicate hard boundaries between immigrants and locals that are not altered by their co-presence within the same nation-state. The distinction made that some of these foreigners are of Japanese descent locates them in problematic ways in relation to the Japanese themselves – separated as foreigners but included as Japanese in the ethnic ideology of Japan. In this way they participate in multiple identities and are simultaneously assimilated within Japanese identity and kept distant from it.

There are relatively few government policy documents dealing with the education of immigrants and those there are take the form of guidelines for educational provision for prefectural governments in responding to a local presence of immigrants. The main policies are:

- 地域における多文化共生推進プラン (Plan for Multicultural Coexistence in Local Areas) (MIC, 2006);
- 日系定住外国人施策に関する行動計画 (Action Plan on Measures for Foreign Residents of Japanese Descent) (Council for the Promotion of Measures for Foreign Residents of Japanese Descent, 2011).

The policy document for the Plan for Multicultural Coexistence in Local Areas (MIC, 2006: 3) covers many areas relating to the integration of immigrants into Japanese society, including education. The plan relates to both adult education and school education and the provisions it outlines are similar for both, although modes of delivery vary. It insists on the need for education in the Japanese language for immigrant groups and for support services for children's acquisition of the Japanese language:

(1) コミュニケーション支援
特にニューカマーの中には日本語を理解できない人もおり、日本語
によるコミュニケーションが困難なことによる様々な問題が生じて
いるため、外国人住民へのコミュニケーションの支援を行うこと。
(1) Communication support
Support communication with foreigners, because various problems have
occurred due to the fact that communication in Japanese is difficult
and particularly there are among the newcomers people who do not
understand Japanese.
(MIC, 2006: 4)

In this quote, communication is problematised in two ways: communication in Japanese is difficult; and many 'newcomers' do not speak Japanese. The construction of communication in Japanese reflects aspects of the *Nihonjinron* ideology. *Nihonjinron* has a strongly linguistic dimension and the Japanese language plays a significant role as one of the fundamental manifestations of distinctiveness (Maeda, 2003; Miller, 1982). Japanese is constructed as a language which has a particular *kotodama* (言霊, 'language spirit'), which forms the basis of its uniqueness:

Japanese language (*koto*) has abiding within it a distinctive spirit (*tama*). At the same time it is this spirit that imparts to the language a character or inner essence that ends up making it radically different from any other language on earth. (Miller, 1982: 132–133)

Kotodama does more than make the language distinctive: it makes it difficult, and this difficulty is again unique. As Miller observes, Japanese 'possesses a characteristic spirit or soul that other languages do not enjoy, and … it is more difficult for everyone, foreigner and native speaker alike, than any other language on earth' (Miller, 1982: 51).

To address problems of communication, the document proposes providing communication support. Communication support is interpreted particularly in terms of developing the ability to communicate in Japanese, and provisions relating to communication support are presented as educational solutions, rather than including other forms of support, such as interpreting and translating. That is, communication support is seen in terms of enabling 'foreigners' to communicate with the Japanese in Japanese. The educational orientation can be seen in later provisions of the same document:

② 日本語及び日本社会に関する学習支援
イ. 日本語および日本社会に関する学習機会の提供オリエンテーショ
ンの実施後も、外国人住民が継続的に日本語および日本社会を学
習するための機会の提供を行うこと。

2   Learning support for Japanese language and Japanese society
b.   Providing foreign residents with opportunities for continuously
learning the Japanese language and about society even after carrying
out the orientation providing opportunities for learning the Japanese
language and about society.

(MIC, 2006: 5)

The policy constructs ongoing learning of the Japanese language and about
Japanese society as a key area of educational need for foreign residents. That
is, the Japanese state has some responsibility to ensure that immigrants are
assimilated in terms of both the language and the culture of the host society.
The policy constructs immigrants as becoming intercultural subjects who
can act within the Japanese mainstream. Their interculturality is represented
as a way to minimise the impact of their presence on Japan as a whole. Their
task is to understand those among whom they live and to adapt to them in
order to prevent possible problems. Immigrants as intercultural subjects are
therefore successful to the extent that they do not disrupt the mainstream
and minimise the visibility of their linguistic and cultural diversity in the
public sphere.

In school education, additional provisions are made for specific programmes in Japanese as a second language in the Action Plan on Measures
for Foreign Residents of Japanese Descent.

d. 日本語教育の機会の充実を図るため、定住外国人の子どもの就学
支援事業（「虹の架け橋教室」事業）について、平成23年度も引
き続き実施する。また、事業の評価や検証を行うとともに、子ど
もの就学状況や新たなニーズの把握に努め、より効果的・効率的
な事業として、平成24年度以降の継続について検討する。

d. Continue to implement the school attendance support programme
for children of resident foreigners (the 'Rainbow Bridging Course'
programme) to allow for better access to Japanese language education
in 2011. Also, consider the continuation of the project after 2012 as
a more effective and efficient programme through an evaluation and
inspection of the programme and endeavouring to understand the
conditions for children attending school and any new needs.

(Council for the Promotion of Measures for Foreign Residents of
Japanese Descent, 2011)

These provisions address a core problem – the high dropout rate of immigrant children from Japanese schools, the main consequence of which is expressed in terms of Japanese language acquisition. The document does not detail other educational consequences of school dropout and the focus on the Japanese language seems to parallel the assimilatory discourse of other documents.

In all of the provisions for Japanese language support, the terminology used to refer to the language is significant. In Japanese, there are two terms used to designate the language: 国語 (*kokugo*, 'national language') and 日本語 (*nihongo*, 'Japanese language').[6] The former term is the one typically used to designate Japanese when the educational context is the learning of the language by the Japanese themselves – for example, school documents relating to literacy development regularly use the term *kokugo*. *Nihongo* is the term typically used for Japanese when the context involves teaching and learning Japanese as a foreign language by non-Japanese. The two terms do not designate different language varieties but rather represent different identity constructions of the users. The term *kokugo* is closely associated with national identity – it is the language of the Japanese for the Japanese. It was coined in the Meiji period as part of a nationalistic concern for the establishment of a common national language which would encapsulate Japanese national identity (Coulmas, 2002). In contrast, *nihongo* marks the language user as other. The use of the term *nihongo* in policy documents relating to foreign residents of Japanese descent therefore emphasises their foreignness over their place within Japan and their Japanese heritage – their acquisition of Japanese is for communication, not identity. In this way, the terminology can be seen as exclusionary, in setting learners of the language apart from the Japanese themselves, as Sugino (2008) argues. As the Japanese monoethnic ideology equates the Japanese nation with the Japanese language and Japanese ethnicity, those of Japanese ethnicity who have abandoned their language have also abandoned their identity as Japanese and have entered the sphere of the other.

Immigrants of Japanese descent constitute a problem for the conceptualisation of Japan as a monoethnic nation (一民族国家, *ichiminzoku kokka*). The term 民族 (*minzoku*) used to designate 'ethnic identity' contrasts with the term 人種 (*jinshu*), meaning 'race'. Murphy-Shigematsu (2000) argues that rather than simply referring to a racial grouping, the term *minzoku* includes psychological, social, cultural and linguistic factors. For foreigners of Japanese descent, it appears that, although at one level such people are associated with the Japanese people in that they are part of the Japanese *jinshu*, they are less a part of the Japanese *minzoku*, as they do not have at least some of the additional dimensions beyond descent which are included in the concept. Again, the foreignness of such people seems to predominate over their Japanese identities in policy discourses.

The original languages of immigrants are largely omitted from the discourse of these policies. The documents construct the language issues almost entirely in terms of the development of Japanese. The single exception is a discussion of Portuguese for ethnic Japanese students from Brazil:

> b. 今後開催される予定の日伯領事当局間協議や、ブラジル教育省との会議等の機会を捉え、日本に在住するブラジル人の子どもへの支援（教科書の無料送付等）をブラジル政府に要請する。
> c. 日本にあるブラジル人学校等の教員にブラジルの正規の教員資格を与えるため、ブラジル政府が同国の大学と日本の大学の連携の下で実施する「在日ブラジル人教育者向け遠隔教育コース」に対し、国際協力関係機関の施設を引き続き無償提供し支援する。
> b. Request that the Brazilian government support (distribution of textbooks free of charge, etc.) the children of Brazilian people living in Japan by taking advantage of future meetings between Japanese and Brazilian consular authorities, meetings with the Ministry of Education of Brazil, etc.
> c. Continue to support the 'Remote Education Course for Resident Brazilian Teachers' which the Brazilian government operates in partnership with Brazilian and Japanese universities in order to issue to teachers at Brazilian schools in Japan official teaching certificates from Brazil by offering the facilities of the International Cooperation Agency without charge.
> (Council for the Promotion of Measures for Foreign Residents of Japanese Descent, 2011)

These provisions are interesting in that they construct the role of the Japanese government as one of facilitating the work of the Brazilian government in providing Portuguese language education to students of Brazilian origin living in Japan. Policy documents therefore construct a place for Portuguese but it is one for which the Japanese state is not primarily responsible. Brazilian schools, like most other ethnic schools in Japan, are not accredited by the Japanese Ministry of Education, as to be accredited they would have to adopt the Ministry's curriculum, which is predicated on Japanese as the language of instruction. Instead, such schools are classified as 各種学校 (*kakushu gakkou*, 'miscellaneous schools'). Some of the schools, however, are accredited by the Brazilian Ministry of Education and so are considered to be foreign schools operating in Japan but not as part of Japanese educational provision. The policy focus for these schools in Japan is one of allowing and encouraging a foreign government to provide education for students in Japan, but its obligation is only to allow and encourage this. Japan's policy does not in itself make provision for languages other than Japanese in the education of immigrant groups. The inclusion of a reference to Brazilian schools is particularly interesting in that it occurs in a document relating to the education of 'foreign residents of Japanese origin'. In documents relating to the general education of immigrants there is no mention of Brazilian schools or of the home languages of immigrants. That is, such schools are not acknowledged in educational policy, although they are acknowledged in more limited domains.

Brazilian schools are in many ways a special case in Japanese policy, as there is no policy recognition of languages other than Japanese as media of instruction in Japan in either public or private schools. Although schools do exist that offer education in Korean or Chinese to children of immigrants, these are not accredited by the Ministry of Education[7] and therefore lie outside accepted educational provision (Heinrich, 2011). Like Brazilian schools, Chinese and Korean schools receive no direct central government support[8] and are privately funded (Hattori, 2005; Nomoto, 2007); however, there is no policy commitment in documents relating to the education of Chinese or Korean immigrants to pursue a programme of facilitating such schools as there is in the Brazilian case.

This indicates that there is a discursive space in policy in which other languages may be allowed but that this space is limited to those for whom Japaneseness is otherwise unproblematic. That is, they are Japanese ethnically but not linguistically. Tsuneyoshi (2004) has found evidence that foreign residents of Japanese origin have been educated in the same classes as children of Japanese nationals who have spent a few years abroad for work reasons in spite of the very different linguistic and cultural profiles and needs of these groups. She argues that this indicates a pervading dichotomy between Japanese and foreigner which ignores actual differentiations in favour of a view of Japaneseness understood in terms of ethnic affiliation. The construction of ethnic affiliation is consistent with the ideology of monoethnic Japanese identity and so, as ethnic Japanese, the Brazilian return immigrants seem to pose a lesser problem than immigrant groups who do not share an ethnic identity with the Japanese mainstream. The Brazilian returnees participate in the shared single racial identity (*jinshu*) of the Japanese, and it seems that, for such people, maintenance of another language, in addition to Japanese, is acceptable. In policies about immigrants more generally, however, provisions include those who are outside the monoethnic Japanese identity and they represent a much more basic form of diversity. For such people, linguistic assimilation represents a reduction of the diversity and a greater conformity to the prevailing ideologies of Japanese identity, although it does not equate with acceptance of these people as Japanese or resolve their presence as diverse others in the monoethnic state.

The documents treating resident foreigners are largely concerned with issues relating to the immigrants themselves, although some mention is made of the educational implications of diversity for the Japanese:

> 住民の異文化理解力の向上
> 多文化共生のまちづくりを進めることで、地域住民の異文化理解力の向上や異文化コミュニケーション力に秀でた若い世代の育成を図ることが可能となること。
> Enhancing the ability of residents to understand different cultures
> By developing a multicultural society, it will be possible to enhance local residents' ability to understand different cultures and to help younger generations to excel in intercultural communication.
> (MIC, 2006: 3)

This statement indicates that the movement towards a policy of multicultural coexistence has made available possibilities to develop new capabilities for younger Japanese people. In this way multiculturalism is framed as a form of benefit for the Japanese in allowing them to develop new capabilities. These skills are designated as *ibunka* (異文化) in collocations such as *ibunkarikai* (異文化理解) or *ibunka komyunikeshon* (異文化コミュニケーション). This term *ibunka* is often translated as 'intercultural', but the translation is misleading as the character 異 (*i*) means 'different' – *ibunkarikai* 'understanding of different cultures', *ibunka komyunikeshon* 'communication with (people from) different cultures'. The emphasis here is on cultural difference and the ability to deal with it rather than on adjustment to diversity. It is a term that positions the interlocutor as 'other' and as 'different' and understands diversity in terms of otherness and difference. In addition, the quote above establishes a dichotomy between 地域住民 (*chiikijuumin*, 'local residents') and 外国人住民 (*gaikokujinjuumin*, 'foreign residents') in which the geographic term 'local' is understood in a cultural and ethnic sense. The capabilities being developed here are those that allow the Japanese to understand and communicate with otherness while preserving difference intact. These capabilities are framed as being developed through the experience of diversity locally but are not framed specifically as responses to local diversity.

The policies relating to *tabunka kyousei*, multicultural coexistence, which are designed to address the internal diversity of modern Japan, are linked at the policy level with *kokusaikakyouiku*, international education (see Chapter 2), which is oriented to engagement with external others. The Plan for Multicultural Coexistence in Local Areas in fact includes as one of its goals the promotion of *kokusaikakyouiku*.

多文化共生の視点に立った国際理解教育を推進すること。
Promote education for international understanding from the point of view of multicultural coexistence].
(MIC, 2006: 7)

In framing educational policy relating to internal diversity in terms of an engagement with external diversity, the plan effectively recasts a concern for engaging with a barely recognised internal diversity in terms of a more dominant and high-profile agenda relating to internationalisation. This means that the provisions for educating immigrants become a version of Japan's programme of engaging with the rest of the world and internal diversity is therefore not valued in its own right but rather in terms of what it may contribute to other, more valued agendas. Given this focus, the goals relating to developing the ability of residents to understand other cultures discussed above can be seen not only in terms of cultural understanding for engaging with diverse others within Japanese society but also in terms of the larger agenda of internationalisation which underlies Japanese language-in-education policy.

The Japanese policies construct a one-way intercultural relationship between immigrants and the Japanese, in which only the immigrant is expected to make any accommodation. The intercultural relationship envisaged is one in which the immigrant adopts the language and culture of the mainstream to become integrated or assimilated into it, although without ever attaining to belonging. It positions the intercultural subject as always being an outsider, but without expressing or enacting outsider status. Immigrants contribute to the development of the Japanese mainstream as intercultural subjects only to the extent that they develop capabilities and practices which can be used to engage with external others – a relationship which, as was said in Chapter 2, is predicated on the expression of a particular Japanese worldview to others. The association of immigrants and external others is strengthened linguistically in policy (and other discourses) because both groups are referred to as 'foreigners' (外国人, *gaikokujin*). They are distinguished primarily in terms of location – immigrants are foreigners living inside Japan instead of overseas. This terminology ultimately allows for little real movement in terms of identity and acceptance for the immigrant in relation to the Japanese mainstream.

Immigrant Language-in-education Policy in Italy

Italy has historically been a country of emigration rather than immigration. However, this began to change when the development of the various precursors of the European Union brought foreign nationals to live and work in Italy, often as temporary migrants who would return eventually to their home countries. Economic immigration on a larger scale, however, developed primarily from the 1980s and brought increasing numbers of people into Italy from outside the European Union, especially from Eastern Europe, and from outside Europe, most notably from Africa, China and Latin America (Ambrosini, 2001).

Italy's immigrant language-in-education policies are presented in a number of laws, circulars and decrees relating to either immigration or education. The principal documents are:

- Presidential Decree of 10 September 1982, no. 722 (PDR 722/1982) (Presidenza della Repubblica, 1982);
- Law of 30 December 1986, no. 943 (Repubblica italiana, 1986);
- Ministerial Circular of 8 September 1989, no. 301 (CM 301/1989) (MPI, 1989);
- Ministerial Circular of 26 July 1990, no. 205 (CM 205/1990) (MPI, 1990);
- Ministerial Circular of 28 April 1992, no. 122 (CM 122/1992) (MPI, 1992);
- Ministerial Circular of 2 March 1994, no. 73 (CM 73/1994) (MPI, 1994);
- Legislative Decree of 25 July 1998, no. 286 (Repubblica italiana, 1998);
- Presidential Decree of 31 August 1999, no. 394 (Presidenza della Repubblica, 1999);
- *Guidelines for the Reception and Integration of Foreign Students* (MIUR, 2006).

The education of immigrants in Italy has evolved as the context of immigration has changed (Liddicoat & Díaz, 2008). The issue was first considered primarily in the context of the European Economic Community's Council Directive 77/486 (Council of the European Communities, 1977), which contained provisions for the education of the children of immigrant workers from other member states. Its specific educational provisions involved both instruction in an official language of the country in which they were living (article 2) and promotion of the teaching of their original language and culture 'in accordance with their national circumstances and legal systems, and in cooperation with States of origin' (article 3). The provision concerning the official language of the host country is therefore a more strongly articulated requirement in the directive than the provision of the original language of the students, as the former is a requirement for all students whereas the latter is determined by local circumstances. The teaching of original languages and cultures was constructed primarily as a maintenance programme, 'with a view principally to facilitating their possible reintegration into the Member State of origin'. That is, the first language provisions were seen as relevant to a life beyond Italy and immigration to Italy was assumed to be temporary. When Council Directive 77/486 was ratified by an Italian Presidential Decree PDR 722/1982 (Presidenza della Repubblica, 1982), the provisions of the European Economic Community document were repeated in article 2:

> Nelle scuole che accolgono gli alunni … la programmazione educativa deve comprendere apposite attività di sostegno o di integrazione, in favore degli alunni medesimi, al fine di:
> a) adattare l'insegnamento della lingua italiana e delle altre materie di studio alle loro specifiche esigenze;
> b) promuovere l'insegnamento della lingua e della cultura del Paese d'origine coordinandolo con l'insegnamento delle materie obbligatorie comprese nel piano di studi.
> The schools which receive students … the educational programme must include appropriate support or integration activities in order to:
> a) adapt the teaching of the Italian language and other subjects to their specific requirements;
> b) promote instruction in the language and culture of the country of origin, coordinating it with the compulsory subjects included in the plan of studies.
> (Presidenza della Repubblica, 1982)

The decree therefore envisages a certain amount of adaptation of the programme to the needs of immigrant students but within the context of mainstream educational programmes for Italian students. It also contained administrative processes for the enrolment of immigrant students and a stipulation about how such students should be integrated into existing classes, which further underline that the model of education is insertion into mainstream classes (article 1):

> L'assegnazione alle classi degli alunni iscritti … è effettuata, ove possibile, raggruppando alunni dello stesso gruppo linguistico che, comunque, non devono superare il numero di cinque per ogni classe.

The allocation of enrolled students to classes ... is to be carried out, where possible, by grouping students from the same language group who, however, should not exceed the number of five in every class. (Presidenza della Repubblica, 1982)

There is no mention of special programmes for immigrant students – other than study of their first language and culture – and little attention to individual needs beyond a call for adapting teaching. In developing the education of immigrant groups, the Italian position in 1982, therefore, offered little in the way of a pedagogical approach to teaching these children, and went little beyond specifying a maximum number of students (five) in mainstream classes. There was little treatment of the rationale for language learning; however, it is clear that the teaching of Italian brings learners into relationship with Italian schooling and society. First language instruction was provided for immigrants from within the European Community and the policy reflects an activity within the context of European integration. Italy is therefore represented as engaged with relationships between member states and is dealing with the consequences of this for education. The focus is on developing relationships between immigrants and the mainstream through Italian while preserving to some extent the capacity of immigrants to continue to engage with their home cultures to facilitate their return.

In the late 1980s, the community orientation of language-in-education policies began to be opened up further, reflecting the evolution of Italy's immigration. In 1986, Law 943 (Repubblica italiana, 1986) applied the provisions for the education of immigrants from within the European Community to those from outside ('extra-Community' immigrants). Article 9 of this law specified that education for these immigrants was to include both Italian language and culture and the original language and culture:

2. Al fine di favorire l'integrazione nella comunità italiana dei lavoratori extracomunitari e delle loro famiglie, le regioni promuovono appositi corsi di lingua e cultura italiana.
In order to favour the integration of extra-Community workers and their families into the Italian community, the regions will promote appropriate courses in Italian language and culture.
5. Analogamente a quanto disposto per i figli dei lavoratori comunitari e per i figli degli emigrati italiani che tornano in Italia, sono attuati specifici insegnamenti integrativi, nella lingua e cultura di origine.
Corresponding to what has been decided for the children of communitarian workers and for the children of Italian emigrants who return to

Italy, specific integrative education in the original language and culture is to be put into effect.
(Repubblica italiana, 1986)

Article 5 associates the education of extra-Community children with that of children from within the European Community and those of returned immigrants. The inclusion of the latter group here is interesting, as it seems to be the first time this group has been included in this policy context, with the implication that principles established for Community immigrants were applied also to Italian returned emigrants. The same collocation, quoted directly from the 1986 law, appears in later documents relating to intercultural education, notably CM 205/1990, CM 73/1994, and Legislative Decree 286 of 1998. Because, through analogy, educational provision for the extra-Community group is constructed as being the same as that which applies to any other type of immigrant group, a single activity applies equally to all immigrants. This means that educational approaches that had originally been developed as a response to European integration have been generalised to all immigrant groups. The education of immigrants is constructed as a reciprocal process involving the development of both the language of the host society and that of the home country. These students are therefore positioned as having educational needs relating to two languages and cultures – those of Italy and those of their country of origin – and the educational system takes responsibility for the development of both.

The education of immigrant children from outside the European Community was further considered at the policy level in the 1989 Ministerial Circular on the inclusion of immigrants in Italian schools, CM 301/1989 (MPI, 1989). The circular primarily covers issues relating to the placement of immigrant students in mainstream classes and some aspects of pedagogy for such students. It distinguishes between the needs of two groups of immigrant children: recent arrivals and those who have been in Italy for a longer period before starting school. The former group is seen as having significant problems in terms of both language and adaptation to the new culture: 'i primi avranno non solo problemi di integrazione linguistica, ma manifesteranno problemi di adattamento alle nuove condizioni di vita' ('The first will have not only problems of linguistic integration, but will manifest problems in adapting to new living conditions') (MPI, 1989). The latter group are assumed to have fewer problems and needs: 'I secondi, di regola, dovrebbero in qualche misura possedere i rudimenti della nostra lingua e dovrebbero non più subire problemi acuti di adattamento ai nuovi costumi' ('The second, as a rule, should to some degree possess the rudiments of our language and should no longer suffer acute problems of adaptation to new customs') (MPI, 1989). While these groups are clearly established, there is little consideration in the document of how the differing needs will be addressed. The concern here is for the adaptation or integration of immigrant children into Italy. Diversity is therefore ideologically constructed as problematic, in that those who are different experience problems in engaging with hegemonic Italian. The text here places a stronger emphasis on intercultural relationships to help adaptation to local ways of living than is the case in previous documents, which mainly treat linguistic needs. Immigrant learners are constructed as people with intercultural problems which come from their separation from Italian society – that is, their immigrant background constitutes a problem which needs to be resolved through engagement with the host culture and adaptation to it. The changing focus of policy seems to relate to a change in the nature of immigration, which moved away from temporary immigration for work purposes to a more permanent form of immigration.

Immigrant children are additionally positioned as an intercultural resource in their own right, as Italian and immigrant children are engaged in activities of cultural mediation, with reciprocity of learning.

> sarà opportuno incentivare attività di manipolazione di materiale, di costruzione e di attività ludiche tramite le quali gli alunni della classe, dell'una e dell'altra etnia, individuino canali comunicativi efficaci, accendendo nel contempo processi di reciproca acquisizione di espressioni linguistiche verbali.
> it will be appropriate to set up use of materials, construction and ludic activities through which the students in the class, from one or the other ethnic group, pinpoint their own channels of effective communication, beginning at the same time processes of mutual acquisition of oral linguistic expressions.
> (MPI, 1989)

The role of the teacher is framed as providing opportunities for students to learn to communicate through activities in which language does not play a major role. In terms of language learning, therefore, CM 301/1989 does not provide for much in the way of support or language development for students integrated into mainstream classes. The circular does, though, make a brief reference to the need to engage with cultural diversity:

> La scuola obbligatoria non può non avere come obiettivo educativo una sempre più acuta sensibilità ai significati di una società multiculturale. Ciò suggerisce attività didattiche orientate alla valorizzazione delle

peculiarità delle diverse etnie. Sollecitare gli alunni ad accettare e capire quelle peculiarità contribuisce a promuovere una coscienza culturale aperta.

Compulsory schooling cannot not have as an educational objective an ever more acute awareness of a multicultural society. This suggests pedagogical activities oriented to the valuing of the particularities of various ethnic groups. Getting students to accept and know these particularities contributes to promoting an open cultural conscience.

(MPI, 1989)

This text emphasises a need to educate students to accept and value difference but it is not clear in the document who is to be educated in this way. The framing here constructs diversity as an external concern – something to be observed and understood – but without necessarily engaging with and in that diversity. The insertion of this text in a document about immigrant children suggests that it is education for them, as no other groups of students are mentioned. However, the intention would seem to be that this education is intended for the whole class in which the students are inserted. The focus here then seems to be on the education of the mainstream and implies a relationship between the mainstream and immigrants in which the diversity of immigrants is observed and accepted by the mainstream, which remains external to it. There is no projected adaptation of the mainstream group to the immigrant group projected in this text beyond acceptance. At the same time, there is an expectation of adaptation of the immigrant group to the mainstream, through the acquisition of Italian and cultural integration. This means that the policy discursively constructs intercultural relationships in Italian society as being unequal – the minority adapts to the majority, which in return accepts their difference.

The directions set by this document were extended in subsequent texts. Ministerial Circular CM 205/1990 (MPI, 1990) sought to deal with problems relating to the education of immigrant children against a background of rising immigration. Immigrants are labelled in this text, and most of the later texts, as *stranieri* ('foreigners') – that is, they are positioned as being external to and remaining external to Italian society. This term was less used in earlier documents, which used alternatives such as *lavatori migranti* ('migrant workers'), which emphasises the purpose of the immigration into Italy, or *lavatori comunitari* and *lavatori extra-comunitari*, which encode the relationship of the individual with the European Community rather than with Italy.

CM 205/1990 treats the education of immigrant children under three main themes. The first of these is administrative, involving the enrolment of immigrant children in appropriate class levels, with recognition of study prior to coming to Italy, and the development of a personalised education programme for these students that will foster their integration into mainstream classes. The second theme is concerned with language and culture. The discourse of this section of the circular draws heavily on the provisions made for immigrant students from within the European Community and adapts these provisions to other immigrant groups. It covers two areas: the linguistic and cultural 'integration' of students into mainstream classrooms (that is, the acquisition of Italian language and culture) and the teaching of the original language and culture of the immigrants. The teaching of Italian language and culture is constructed within a framework of adapting learners to Italian schooling. There is little emphasis in the document on Italian language programmes for such students; instead, the document requires the integration of immigrant students into mainstream classes for at least part of their time:

> Di immediata evidenza è il problema dell'integrazione linguistica. Nelle esperienze in atto è risultata assai proficua l'alternanza di periodi di presenza degli alunni stranieri nelle classi con momenti di applicazione e attività di laboratorio linguistico in gruppi di soli stranieri.
> In direct evidence is the problem of linguistic integration. In practical experience, the alternation of periods during which the foreign pupils are present in class with times for practical work and activities in language laboratories in groups of foreigners only has been quite successful.
> (MPI, 1990)

The interaction of immigrant students with Italian students is seen as a device for facilitating the linguistic integration of immigrant students. That is, interaction between immigrants and mainstream students is represented as a way of enculturating immigrants. Intercultural relationships therefore become ways of socialising immigrants into the mainstream.

The third theme involves the introduction of 'intercultural education' as the pedagogical response to linguistic and cultural diversity within Italy. The circular sets out guidelines for intercultural education that were intended to apply to the period of compulsory education in all schools, whether they were attended by immigrant children or not. It identified intercultural education as a structural condition or feature of a multicultural society and as one of the key elements in achieving immigrant students' integration. In the document, intercultural education is constructed as a dynamic mediation between cultural perspectives:

Il compito educativo … assume il carattere specifico di mediazione fra le diverse culture di cui sono portatori gli alunni: mediazione non riduttiva degli apporti culturali diversi, bensì animatrice di un continuo, produttivo confronto fra differenti modelli.

The educational task … takes on the specific character of mediation between the diverse cultures of which the students are bearers: mediation which is not reductive of the diverse cultural contributions, engendering a continuous, but a productive encounter between different models.

(MPI, 1990)

In intercultural education, then, relationships between immigrants and the mainstream are articulated as a productive engagement with diversity. This mediation seems to stand in contrast to the enculturating aim of interactions for linguistic integration discussed above, in that it appears to allow for a mutual influence of cultures on each other. These interactions, given the context in which they are discussed, will be performed in Italian and so Italian becomes a way of enculturating immigrants into the dominant culture but also of communicating immigrant realties to members of that culture. The role of Italian as a vehicular language across groups, and consequentially its hegemonic position in society, is thus normalised.

In this document, there is a perspective articulated in which cultural diversity is valued as a resource for social and personal development:

L'educazione interculturale … avvalora il significato di democrazia, considerato che la 'diversità culturale' va pensata quale risorsa positiva per i complessi processi di crescita della società e delle persone. Pertanto l'obiettivo primario dell'educazione interculturale si delinea come promozione delle capacità di convivenza costruttiva in un tessuto culturale e sociale multiforme. Essa comporta non solo l'accettazione ed il rispetto del diverso, ma anche il riconoscimento della sua identità culturale, nella quotidiana ricerca di dialogo, di comprensione e di collaborazione, in una prospettiva di reciproco arricchimento.

Intercultural education … confirms the meaning of democracy considered as 'cultural diversity' to be thought of as a positive resource for the complex processes of social and personal growth. Therefore, the primary objective of intercultural education is defined as the promotion of the capacity for constructive cohabitation in a multiform social and cultural fabric. It involves not only respect for diversity, but also the recognition of one's cultural identity, in the daily pursuit of dialogue, understanding and collaboration with a target of mutual enrichment.

(MPI, 1990)

The main goal is to promote the capacity for constructive cohabitation in a culturally and socially diverse environment. The term *convivenza costruttiva* reflects an ideological construction of diversity as potentially problematic (a cohabitation which is other than constructive) and intercultural education is seen as the way of resolving the potential problems. Intercultural education is concerned with the development of a capacity which is predicated both on valuing diversity and on understanding one's own identity as a cultural being:

> Ponendo gli alunni a contatto con i problemi e le culture di società diverse da quella italiana, la scuola media favorirà anche la formazione del cittadino dell'Europa e del mondo.
> Placing students in contact with the problems and cultures of diverse societies, of which Italy is one, middle schooling will also favour the development of European and global citizens.
> (MPI, 1990)

Intercultural education is contextualised within the objectives of European cooperation, in particular with ideas of European citizenship. Thus, while the circular deals with the education of extra-Community immigrants, it does so within the broader context of Europe itself and ties the education of immigrant minorities to the diversity and internationalisation agendas of European education (Liddicoat, 2002). In this way, the education of immigrants becomes just one manifestation of education for diversity within the European context. In CM 205/1990, the educational focus moved from the education of immigrants in order to foster greater integration into Italian society to social transformation in response to diversity. The intercultural education approach as it is presented in policy documents presumes the education of Italians as intercultural citizens engaging with the cultures and identities manifested in multicultural Italy alongside the education of immigrants for life in Italy.

What is striking about the text referring to intercultural education is that immigrants themselves are no longer present in the discussion of education. In fact, they provide only the context in which intercultural education becomes necessary: 'La realtà della presenza di stranieri... rende di particolare attualità una nuova e mirata attenzione della scuola alle tematiche connessse alla educazione interculturale' ('The reality of the presence of foreigners ... renders a new and focused attention by the school to the themes connected to intercultural education of particular present relevance') (MPI, 1990). Intercultural education is therefore constructed as the same process for all students and, hence, the contextualising of such education around the objectives of the European Community, as in the preceding quote. Interactions between members of the dominant culture and immigrant cultures are therefore constructed as a field of practice in which to develop the intercultural abilities that are the aim of such education. The contextualising of intercultural education in terms of European citizenship implies that the purpose of such intercultural learning relates to interactions with people from the European Community. That is, the intercultural relationships established between mainstream Italians and immigrants are not so much valued for their own sake as for what they contribute to another agenda. The discursive construction of the primary focus of intercultural relationships for Italians is Europe rather than the internal linguistic and cultural diversity produced by immigrants. The discourses of European integration and immigration have therefore been conflated.

This extension of intercultural education to all students is foreshadowed earlier in the documents in the context of valuing the original language and culture. In CM 205/1990, it is argued that courses on the original language and culture can have a twofold purpose: 'si cerca di includere la "valorizzazione della lingua e cultura d'origine" in progetti di educazione interculturale validi allo stesso tempo per gli alunni italiani e per gli alunni stranieri' ('"valuing the original language and culture" may be included in intercultural education projects, which are equally valuable for Italian students and foreign students') (MPI, 1990). In this text, the purposes of courses relating to immigrant language and culture have been shifted from support for immigrant students to being a resource for general learning. It would appear that two educational needs are conflated here: continued learning of a first language and culture; and learning about a foreign language and culture. Further, there is a potential for the immigrant students' learning of their own language and culture being subordinated to the learning needs of mainstream students, who, because of the limitations placed on the numbers of immigrant students in classes, will always be the majority in any class. In this way, provisions for immigrant groups can perform a double service by responding to mainstream learning goals. Immigrant languages are not seen as specifically immigrant but are collapsed into a broader agenda of language learning, similar to that discussed in the case of Australia in the preceding chapter.

CM 205/1990 therefore appears to be a dichotomous document in that throughout most of the text the focus is on, and only on, *stranieri* ('foreigners'), with the exception of the fragment quoted above in the discussion of courses in immigrants' original language and culture. In the section on intercultural education, however, it is the immigrant children themselves who are absent from the discussion. The specific provisions for immigrant students talk of the 'integration' of these students into the school, into schooling and into Italian society, language and culture. That is, the focus is on bringing immigrants into the mainstream through Italian language and culture – their relationship to the dominant group is one of adaptation, preserving therefore the hegemonic position of the dominant group. The relationship between immigrants and members of the dominant group is essentially a one-way one in which interculturality provides a way for diverse others to adapt to the dominant group but is less required of the dominant group in responding to internal linguistic and cultural diversity. Instead, the dominant group is represented as needing to establish intercultural relationships with external, European, others. Where issues move from a perspective of integration to a perspective of explicit interculturality, this is no longer constructed as being about the learning of immigrants. In intercultural education it appears that the immigrant students become the objects of study rather than the agents of learning and their presence contributes to an intercultural agenda which does not explicitly include them, especially if they are immigrants from outside the European Community.

In 1992, a Ministerial Circular on intercultural education (CM 122/1992) (MPI, 1992) expanded the provisions of CM 205/1990 to include post-compulsory schooling. In so doing, some elements and trajectories found in CM 205/1990 were further strengthened. The 1992 document devotes much attention to the rationale for intercultural education and it is here that much of what has been discussed above becomes concretised. In particular, it is clear that CM 122/1992 is not a document specifically about the education of immigrants, but rather a document about general education, of which the education of immigrants is just one part. This document contextualises intercultural education within the framework of European Union goals, as articulated in the Maastricht Treaty.

> Il cambiamento investe la vita sociale, nazionale e internazionale, la vita economica e produttiva, le relazioni tra i paesi, il disegno e gli equilibri politici delle regioni del mondo: quest'ultimo versante ci chiama direttamente in causa attraverso il processo di unificazione europea definito di recente a Maastricht.
>
> The change [in the modern world] affects social, national and international life, economic and productive life, relations between countries, the design and the political equilibria of the regions of the world: this last consideration affects us directly because of the process of European unification recently defined at Maastricht.
> (MPI, 1992)

Intercultural education is now no longer a process of immigrant education, but rather a process of generalised, internationally oriented education designed to confront the emerging issues of internationalisation and globalisation, especially as they are manifested in a uniting Europe, intersecting with the ideology of European communality and mobility discussed in Chapter 2. Within the context of generalised intercultural education, migration is only one of the considerations: it provides one context for interculturality.

> I processi migratori e la conseguente necessità di trovare nuove forme di convivenza, destinati tra l'altro ad accrescersi perché legati a profondi sommovimenti che attraversano, scompongono e ricompongono popoli, culture e stati, rivelano concretamente lo spessore dei problemi attuali e le gravi ingiustizie di cui sono spesso espressione.
> Migratory processes and the consequent necessity of finding new forms for cohabitation are destined among others to grow because they are tied to profound disturbances that cross, decompose and recompose people, cultures and states; they reveal concretely the extent of the current problems the serious injustices of which they are often the expression. (MPI, 1992)

The terminology here – 'I processi migratori' – does not make it explicit whether the issues involved are immigration or emigration. Migration is more generalised than in the earlier documents, referring to an abstract process of mobility, with attendant social consequences which need to be addressed, rather than focusing, as the other documents do, on the concrete situation of immigration to Italy.

The focus on general education in CM 122/1992 backgrounds questions of language and foregrounds questions of culture. The text has no mention of language education as an element of an intercultural approach, even in the section of the document which specifically addresses the education of immigrants. In fact, in this section, the key issue is not the education of immigrants but rather the ways in which immigrants can be used to foster more general education. Again, immigrants are represented as providing a way to develop a wider, externally focused agenda:

> Tale presenza, con la sua concreta fisicità e con le altrettanto concrete motivazioni al confronto con una o più culture può essere considerata una situazione privilegiata, in cui la piena consapevolezza della propria identità quale base per la apertura alla diversità, il rispetto delle reciproche identità, la comprensione reciproca dei bisogni, costituiscono

un arricchimento e fondano una reale possibilità di conoscenza di una cultura diversa.

This presence [of immigrant students], with its concrete physicality and the equally concrete reasons for comparison with one or more cultures, can be considered a privileged situation, in which the full knowledge of one's own identity, which is the basis for the opening up to the diversity, respect of each other's identities, and mutual understanding of needs, constitutes an enrichment and provides a real possibility for knowledge of a different culture.

(MPI, 1992)

Here immigrant students provide a learning opportunity for intercultural education: they are positioned even more centrally as objects of study than in previous documents. While intercultural education in CM 122/1992 continues to be asserted as a benefit for immigrant children, these children as learners have been subordinated to a broader internationalised objective of which they represent an instance. Intercultural education is constructed as being less for them than about them: they provide a cultural focus on which to base intercultural education, a starting point for the process of valuing diversity which will be applied elsewhere. CM 122/1992 was a statement of the first policy to attempt to define culture in the context of the education policies, and it also tried to distinguish the difference between 'multicultural' and 'intercultural' viewpoints:

Secondo il punto di vista multiculturale, le culture antropologicamente intese sono come una seconda natura, come la atmosfera che circonda i viventi e consente loro di respirare: di qui la necessità di rispettarle di assicurarle ai nuovi nati come un indispensabile corredo per il loro sviluppo, essendo la trasmissione dei modelli culturali funzionale non solo alla sopravvivenza dei gruppi, ma anche a quella degli individui.

Secondo il punto di vista interculturale, le culture non debbono essere intese come corazze che impediscono la crescita né venerate come santuari intoccabili, perché esse sono pur sempre prodotto umano e la loro funzione non è solo quella di proteggere, ma anche quella di sorreggere lo sforzo che ogni uomo deve fare per affrancarsi dalle condizioni di partenza, allargando lo sguardo non solo alla varietà dei modelli di umanità esistenti, ma anche a quelli possibili. La presenza di culture altre nella esperienza diretta dei ragazzi, o nell'atmosfera sempre più pluralistica e variabile che comunque avvolge le scuole, offre nuovi scenari e nuove ragioni per quella elaborazione della cultura di cui parla la legge.

According to the multicultural viewpoint, cultures understood anthropo-
logically are like a second nature, like the atmosphere that surrounds living
beings and allows them to breathe: hence the necessity of respecting them
and assuring them to the newborn like an indispensable endowment for
their development, being the transmission of cultural models functioning
not only for the survival of groups, but also for that of individuals.

According to the intercultural viewpoint, cultures do not have to
be understood like armour that prevents growth nor venerated like
untouchable sanctuaries, because they are also always a human product
and their function is not only that of protecting, but also that of supporting the effort that every man must make in order to free himself
from his starting points, enlarging the focus to include not only the
variety of existing models of humanity, but also those which are possible.
The presence of other cultures in the direct experience of children, or in
the more and more pluralistic and variable atmosphere that envelops
schools, offers new scenarios and new reasons for the elaboration of
culture about which the law speaks.
(MPI, 1992)

Here, the divide between the multicultural and the intercultural is framed
in such a way that multiculturalism is conceptualised as an entrenchment
of an immutable prior cultural heritage, while interculturalism is a dynamic
investigation of cultures which decentres the learner from his/her prior
cultural starting point and moves towards creative engagements with
culture. In this way, the interactive agenda of the education of immigrants
in earlier documents is articulated in a new way – it is the antithesis of
multiculturalism. That is, the adaptation of immigrants to Italian society
is constructed as intercultural, in that it moves away from entrenched
positions, but without a necessary compensatory movement from the
dominant culture and so preserving existing hegemonic relations.

This idea is further developed by a Ministerial Circular on intercultural
dialogue (CM 73/1994) (MPI, 1994), which elaborates on the 'multicultural
society' issue. CM 73/1994 also provides an elaboration of intercultural
education as well as a new construction of immigrant students within
the context of interculturality. In this document, the focus is placed on
minorities in education, whether these are indigenous ethnic minorities, immigrants or other groups. The document examines intercultural education
as the solution to 'multiculturalism' – that is, the problem of diversity. The
document has two key emphases. The first is the prevention of racism and
anti-Semitism, which is to be addressed in intercultural education through
an examination of prejudice and stereotyping. The focus here appears to

be on the education of mainstream Italian students and their reactions to diversity. Immigrant children have become just one element of the multi-cultural school community who are potential victims of prejudice and they, together with other minorities, are again cast primarily in the role of objects of learning rather than learners. The second focus is on the nature of Europe and the world as multicultural societies and on learning to live in supranational contexts based on mobility. The aim is to foster a sense of belonging at supranational levels and engagement with the supralocal. In this section of the document, the place of minorities is further backgrounded against the European agenda of unification.

The change in focus starting from 1994 does not constitute a total redirection of policy in intercultural education from a general programme aimed at all students but rather a re-emphasising in which immigrant education becomes the normal context in which intercultural education is discussed. That is, the nature of the relationship between immigrants and the mainstream receives a new focus. The change is therefore more one of reframing policy. The change in framing can be very clearly seen in Legis-lative Decree DL 286/1998 (Repubblica italiana, 1998), which deals with several aspects of immigration law. In this document, article 38 is headed 'Istruzione degli stranieri. Educazione interculturale' ('Teaching of foreigners. Intercultural education'), that is, it equates intercultural education specific-ally with immigrant education. The document makes two key provisions for education: teaching of the Italian language and dealing with diversity.

1. L'effettività del diritto allo studio é garantita dallo Stato, dalle Regioni e dagli enti locali anche mediante l'attivazione di appositi corsi ed iniziative per l'apprendimento della lingua italiana.
2. La comunità scolastica accoglie le differenze linguistiche e culturali come valore da porre a fondamento del rispetto reciproco, dello scambio tra le culture e della tolleranza; a tale fine promuove e favorisce iniziative volte alla accoglienza, alla tutela della cultura e della lingua d'origine e alla realizzazione di attività interculturali comuni.
1. The implementation of the right to schooling is guaranteed by the state, the regions and also by local bodies providing appropriate courses and initiatives for Italian language learning.
2. The school community welcomes different languages and cultures as values which give a basis to mutual respect, cultural exchange and tolerance; to this end it promotes and favours initiatives directed to reception, protection of the original language and culture and the undertaking of common intercultural activities.

(Repubblica italiana, 1998)

The second paragraph here, through terms such as 'rispetto reciproco' (mutual respect) and 'attività interculturali comuni' (common intercultural activities), implies that intercultural education is a dimension of general education. However, at the same time, its location in a document concerning immigration and in an article which treats the education of immigrants specifically weakens such an interpretation and the focus on immigrants is foregrounded. The emphasis here is on the teaching of Italian in paragraph 1 and on the toleration of, but not necessarily educational support for, other languages in paragraph 2. Languages and cultures are therefore constructed ideologically as a private attribute which is brought to school and which is accepted by the school and the school community, but which is not something that is addressed in education, except through intercultural activities aimed at developing acceptance of existing diversity.

In 1999, Presidential Decree DPR 394/1999 (Presidenza della Repubblica, 1999), which was broadly concerned with questions of vocational education, placed a clear emphasis in article 45 on establishing initiatives for the education of immigrants and its provisions are clearly located within a context of the immigrant community itself, as is shown in paragraph 8:

> 8 Il Ministro della pubblica istruzione, nell'emanazione della direttiva sulla formazione per l'aggiornamento in servizio del personale ispettivo, direttivo e docente, detta disposizioni per attivare i progetti nazionali e locali sul tema dell'educazione interculturale. Dette iniziative tengono conto delle specifiche realtà nelle quali vivono le istituzioni scolastiche e le comunità degli stranieri al fine di favorire la loro migliore integrazione nella comunità locale.
>
> The Ministry for Public Education, by issuing the directive on education for in-service education of inspection, administration and teaching personnel, (laid) such plans to establish national and local projects on the theme of intercultural education. Such initiatives take into account the specific realities in which scholastic institutions and communities of foreigners exist in order to facilitate their best integration in the local community.
> (Presidenza della Repubblica, 1999)

This document presents intercultural education as a way of integrating immigrants (foreigners) into the local community. Intercultural relationships for immigrants are therefore focused towards developing an accommodation with the mainstream. Moreover, intercultural education in this document has moved beyond a school context, in which case it is possible that whole school populations are to be included in intercultural education, regardless of policy constructions, and the decree includes it as a dimension of the education of adult immigrants, as seen in paragraph 6:

> 6. Allo scopo di realizzare l'istruzione o la formazione degli adulti stranieri il Consiglio di circolo e di istituto promuovono intese con le associazioni straniere, le rappresentanze diplomatiche e consolari dei Paesi di provenienza, ovvero con le organizzazioni di volontariato iscritte nel Registro di cui all'articolo 52 allo scopo di stipulare convenzioni e accordi per attivare progetti di accoglienza; iniziative di educazione interculturale; azioni a tutela della cultura e della lingua di origine e lo studio delle lingue straniere più diffuse a livello internazionale.
>
> In order to undertake instruction or education of foreign adults the district council for primary and secondary schooling promotes agreements with foreign associations, diplomatic and consular representations from the countries of origin ... for establishing plans for reception; intercultural education initiatives; activities to protect the home culture and language.
> (Presidenza della Repubblica, 1999)

When the target population moves from children to adults, the emphasis is clearly placed on intercultural education only for those who are not members of the mainstream Italian culture. That is, intercultural education here is designed to integrate those from outside Italy into Italian society and not as a general educative programme for all adult Italians, who are not subject to the educational system and to the provisions of educational policy.

In *Linee guida per l'accoglienza e l'integrazione degli alunni stranieri* (*Guidelines for the Reception and Integration of Foreign Students*) (MIUR, 2006), the use of intercultural education as a means for integrating immigrant students into the Italian mainstream is stated at its strongest:

> L'educazione interculturale costituisce lo sfondo da cui prende avvio la specificità di percorsi formativi rivolti ad alunni stranieri, nel contesto di attività che devono connotare l'azione educativa nei confronti di tutti. La scuola infatti è un luogo centrale per la costruzione e condivisione di regole comuni, in quanto può agire attivando una pratica di vita quotidiana che si richiami al rispetto delle forme democratiche di convivenza e, soprattutto, può trasmettere le conoscenze storiche, sociali, giuridiche ed economiche che sono saperi indispensabili nella formazione della cittadinanza societaria.
>
> Intercultural education constitutes the background against which the specific nature of a developmental process relating to foreign students

begins, in the context of activities which should influence educative action for all. School in fact is a central place for the construction and sharing of common rules; as such it can activate a practice of daily life which is enriched with respect to democratic forms of cohabitation and, above all, it can transmit the historic, social, legal and economic knowledges which are indispensable in the development of social citizenship. (MIUR, 2006: 3)

Here, intercultural education is linked specifically with the educational development of the immigrant child and is located within the context of the development of common rules and practices of daily life. It is associated with the acquisition of information about the society in which the immigrant will live and which will be the basis of his/her citizenship. That is, it seeks to develop a shared common knowledge between immigrants and their Italian hosts. The document includes a possible idea of a more generalised intercultural education, but remains nonetheless fundamentally directed at the education of immigrant children (which is, after all, the area covered by the document) and aimed at their integration into society. There is a fundamental tension in the document between education to adapt immigrants and integrate them into Italian society and a pluricultural understanding of the society which will result from such education. Interculturality is therefore a tool which will allow immigrants to participate within the mainstream, adapting to it, while having the possibility of preserving private cultural differences. The guidelines are at pains to argue against an assimilationist interpretation of its provisions:

L'educazione interculturale costituisce lo sfondo da cui prende avvio la specificità di percorsi formativi rivolti ad alunni stranieri, nel contesto di attività che devono connotare l'azione educativa nei confronti di tutti. Percorsi che rifiutano sia la logica dell'assimilazione, sia la costruzione ed il rafforzamento di comunità etniche chiuse ed è orientata a favorire il confronto, il dialogo, il reciproco arricchimento entro la convivenza delle differenze.

Intercultural education constitutes the background from which the specificity of the educational pathways aimed at foreign students begin, in the context of activities which should connote educational action for all. Pathways which reject the logic of assimilation and the construction and reinforcement of closed ethnic communities and are oriented to favour comparison, dialogue, reciprocal enrichment in the coexistence of differences.

(MIUR, 2006)

Thus, intercultural education is a non-assimilatory education practice addressed to foreign students, but which has a relevance to education for all students and which takes place in a context of exchange.

Collectively, these documents show a movement in the development of intercultural education as a concept in Italian educational policy, from a focus on the education of immigrant children, through a widely focused educational approach for all children in Italy and back to a more strongly immigrant focus. This cycle represents two different orientations to education in response to emerging linguistic and cultural diversity as the result of immigration: the education of immigrants for participation in society; and the education of the society in which the immigrants will live. These orientations are not necessarily mutually exclusive; however, the development of policy over time in Italy shows that emphasising one dimension may de-emphasise another. They construct intercultural relationships between immigrant groups in which the immigrant group is positioned as requiring interculturality as a way of integrating into the mainstream – that is, interculturality for immigrants is to some extent assimilative and represents the cost of maintaining linguistic and cultural diversity in the host society. Intercultural relationships for the mainstream are not directed to the minority but rather the external others – the interculturality of immigrants is therefore not directly reciprocated. To the extent that an intercultural relationship is envisaged between members of the dominant culture and members of immigrant minorities, it is one of acceptance of diversity by the mainstream. That is, immigrants integrate and establish relationships with the mainstream, and the mainstream responds by accepting the diversity they retain.

Conclusion

These three polities reveal a number of common themes in how they respond at the policy level to the presence of immigrant ethnolinguistic minorities, although there are also different responses to the diversity brought by such groups to the host society.

All three polities present as the main language-in-education issue the teaching and learning of the official language to immigrants, and this concern is one which is present to some extent in both school education and adult education. The policies therefore construct command of the dominant language of the society as the key language need for immigrants. The dominant language is emphasised for a variety of reasons: access and participation, employment, the reduction of problems, maintaining social cohesion, and so on. These reasons orient both to issues concerning the welfare of the immigrant in the host society and also to the social goals of the host society itself. Notably, the focus on social cohesion orients to diversity itself as inherently problematic and constructs the acquisition of the dominant language, and its associated culture, as the solution to the problem of diversity. Immigrant languages are always depicted in a way that maintains the hegemonic position of the dominant language and culture and therefore of the dominant group. In this way, in responding to the presence of diversity in society, the dominant group is able to maintain moral, political and intellectual leadership by diffusing its own beliefs about the role and nature of its own language and culture in such a way that its own interests become equated with those of society at large, and of all sectors of that society (Gramsci, 1975). The policies typically make reference to the needs of non-elites and, as Condit notes, 'hegemony is a negotiation among elite and nonelite groups and therefore always contains interests of nonelite groups, though to a lesser degree' (Condit, 1989: 119). Effectively, the discourses of policies for linguistic minorities shape the interests of minority groups in terms of the interests of the majority.

The focus on immigrant languages in education is much less developed in all three polities, and in Japan it is almost non-existent. In both Australia and Italy, the earlier periods of language-in-education policy for immigrants appear to have given greater emphasis to the languages of immigrants. In Australia, this seems to have been associated with the move from assimilation to multiculturalism in settlement policy and a desire to distance policy from assimilationist discourses. In Italy, it seems rather to stem from the construction of immigration as temporary, work-related sojourns by people from within Europe and policy was concerned with facilitating the return of immigrants to their home countries and recognition of commitments within the project of uniting Europe.

The languages of immigrants in education in all three policy contexts tend to be marginalised or at best their role ambivalent. In Australia, the teaching of some immigrant languages as additional languages is maintained in policy discourses often because of their role as official languages of other polities rather than as immigrant languages in Australia. This means that many immigrant languages are passed over in silence in policy texts. Language maintenance programmes have largely been allocated to complementary education, which is financially supported by the government but which exists outside the normal parameters of the educational system. Such programmes typically involve additional time commitments for immigrant children after school or at weekends. In Italy, policy documents are increasingly silent about the place of immigrant languages as they shift the educational emphasis more to Italian. Nonetheless, more language-in-education policies do include languages of the European Union as additional languages and so some languages of immigrant groups are given a place in a broader, externally oriented policy (Cignatta, 2007). In Japan, language maintenance is outside the Japanese education system, having been allocated to unaccredited or foreign schools, and the main policy role of the Japanese government involves facilitating the work of the Brazilian government in Japan.

One common discourse across the polities, although much more weakly articulated in Japan than elsewhere, is the role of education in the immigrant language in securing broader national goals in education. There is some acknowledgement of the issue of educational success for immigrant children studying in a new language and also emphasis on the role which learning of the first language may play in acquiring the dominant language. This means that where immigrant languages are included, this is often as part of the project to develop the dominant language rather than being attributed educational value of their own.

One of the issues that emerge from the study of these policies is that the intercultural relationship being envisaged can involve either a relationship of accommodation of the immigrant to the mainstream – that is, interculturality can be seen as a device for integration – or as a mutual accommodation of groups. The intercultural subject here is therefore either a person who accommodates to the culture of others, or one who integrates into the mainstream while maintaining a personal, private cultural distinctiveness. Both possibilities exist in the policies from Australia and Italy, but the prominence given to the dominant language in language-in-education policies and the marginalisation of the immigrant languages serve to construct a particular view of intercultural relationships between immigrants and members of the dominant group which is similar across all three polities. Firstly, intercultural relationships are expressed largely in terms of an accommodation of the immigrant group to the mainstream. It is therefore a largely monodirectional relationship. This is the dominant policy discourse in all three polities, although it is articulated with different force in each. In Japanese policy texts, it is almost the only possibility which is presented for intercultural relations, although it is acknowledged that Japanese people do need to understand and tolerate difference. In Italian policy texts, accommodation to others is acknowledged where the focus of policy primarily involves immigrants from the European Union, in which case it meshes with other foreign and social policy goals, but it is backgrounded in discussion of other immigrants and eventually lapses as a policy position. Italian policy also articulates the role of intercultural relationships in socialising immigrants into Italian society through contact with the mainstream (e.g. CM 205/1990) – that is, intercultural relation-ships can have an assimilatory purpose that supports the hegemony of the official language. Australian policy holds open the possibility of a reciprocal engagement between members of the immigrant and dominant groups, but presupposes adaptation of immigrants to the mainstream as the norm.

The intercultural relationship between immigrants and the mainstream is constructed as an asymmetrical one. It is asymmetrical in a number of ways. Firstly, as argued above, it is asymmetrical in that it involves an accommodation of the immigrant to the mainstream rather than an accom-modation of the mainstream to the immigrant. It is also asymmetrical in the role languages have in this relationship. All of the policies discussed assume that intercultural relationships will normally be conducted in the dominant language. Members of the mainstream are not positioned as needing to acquire the languages of immigrants, although in Australia and Italy languages acquired for other purposes may also be used with some immigrant groups. In Japan, opportunities for acquiring immigrant minority languages such as Portuguese, Chinese or Spanish are negligible in school education, in which English predominates. Thirdly, it is asymmetrical in the ways in which the intercultural subject is established. Where the intercultural subject is a member of an immigrant group, he/she is expected to participate fully in the language and culture of the mainstream and background cultural distinc-tiveness. The immigrant intercultural subject therefore deploys a range of practices relating to social integration, cultural mediation and linguistic per-formance to achieve membership of the mainstream culture. The mainstream intercultural subject is constructed differently, as an individual who knows about and accepts the diversity of others but does not necessarily participate in it. This means that the mainstream intercultural subject is constructed as an observer and interpreter of cultural difference and can use these practices to maintain social cohesion through tolerance and understanding. Where policies do discuss intercultural engagement between the mainstream and immigrants, they may construct the purpose of this relationship as being preparation for intercultural relationships with international others. That is, the main locus of value in engaging with immigrants is placed not on the development of relationships with linguistically and culturally diverse others within the polity but on practices this can develop for deployment outside. The intercultural subject in each polity is therefore an individual who can deploy certain practices in the dominant language to achieve relationships across cultures, but the practices used are different. These language-in-education policies typically construct immigrants as moving from existing identity and cultural positions towards the mainstream, which does not reciprocate and thereby maintains its hegemonic position.

By establishing such asymmetries in discourse, language-in-education policies, even when superficially sympathetic to linguistic and cultural diversity, project a future in which the power relationships between immigrant and mainstream are preserved. In this future, immigrants adapt to the mainstream, although maintaining private linguistic and cultural distinctiveness, while the mainstream is left relatively untouched by the diversity within its midst. Such interculturality is represented as a cost to the immigrant who wishes to maintain linguistic and cultural distinctiveness – it requires the development of practices and capabilities which are in addition to those required by the mainstream.

Notes

1. The term 'community languages' in the Australian context does not include indigenous languages (other than Australian Sign Language, which constitutes a special interpretation of indigeneity) and indigenous languages constituted a separate category, subject to different policies and programmes (Liddicoat, 2009).
2. Multiculturalism was further constructed as a policy for immigrants in that the place of indigenous Australians in multicultural Australia has not been clearly articulated. The languages and cultures of indigenous Australians were largely absent from the core policy documents and educational programmes. In cases where indigenous Australia is recognised within multiculturalism, it is often as an added afterthought (Liddicoat, 2009).
3. Although the NESB group does include indigenous people, the policies relating to language maintenance discussed here seem to relate more to immigrants than to indigenous people, as much of the discourse focuses on communication outside Australia.
4. In this discussion, only policy statements relating to language maintenance are discussed as policies for new learning do not distinguish immigrants with a heritage connection to the language from those without. Policies for new learning are discussed in Chapter 2.
5. This advantage has also been constructed in terms of 'unfairly advantaged' in language learning, in that learners with a heritage connection to the languages are seen as having possibilities for successful learning that are not available to the 'normal' language learner (Clyne, 2011).
6. For a discussion see Miller (1982, 1986).
7. Korean schools were initially allowed to be registered by prefectural authorities in the years following the Second World War; however, in 1948 Korean schools were required to conform to the 1947 School Education Law, which involved using Japanese as the medium of instruction, and those which did not conform were closed (Okano, 2009; Tai, 2007).
8. Some schools do receive support from prefectural governments and Nomoto (2007) estimates that 12.8% of Brazilian schools receive such funding.

4 Languages in the Education of Indigenous People

Introduction

The term 'indigenous' has as its starting point a geographical and a historical dimension: 'The idea of indigenous people must have some basis in the territory inhabited by them in the past and the present' (Béteille, 1998: 190). The term implies the existence within the same polity or geographical area of a group which is not indigenous – that is, an exogenous group. As Béteille (1998: 188) notes: 'The designation of any given population in a region as "indigenous" acquires substance when there are other populations in the same region that can reasonably be described as settlers or aliens'. Moreover, Béteille argues that the designation is of significance when the group designated as indigenous comes into contact with the exogenous group through a historical process of occupation or usurpation. Thus, the designation of a group as indigenous indicates something not only about the historical origins of a group within a particular place but also about power relationships between that group and other groups, in which the indigenous group is or has historically been subordinated in some way. Thus, the 'French', 'Spanish' or 'Japanese' ethnic group may be indigenous to parts of the countries that they occupy in the sense of having a historical origin within those countries, but they are not considered to be indigenous groups because they are the dominant and dominating ethnic groups within those countries.

The processes of occupation and usurpation that can be taken to be definitional for identifying an indigenous group result from territorial expansion of one polity at the expense of another. This can involve the incorporation of neighbouring territory into a polity, as was the case in the expansion of European nation-states, Japan, China and many others. In this situation, ethnolinguistic minorities come to be included within an existing polity as the boundaries of the polity change, resulting in increased linguistic and cultural diversity within the polity. This process can be considered to be colonisation by annexation. Alternatively, colonisation can involve the political, economic and social control by one polity of another which remains external to the colonising polity. In this case, the occupied territory is not incorporated into an existing polity but retains a form of subordinated identity. In the former type of colonialism, inhabitants of the new territory are typically considered to have become citizens of the colonising power and are subject to the laws, policies and practices of the polity into which they have been incorporated. In the latter case, the colonised people are not usually considered to be citizens of the colonising power, although they may be considered subjects of it, and may be governed by different laws, policies and practices from those in the colonising polity.

Colonisation may involve substantial immigration of members of the colonising group into the colony. This may result in a substantial change in the demographic profile of the colonised territory – the colonising group may even become the demographically dominant ethnic group, as has been the case in Australia and North America. Alternatively, a smaller number of colonisers may remain a demographic minority but exert disproportionate social, political or economic power over the indigenous majority. This was the case in South Africa, where the dominant European group remained separate from the indigenous peoples and reinforced that separation through the policies of apartheid, and in South America, where the colonisers and indigenous people blended to create a new dominating ethnic group, the mestizos, who were neither strictly indigenous nor exogenous, although they adopted the language of the colonisers.

One consequence of the process of colonisation, regardless of the form it takes, is that a new language is introduced into the linguistic ecology of indigenous people – the language of the colonising group. Over time, the presence of this language usually leads to language shift in indigenous communities from the indigenous language to the language of the dominant or dominating group. This may be the result of an explicit official policy aimed at reducing internal linguistic diversity or it may be the result of implicit policies and social, political and economic pressures (Hornberger, 1998) within the polity which undermine the value of local languages in favour of the language of the dominant group. Crawford (1995: 22) argues that indigenous groups are under pressure from modern cultures and the development of new technologies which threaten not only languages but also other aspects of society and culture: 'destruction of lands and livelihoods; the spread of consumerism, individualism, and other Western values; pressures for assimilation into dominant cultures; and conscious policies of repression'. One of the consequences of colonialism has been language shift away from local languages to the language of the dominating group and discussions of indigenous language policy frequently highlight the loss of languages which has resulted from colonisation (for example, Crawford, 1995; Hornberger, 1998; Walsh, 2005). Indeed, in many cases, language shift in indigenous contexts involves 'language death' (Campbell, 1994; Crystal, 2000; Dressler, 1988) as the language concerned is not spoken outside the polity or, if it is spoken, it is usually a subordinated language in other polities as well.

There is no simple correlation between colonisation and language policy. As Ricento (2003) notes, the same ideological imperative – imperialist control of economic resources – may be manifested in very different forms of policy, from support of the indigenous language to restrictions on its use. For example, Pennycook (2002) argues that the inclusion of Cantonese in British language-in-education policy in Hong Kong amounted to an attempt to control the indigenous population by inculcating ideals of docility through the manipulation of Confucian principles. Vernacular language education aimed to develop loyalty, obedience and acceptance of colonisation and kept the Chinese population in a form of tutelage to Britain. Conversely, Diallo (2010) argues that in West Africa, French colonial educational policy introduced French language education in order to inculcate a sense of connection between colonised people and the French state, which emphasised the inclusion of African people within the ambit of French culture, marginalised and devalued local languages and cultures and constructed a sense of inferiority for them.

The rights of indigenous communities began to be recognised in policy in the latter decades of the 20th century. Indigenous rights have been a focus of international attention, notably in the work of the United Nations (UN). The UN declared the decade 1994–2004 as the first World Decade on the Rights of Indigenous Peoples and 2005–2015 as the second. The Declaration on the Rights of Indigenous Peoples (United Nations Organization, 2008) was adopted on 13 September 2007 by the UN General Assembly. The adoption of the Declaration completed a long process that began with the development of a Draft Declaration which was adopted by the Human Rights Council in 1994. Article 13 of the Declaration identifies the revitalisation, use and transmission of an indigenous language as a right, while article 14 includes a right relating to the inclusion of indigenous languages in education. These developments at international level have been paralleled in some case in individual polities, whose language policies have tended to focus on issues of language maintenance in such communities (Hornberger, 1998).

Indigenous Language-in-education Policy in Australia

The history of indigenous[1] languages in Australia has been one of continued language loss since the arrival of Europeans in 1788. For most of this period, little attention has been paid to the place of indigenous languages in education except insofar that it was the case that indigenous people were routinely educated in a monolingual English classroom environment, regardless of their own language background, as a part of an assimilationist programme (Welch, 1988).

The first Commonwealth government language-in-education policy relating to indigenous languages was the introduction of bilingual schools in the Northern Territory announced in 1972. Although the policy was a national document, its scope was limited to the Northern Territory, for which the Commonwealth government was at the time responsible. The introduction of bilingual programmes was designed to address the school needs of students who spoke an indigenous language at home and were acquiring English as an additional language in the school system. The first policy with a national scope was the National Policy on Languages (NPL) (Lo Bianco, 1987), introduced in 1987. This policy was the first of a number of broadly focused language policies which included an educational component relating to indigenous languages and a number of policies on the education of indigenous people which included a language component. Language-in-education policy for indigenous languages in Australia has therefore been spread over two distinct domains of policy-making: policies for language education and policies for indigenous education. The relevant policies are outlined in Table 4.1.

Table 4.1 National language-in-education policy for Australian indigenous languages

Language policies	Indigenous education policies
National Policy on Languages (1987)	
	Aboriginal Education Policy (1989)
Australian Language and Literacy Policy (1991)	
National Statement and Plan for Languages Education in Australian Schools (2005)	
Indigenous Languages – A National Approach (2009)	
	Aboriginal and Torres Strait Islander Education Action Plan (2011)

The NPL identified three distinct groups for whom indigenous languages education programmes were needed, each with different needs (Lo Bianco, 1987: 107): 'traditional Aborigines'; 'urban Aborigines'; and 'the non-Aboriginal community generally'. This formulation constructs a dichotomy between indigenous people but with one pole based on time ('traditional') and the other on location ('urban'):

> For the present purposes, two main groups can be identified: those whose background, living patterns and language situation are primarily traditional or traditionally oriented; and those for whom these characteristics are primarily urban. (Lo Bianco, 1987: 107)

Thus, the dichotomy between unlike dimensions is reconciled in the NPL through an equation of the two which is essentially cultural: a traditional culture and an urban culture, the former being indigenous and the latter more assimilated to the mainstream. This is borne out when the document moves on to characterise these groups linguistically. Traditional Aborigines are 'characterised linguistically by their use of an Aboriginal language rather than English in their homes and family situations' (p. 107), while urban Aborigines are defined as 'linguistically distinct in that they regularly speak a variety of English in their home and family situations' (p. 107).

This categorisation is based on sets of terms which entail an unvoiced other dimension. The classification 'urban' is one which involves dichotomies between 'urban' and 'rural' (agricultural), or between 'urban' and 'regional/remote' (isolated by distance), which are a common classificatory feature in Australian policy discourses more generally. The urban–rural/remote dichotomy is an asymmetrical one in economic and social terms, as non-urban communities are understood as lacking in facilities, losing access to services, unable to sustain populations because of outmigration and influenced by unpredictable ecological events (Hugo, 2002; Lockie, 2000).

The majority of speakers of indigenous languages reside in areas which are classified as rural or regional/remote, while many people who identify as indigenous living in cities are speakers of an English variety. However, the opposition here implies that indigenous languages and cultures are not a feature of urbanised life, which correlates with speaking English in home and family situations. Indigenous languages have therefore been represented as the languages of indigenous spaces, not the languages of urbanised spaces, which expect a shift to English as the language of the home as a part of an engagement with the linguistic and cultural mainstream.

The classification 'traditional' entails an opposition with 'modern' in which modernity implies beneficial progress towards the norms of the west in which the traditional is understood as backward or deficient according to valued dimensions of economic and social life (Phillipson, 1996). The traditional is therefore at variance with the wider world: it is 'a "closed circle" which integrates social and cultural practices that look inward and downward, not upward and outward' (Petras, 1994: 2073). Moreover, 'tradition' implies a static construction of the past in which the traditional is always the same – when traditions evolve they are no longer traditional – and engagement with the modern is necessarily at odds with tradition. The terms used to characterise indigenous languages are therefore not neutral but entail ideological constructs of their signification and these ideologies tend to cast indigenous languages as marginal.

The utility of indigenous languages is represented in terms of knowing more about the indigenous past:

> Aboriginal languages represent a way for non-Aborigines seeking to increase their knowledge of traditional Aboriginal history and culture to gain insight, understanding and knowledge. Aboriginal languages, through their sociolinguistic patterns of use, and their rich store of ideas and stories, can reveal Aboriginal cultural values in unique ways. (Lo Bianco, 1987: 117)

Indigenous languages are therefore presented as granting the capacity to develop an intercultural relationship between non-indigenous people and the indigenous past rather than the indigenous present. The domain of engagement is history and culture, but both qualified as 'traditional', positioning them outside the norms of history and culture; furthermore, the stipulation of 'ideas and stories' hints at a fictional and folkloric nature of the knowledge to be accessed through these languages. Aboriginal culture is characterised as pre-modern – as 'predominantly a non-material, spiritual culture' (p. 75) – which inevitably contrasts with the material and scientific culture of the mainstream.

The NPL renders the introduction of indigenous languages into the realm of modernity problematic in both cultural and linguistic terms:

> The use of the traditional language to impart knowledge which is not historically part of the discourse conducted in such languages raises problems of a linguistic and sociological nature. Family relationships can be affected when children have their knowledge of language extended beyond what their parents are able to discuss in the language, and lin-guistically careful and systematic work is required to utilise the internal resources of the language concerned to extend its capacity to deal with new concepts and skills. (Lo Bianco, 1987: 113)

In this text, the possibility of using traditional languages for modern discourses raises problems that are linguistic – the need for corpus planning to develop the necessary linguistic tools for such discourses – and disruptive of family relationships by introducing new discourses into traditional languages and so disrupting the stasis of the past.

The NPL constructs the area of value for indigenous languages in terms of their ability to connect with the static past rather than as resources for new ways of engaging with and among indigenous people. In discussing the value of indigenous languages to urban Aborigines and non-Aboriginal people the text again is oriented to connections with a traditionalised past:

> In addition, it is of wider symbolic and practical importance to Aborigines who do not speak a traditional language, and to non-Aborigines, to support these languages, as sources of knowledge about the primarily orally-transmitted cultural values and world view of Aboriginal society. (Lo Bianco, 1987: 108)

Here the 'cultural values and world view of Aboriginal society' are those of traditional Aborigines and not of those who do not speak the languages. Urban Aborigines are therefore de-indigenised as not having access to the values and worldview of 'traditional' Aborigines. Instead, they are positioned in the same relationship to these values and worldviews as non-indigenous people, who will 'support' these languages because of their connection to an otherwise inaccessible indigenous past.

The document does, however, also suggest that access to indigenous languages may have a role in connecting people with contemporary Aboriginal Australia:

> Much of non-Aboriginal Australia is ignorant of the needs, aspirations and culture of the original inhabitants of the continent and of the fact that many Aboriginal people use traditional languages to fulfil all their needs.… Knowledge about Aboriginal languages, and the ways they are used, may be vital to the appreciation and understanding of Aboriginal culture. (Lo Bianco, 1987: 75)

While this focus on needs and aspirations seems to indicate the contemporaneity of what can be learnt about indigenous Australians from their language, it is in this context that their culture is described as 'non-material and spiritual' and it appears that it is the grounding of indigenous realities in tradition which creates the problem of lack of understanding. Ignorance is therefore distanced from the impact of contemporary processes in the mainstream (colonisation, discrimination, prejudice, etc.) and located within the static past of indigenous people.

A further traditionalising ideology of indigenous languages can be seen in the way the text treats the creole languages of indigenous people, which result from accommodations to the arrival of English in Australia:

> Kriol and Torres Strait Creole, though not indigenous languages, express identity in similar ways and tend to be regarded by their speakers as markers of group identities. (Lo Bianco, 1987: 73)

Creoles, although used almost exclusively by indigenous people, are therefore not considered to be indigenous languages because they have disrupted the linguistic tradition of indigenous Australia. If tradition is a static construction of the past, creoles are a departure from this past resulting from accommodation with the new. Indigenous creoles – Torres Strait Creole and Kriol – are in fact the two most widely spoken indigenous languages recorded in the Australian census (DIAC, 2008).[2] Speakers of creoles appear to be absent in the traditional/urban dichotomy established in the policy. They are not traditional because they have abandoned traditional languages, but they are neither geographically nor culturally urban. The realities of those indigenous people who have experienced language shift but have not shifted to a variety of English are therefore marginal in the policy context, having lost the claim to value which is associated with tradition.

The educational provisions of the NPL envisage forms of learning of indigenous languages by indigenous people, either as first or as additional languages, and also by non-indigenous people. Most emphasis is, however, given to the education of those for whom these are first languages, especially those who do not speak English. The starting point for its consideration of the role of these languages in education is that there should be some form of affirmation of the languages and cultures indigenous children bring to school:

> Since schooling is compulsory, children of non-English-speaking Aboriginal background are entitled to expect the positive affirmation of their linguistic and cultural background, and effective education will require this. (Lo Bianco, 1987: 73)

This quote creates a new category of speakers of indigenous languages, those who do not speak English, and singles out these students as the ones whose language and culture should be positively affirmed in the school system. This construction is interesting in that the document makes frequent reference to the multilingualism of indigenous Australians but does not appear to construct this multilingualism as involving English. Moreover, those indigenous children who speak English and an indigenous language are not included among those whose background needs affirmation.

For children who speak an indigenous language, the policy presents bilingual education as desirable:

> Since schooling is compulsory, and contact with the wider community probably inevitable, the issues of bilingualism and bilingual/bicultural education for speakers of these languages arises. (Lo Bianco, 1987: 108)

The framing here again suggests that the population under consideration is not one which uses English or has contact with the wider population. This seems to be related to the idea that speakers of traditional languages are those who live in remote areas of the country with little external contact and that their need for English is one of engagement outside their remote communities. The construction of speakers of indigenous languages as recipients of education therefore appears to take a rather monolingual view of such students and sees isolation from others as the normal context in which such languages will be maintained. English, then, is needed to allow indigenous people to establish relationships across groups and move out of their linguistic and cultural isolation.

Bilingual education is represented as having two goals – the development of proficiency in the indigenous language in its own right and as a basis for the acquisition of English:

> bilingual education ought to aim to extend the children's knowledge of their first language, to maintain and develop their proficiency in this language, and to inculcate positive values towards their language and culture. As far as English is concerned, these programs ought to provide a sound basis in the first language for the acquisition of English and the development of the highest standards of literate and spoken Standard Australian English. (Lo Bianco, 1987: 109)

In this representation of the objectives of bilingual programmes the focus is very much on language maintenance programmes in which both languages have a strong and sustained place. The learning of the indigenous language is given value here not simply because of its own relevance to the lives of children but also as a starting point for the acquisition of the language of the mainstream. That is, the education of students who speak an indigenous language as a first language aims at developing a capacity to connect through English with diverse others in the Australian mainstream. In this policy text, bilingualism, in reference to indigenous languages, is used only in the context of the learning of English by indigenous people who speak an indigenous language: the learning of indigenous languages by those who do not already speak them, whether indigenous or not, is not included. That is, bilingualism is a feature of minorities – it is the continued maintenance of a first language while acquiring the language of the dominant group.[3]

Bilingualism involving an indigenous language is not presented as a goal for non-indigenous people. The focus is instead on language awareness programmes located within other forms of educational provision:

> the policy addresses the development of Aboriginal language awareness programs for all Australian students as an integral part of Aboriginal Studies programs and general language awareness. (Lo Bianco, 1987: 105)

This implies that the mainstream will not normally learn indigenous languages for the purposes of communicating with indigenous people; rather, the policy seems to project that such communication will be done in English, the language of the mainstream. Instead, the mainstream will know about the languages that indigenous people will use among themselves as a way of understanding them, as an external lens through which to view indigenous people. In fact, bilingual education for the mainstream is usually understood in the policy in terms of the learning of a language which originates from outside Australia, although indigenous languages are not specifically excluded from such bilingualism.

The construction of the language learning for indigenous people who do not have an indigenous language has parallels with the provision of indigenous languages for the mainstream:

> Many urban Aborigines wish to become familiar with a traditional language. It is highly desirable that opportunities be made available for the teaching of accredited school courses and adult education programs in some Aboriginal languages and that components concerning Aboriginal languages and their cultural significance be designed and offered as part of Aboriginal Studies. (Lo Bianco, 1987: 116)

Language awareness is offered as a way of connecting indigenous people with the indigenous past; however, there is also consideration here of programmes of language learning for such groups, either within school provision or in adult education. The policy seems to place much emphasis on Aboriginal studies as the location of normal learning about Aboriginal languages; however, it also notes that not all Australian students have access to such programmes and that they need to be provided as a normal part of schooling (p. 117).

The NPL does project a scenario in which the learning of indigenous languages is an educational possibility for all the groups it identifies. Nonetheless, the focus is certainly on the learning of indigenous languages by first language speakers and this learning is coupled with the acquisition of English. Less focus is placed on the learning of these languages by other groups. There is specific mention of the need for language programmes for other indigenous people but not for non-indigenous people, for whom the focus is placed on language awareness. In addition, of the actions identified within the policy for the National Aboriginal Languages Project (NALP) the focus is on the teaching of languages in indigenous communities where the language is spoken, while other actions relate to the provision of ESL programmes. This is an ideological position that constructs the normal speaker of an indigenous language as an indigenous person and locates indigenous languages as languages of communication among indigenous people, primarily within indigenous communities in remote areas. This means that indigenous languages are not constructed as languages of intercultural communication, except potentially among indigenous people who have lost a linguistic/cultural connection with traditional indigeneity. Instead, English is constructed as the language of communication across the divide between indigenous and non-indigenous people, reinforcing the hegemonic place of English through its unifying role.

In 1989, the education of indigenous Australians was addressed in a brief policy document agreed by the Education Ministers of the Commonwealth and all States and Territories (DEET, 1989a). The Aboriginal Education Policy (AEP), which existed alongside the NPL, addressed the whole scope of the education of indigenous people and language-in-education policy constituted only a small part of the document. The education of indigenous people was felt to be in crisis because of low participation and achievement levels and the AEP sought to address this at national level.

One notable feature of the AEP is that it does not use the word 'traditional' to describe indigenous languages and cultures, using instead the word 'Aboriginal'.[4] This means that the languages and cultures involved are here constructed in ethnic terms rather than in terms of their relationship to a view of indigenous authenticity as being located in a past reality. Nonetheless, some of the ideological opposition between indigenous languages and English (the traditional/modern dichotomy) remains in the policy. For example, although the policy emphasises the place of indigenous participation in decision-making and includes a section detailing indigenous people's needs and aspirations for education, it formulates these within its own discursive domain. In discussing indigenous people's aspirations for language education, the policy document states:

> Many Aboriginal people seek 'two-ways' education of a bi-lingual and bi-cultural nature, in order for them to maintain or restore their cultural identity and acquire useful skills for their participation in Australian social and economic life. (DEET, 1989a: 9)

This statement takes up the NPL's focus on bilingual education as a specifically indigenous concern and reframes its focus. The NPL had seen bilingual programmes as being related to language maintenance for people who spoke indigenous languages but here there is an expressed need for bilingual programmes for new learning of indigenous languages, presumably by indigenous people who speak English. The discursive construction of the relative roles of the languages here involves a contrast between indigenous languages for identity purposes and the development of 'useful skills for ... participation', which can be read as the contribution of English in such programmes. This means that, in framing indigenous people's aspirations for language education, the policy constructs a distinction between the personally desirable and the externally useful, with usefulness being seen as fitting people for mainstream society. Thus, it locates value and usefulness within the value system of the hegemonic mainstream culture and assumes that this is the natural understanding of value. In this way, this statement replicates the emphasis on indigenous languages as local and internal and English as the language of connection with others. By producing this construction of the relative values attached to each language in a section on indigenous people's needs and aspirations, the policy locates this perception not as one of government (and thus of the mainstream), but as that of indigenous people themselves, by presenting the statement as something that the policy voices on behalf of others (Luke *et al.*, 1993). This claim therefore becomes on the surface the inclusion of a minority voice, but it is a voice that supports the hegemony of the dominant group (see Condit, 1989).

Language, when it appears in statements of the official agenda, appears primarily as a problem in need of resolution. For instance:

> participation, in the sense of effective learning, is hampered by inadequate sensitivity and relevance to cultural differences in: curriculum, teaching strategies, student grouping, relations with students and their communities, learning schedules and organisational arrangements.

The health, housing and economic conditions of communities are also significant factors as are language differences.... (DEET, 1989a: 11)

Here, two sets of conditions are presented which limit effective learning by indigenous students. The first of these is attributed to the defects of an unstated external agent (teachers, schools and education systems) in their sensitivity to cultural difference in the delivery of education. Luke *et al.* (1993) argue that the discourse of the AEP constructs the role of schools in undermining or marginalising indigenous cultures as one of misunderstanding of indigenous culture by actors within the education system rather than in the nature of schooling as an institution for the reproduction of the dominant culture. The second set of conditions is a series of deficiencies in the students which prevent them from receiving what is delivered and it is here that the presence of indigenous languages is located, in the form of 'difference'. This difference could be read either as the presence of an indigenous language equating with a perception of inadequate English for participation in education or as a lack of capacity to use those languages in delivering education. Later this difference is unambiguously constructed as a 'disadvantage' for indigenous students in terms of their lack of English proficiency:

The effectiveness of educational services in several areas is likely to be increased when measures are taken to address particular student disadvantages, including programs to improve student nutrition, to cater for students with visual and hearing impairments, to provide tutorial assistance, homework centres and transport services, and to improve the teaching of English as a second language. (DEET, 1989a: 13)

The ability to speak an indigenous language has disappeared from the profile of the indigenous student as it is configured as a deficit in English, which is equated with a range of health and social disadvantages which can be remedied by better provision. Indigenous languages are therefore represented as having limited relevance for issues of educational attainment, except as impediments to be overcome, and English is constructed as the sole language of connection with valued social and economic domains, which exist beyond the indigenous world.

From the starting point of indigenous aspirations for bilingualism and governmental aspirations for English, the AEP formulates two activities as part of the overall approach to indigenous education: the development of bilingual and bicultural programmes; and ESL and other language programmes (DEET, 1989a: 11). The formulation of other language programmes is unexplained and not developed elsewhere in the document; however, the inclusion of these with ESL would seem to suggest that the reference was to other English programmes rather than indigenous language programmes. The focus of these two activities is further developed in a list of long-term goals (DEET, 1989a: 15), of which two specifically mention languages:

> To develop programs to support the maintenance and continued use of Aboriginal Languages.
> To enable the attainment of proficiency in English language and numeracy competencies by Aboriginal adults with limited or no educational experience.

The second of these moves the focus on English beyond schooling into the domain of adult education as a way of responding to educational failure, which is constructed as educational failure in English. The first goal, which relates to the place of indigenous languages, is interesting if taken as a statement about the purpose of bilingual programmes, in that it seems to exclude the reclamation of indigenous languages, which had in fact been mentioned earlier in the document as one of the needs and aspirations of indigenous people. The focus of indigenous languages in bilingual education seems to be the same as that in the NPL – the provision of programmes for those who already speak indigenous languages. Most of the educational goals do not explicitly mention English, although in reality English is present as the unstated norm in most of the goals of the policy, in that there is an underlying ideological assumption that educational attainment is educational attainment in English. For example, the goal of equity in education is stated in the following terms:

> To enable Aboriginal attainment of skills to the same standard as other Australian students throughout the compulsory years of schooling. (DEET, 1989a: 15)

The skills of other Australian students are English language skills, not indigenous language skills, and it these English language skills that the policy has as its central focus. The adoption of a policy for Aboriginal education has a potential consequence of removing Aboriginal languages from the broader language-in-education policy agenda. As the provisions of the NPL primarily related to speakers of indigenous languages, the same group which appears to be targeted by the language provisions of the AEP, the educational provision of these languages as second languages for indigenous and non-indigenous people becomes more tenuous.

If the NPL had sought to balance the place of indigenous languages and English at least for indigenous people who spoke an indigenous language as a first language, the AEP can be understood as privileging English over indigenous languages as the valued language of education; that is, the AEP sought to fit indigenous children for participation in mainstream society through attainment in English.

The focus on English as the necessary language of education became yet stronger in the Australian Language and Literacy Policy (ALLP), introduced in 1991. In fact, in the policy document there is no mention of indigenous languages in the section (in volume 1) relating to the education of indigenous people (DEET, 1991a). The title of this section, 'Aboriginal and Torres Strait Islander Literacy and ESL', explicitly excludes indigenous languages from its focus, as 'literacy' is defined in the policy as literacy in English. Under this national goal, funding was allocated only to programmes to 'improve the spoken and written English skills of Aboriginal primary and secondary students, particularly those whose first language is not English, and to improve English literacy courses for adults' (DEET, 1991a: 11). English is therefore presented as the only language of relevance for indigenous people.

Indigenous languages are, however, not entirely absent from the ALLP and the policy document later states a goal in relation to indigenous language maintenance:

> Aboriginal and Torres Strait Islander languages should be maintained and developed where they are still transmitted. Other languages should be assisted in an appropriate way, for example through recording. (DEET, 1991a: 19)

As in previous policies, the emphasis here is on languages which are spoken as first languages rather than on the potential role of education to reclaim languages that are no longer spoken. Languages which are not being transmitted intergenerationally are less likely to be included in educational provision but rather will be documented – that is, they are to be preserved in some non-communicational way. In relation to its educational goal, the ALLP allocates funds to activities such as curriculum development and the professional education of indigenous people to work in schools. There is no mention in the policy itself of bilingual programmes as a policy objective and such programmes are therefore no longer explicitly included in the projected world envisaged by the ALLP.

These limited statements on indigenous languages are further developed in volume 2 of the ALLP policy document. In that volume the Aboriginal

Language and Literacy Strategy is outlined. This strategy identifies three areas of focus for language-in-education work:

> The development of effective arrangements to allow Aboriginal people to make decisions about Aboriginal language and literacy issues;
> Measures aimed at ensuring Aboriginal literacy in English is raised to a level commensurate with all other Australians, to allow Aboriginal people to participate effectively in the social, cultural and economic life of Australia; and
> Measures aimed at encouraging the use of Australia's Aboriginal languages.
> (DEET, 1991b: 94)

In this listing, indigenous languages are placed last and are the least developed in terms of their educational focus. The most developed text is that for the teaching of English, which equates participation in the social, cultural and economic life of Australia with the use of English. This framing removes social, cultural and economic life conducted in indigenous languages from the sphere of Australian life and locates it in a marginal space which is other than 'Australian'. The culture in which indigenous people need to participate is therefore framed in terms of the mainstream and only that culture is ratified in the policy text.

The emphasis in language learning is predominantly placed on English, although there is some concession to the idea that the acquisition of English is not intended to replace indigenous languages:

> The most common reason for the extinction of languages is domination by another language and consequential shift, perhaps over several generations, to the language which is politically and economically dominant. However, the promotion of English language and literacy alongside support for maintenance and development of Aboriginal languages is not inconsistent, as Aboriginal people have a history of multilingualism.
> (DEET, 1991b: 96)

The policy acknowledges the possibility of language shift and the role of dominant languages in this shift. That is, it articulates the problem of the propagation of a dominant language in a minority language context. It then dismisses the problem as a legitimate one by invoking the historical context of indigenous multilingualism. In so doing it represents indigenous multilingualism as a static past that will problematically continue in the future. English will simply become a feature of the practices of the static past.

The Aboriginal Language and Literacy Strategy is divided into an Aboriginal Literacy Strategy and an Aboriginal Languages Education Strategy. The literacy part is framed in terms of overall development of literacy in English, with recognition of the specific needs of 'students whose first language is not English' (DEET, 1991b: 96) and adult education in ESL and English literacy. The languages education part sets out possibilities for the teaching of indigenous languages in schools and in post-secondary education. The provision in schools is specific in identifying the contexts in which indigenous languages are to be supported:

> develop strategies geared towards the teaching of Aboriginal languages in schools, including special languages other than English programs in Aboriginal languages for children in Aboriginal schools, bilingual/ bicultural programs, measures for Aboriginal languages curriculum development and materials production, and the provision of Aboriginal bilingual language teaching and para-professional staffing resources. (DEET, 1991b: 96)

The recipients of indigenous languages education are identified as 'children in Aboriginal schools', that is, children in schools with predominantly or exclusively indigenous populations. In this way, indigenous languages are constructed as being relevant primarily for indigenous people and only in indigenous contexts. This is also the case in bilingual/bicultural programmes, which are now mentioned in the text for the first time. These too are programmes designed for indigenous children. Indigenous languages education is therefore primarily constructed as being for indigenous people and the languages are represented as having value within the local contexts of Aboriginal communities. The possibilities for some form of learning of or about indigenous languages by other groups, which was present in the NPL, has been removed from the policy discourse as a specific focus for the learning of indigenous languages. The closest the policy comes to indicating another audience for indigenous languages is in the listing of undifferentiated 'Aboriginal languages' as one of the priority languages which would receive specific funding for language learning programmes.

The 2005–08 Statement and Plan policy (MCEETYA, 2005) makes few mentions of indigenous languages specifically but instead integrates them into general language learning. In so doing, it reframes the student base for the study of indigenous languages, providing a rationale for their study by both indigenous and non-indigenous students:

> Australian Indigenous languages have a unique place in Australia's heritage and in its cultural and educational life. For Indigenous learners,

they are fundamental to strengthening identity and self-esteem. For non-Indigenous learners, they provide a focus for development of cultural understanding and reconciliation. (MCEETYA, 2005: 7)

In this statement, indigenous languages have been given a place within the cultural and educational life of Australia, which in the ALLP had been framed in terms of English. The rationale for learning for indigenous people is an essential and internal one relating to identity, while for non-indigenous people it is external – intercultural engagement through language. This focus is consistent with the overall direction of the policy document, which argues for language education for improving intercultural understanding and communication between cultures. As a general policy on language education it locates the learning of indigenous languages in the same context as the learning of foreign languages and so does not address many of the issues that are found in other policy documents.

In 2009, the Commonwealth government released an indigenous languages policy document entitled *Indigenous Languages – A National Approach* (Office for the Arts, 2009). The policy is unusual in the Australian context in that it is not under the responsibility of the Department of Education but rather of the Office for the Arts, which deals with issues of heritage. The focus of the policy is on the preservation of indigenous languages as elements of heritage, and thus involves a return to the idea that indigenous languages are part of a link to the past. The policy involves a number of education and other language planning activities. There are two educational dimensions. The first is the teaching of indigenous languages in schools. This section of the policy does not actually make specific provision for indigenous languages but notes instead that they are included in other educational provision for language learning – the policies relating to foreign language learning (see Chapter 2). This means that this document conflates issues concerning indigenous languages in education with all other forms of language education under the general umbrella of foreign language education. The policy acknowledges that 'Funding can be used to support and maintain Indigenous language programs operating in government schools'. This means that in the education section of a policy of indigenous languages there is no specific provision made for indigenous languages in schooling. The second dimension is 'indigenous languages and literacy and numeracy', although in the policy document the focus is primarily on the teaching of English to indigenous students. The complete text of this part of the policy reads:

The Government is committed to languages education and recognises the important role that Indigenous language learning plays in some schools, particularly bilingual schools.

The learning of English is also a fundamental skill that all Australians, including Indigenous Australians, must have in order to maximise their learning opportunities and life chances.

All Australian governments through the Council of Australian Governments (COAG) processes have committed to halving the gap in the reading, writing and numeracy achievements between Indigenous and non-Indigenous students within a decade.

The Government is providing $56.4 million over four years to provide extra assistance to schools to enable them to expand intensive literacy and numeracy approaches that have been successful with Aboriginal and Torres Strait Islander students and provide professional development support to assist teachers to prepare Individual Learning Plans for Indigenous students. (Office for the Arts, 2009)

The document acknowledges the importance of indigenous languages in some schools but this is not developed. Instead, educational activity is articulated only for the teaching and learning of English by indigenous students. English is represented in terms of its utility for learning opportunities and life chances, and the document presents a view that neither of these can be fully developed through an indigenous language. English is therefore presented as of more utility than indigenous languages in the lives of indigenous people because that which has value is obtained only through participation in English-speaking society. In this policy text, indigenous languages are largely sidelined in the educational domain. The focus on indigenous languages in the policy is therefore located mostly outside education – interpreting services and community activities. This means that in a policy with a broadly language maintenance agenda, education is not seen as a mechanism of maintenance but rather as a mechanism for the teaching of English, entrenching a hierarchical positioning of indigenous languages and English which frames value in terms of engagement with the mainstream society on its own terms and thereby preserves the existing hegemony.

The most recent language-in-education policy statements relating to indigenous languages are found in the Aboriginal and Torres Strait Islander Education Action Plan (2010–2014) (MCEECDYA, 2011). In the Action Plan, however, indigenous languages are almost entirely absent from the policy discourse. Where they are included they are usually mentioned as the policy context for education. There are two statements which acknowledge the first languages of indigenous students. The first is framed in terms of diversity:

Aboriginal and Torres Strait Islander children and young people reflect the linguistic and cultural diversity of the communities in which they live. While some speak Standard Australian English at home, many speak Aboriginal English (a non-standard dialect of English), a creole, one or more Aboriginal or Torres Strait Islander languages, or any combinations of these as their first language. (MCEECDYA, 2011: 6)

The second is framed in terms of a lack of English language.

Some Aboriginal and Torres Strait Islander students do not speak Standard Australian English as their first language. Their home language is often Aboriginal English, a creole, or one or more Aboriginal or Torres Strait Islander languages, or any combination of these. In addition, many parents and relatives may not speak Standard Australian English at home. (MCEECDYA, 2011: 19)

The first is a description of linguistic abilities, expressed in terms of what students are able to do linguistically; the second frames the ability to speak a particular variety of English as a norm and constructs the ability to speak other languages through an ideology of deficit in that it entails an inability to speak English adequately. In fact, the policy explicitly treats multilingualism not as the ability to speak more than one language but as a deficit in English:

Education providers will ensure that teachers working in remote schools with multilingual students are appropriately prepared with English as a Second Language (ESL) strategies, including the means by which to assess student progress in the acquisition of skills in Standard Australian English. (MCEECDYA, 2011: 21)

In this quote, the multilingualism of students is something that teachers need to be prepared for, with the preparation involving ways of dealing with a deficit in English, rather than a capacity to engage with the languages that students bring to school. Teachers are therefore charged with enabling indigenous students to interact in the language and culture of the teacher as the means of entry into an intercultural relationship with the teacher, and by implication broader society.

These two perspectives on indigenous languages – linguistic ability and linguistic deficit – persist side by side in the document. The presence of other languages is represented as a form of linguistic diversity which needs to be engaged with in education and this engagement is usually framed in terms of 'sensitivity' to or 'engagement' with diversity and the 'active recognition and validation of Aboriginal and Torres Strait Islander cultures and languages by schools' (MCEECDYA, 2011: 12). Educational action in response to linguistic and cultural diversity is not constructed in terms of language education but rather as pedagogical adjustment: 'supporting the use and development of pedagogies that are sensitive to and engage with Aboriginal and Torres Strait Islander students' languages and cultures' (MCEECDYA, 2011: 19). This means that the educational strategy for dealing with indigenous languages is one of acknowledgement of their presence and its implications rather than the active teaching of these languages. The educational response to students' lack of English is more active. It includes work in curriculum development, teachers' professional learning, and pedagogy, normalising English as the language of value. In the policy text, language development is explicitly understood as the development of English, especially literacy in standard Australian English, and not in indigenous languages. Indigenous languages are seen, however, as a possible starting point for the development of English literacy, as teaching is required that 'builds from students' home language(s) where Standard Australian English is a second or further language' (MCEECDYA, 2011: 21). Indigenous languages themselves are present in the projected educational provision only to the extent to which individual schools may address them:

School principals will have the flexibility to tailor operations to meet the needs of the local Aboriginal and Torres Strait Islander community. This might include extending operating hours and providing onsite or co-located services such as health care, after hours' study support, multi-lingual and English as a Second Language programs, sporting programs, child care, and family support programs. (MCEECDYA, 2011: 25)

There is no explicit mention of indigenous languages, which are at most implied in 'multilingual … programs', although what such programmes are is not indicated. These programmes are, however, framed as forms of support for the development of the core educational programme, which is expressed throughout the document in terms of English. In the policy, indigenous languages are positioned as being secondary to English as the language of the mainstream. The role of education is to adapt indigenous people who may speak an indigenous language to the language of mainstream society.

Australia's language-in-education policies largely construct indigenous languages as an aspect of intracultural relationships (that is, within indigenous communities). This means that these languages are not represented as having a function in broader relationships and interactions in Australia;

all significant intercultural relationships between indigenous people and the dominant mainstream group are seen as being mediated through English. The hegemonic position of English in Australian society is therefore maintained and the roles of indigenous languages are understood as additional to, or subordinate to, English. The relevance of English to indigenous lives is asserted in texts even where the ostensible focus is on the indigenous languages themselves, which, as a result, are understood always in the context of English as the dominant language of society and as the dominating language in indigenous realities. The provisions for indigenous languages therefore are framed within an ideology that sees their relevance as limited and internal.

As learners of English, indigenous people are represented as developing the capacity to engage with and participate in the life and culture of the mainstream. As intercultural subjects, therefore, they engage in both their own culture and that of the other. Members of the dominant mainstream, however, are constructed as intercultural subjects in a much more reduced way – as observers of difference who have the capacity to understand and accept this difference, but who do not engage actively in it and do not require language abilities other than their own first language. This construction preserves the hegemonic position of the language. In terms of language-in-education policy for indigenous people and their languages, the intercultural subject is constructed as a person who participates in mainstream society while maintaining an additional language and culture as an element of his/her private, intragroup life. This construction still maintains the domination of English as indigenous language and culture do not compete for public space. Interculturality is therefore a requirement for those who maintain distinctiveness from the mainstream. There is an ideological construction of linguistic and cultural diversity as something that coexists with English and is additional to a fundamental English linguistic and cultural norm.

Indigenous Language-in-education Policy in Japan

Japanese policy has rarely acknowledged the presence of indigenous people within the Japanese state. If the presence of immigrants is considered problematic in terms of the Japanese monoethnic ideology, as discussed in Chapter 3, then recognising the presence of indigenous groups in Japan represents an even more fundamental problem. Any recognition of an ethnic minority as an indigenous minority group within Japan of necessity contests the understanding of Japan as a monoethnic nation and challenges fundamental discourses of nationhood within Japan. As a result, there has been little recognition of indigenous minorities in Japanese language or education policies and the status of groups as indigenous minorities has typically been downplayed. Nonetheless, there are indigenous linguistic minorities in Japan. There are two groups in Japan who can be considered indigenous, with their own indigenous languages: the Ryukyuans of Okinawa prefecture and the Ainu of Hokkaido. Both were incorporated into the Japanese state during territorial expansion of Japan and have been considered as citizens of Japan. There are few Japanese government policies which particularly relate to indigenous people, and in fact none for the Ryukyu Islands. The only policies that do acknowledge the Ryukyuan languages stem from the American administration of the islands following the Second World War. There have, however, been two significant documents relating to the Ainu:

- 北海道旧土人保護法 (Hokkaidou Kyuudojin Hogohou, Hokkaido Former Aborigines Protection Act) (Japanese government, 1899);
- アイヌ文化の振興並びにアイヌの伝統等に関する知識の普及及び 啓発に関する法律 (Ainu Bunka no Shikou Narabi ni Dentou nado ni Kansuru Chishiki no Fukyuu Obyobi Haihatsu ni Kansuru Houritsu, Ainu Cultural Protection Act)[5] (Diet of Japan, 1997).

Apart from these documents, both the Ryukyuans and the Ainu were covered by general Japanese education policies which mandated the use of Japanese as the only language of instruction in Japanese schools.

The indigenous people of the Ryukyu Islands have been the less recognised in Japanese educational policy and there is no provision in policy documents for the six languages of the islands. The genetic relationship between the languages of Ryukyu and Japanese has been used to classify the Ryukyuan languages as dialects of Japanese. This means that the Ryukyuan people have been discursively assimilated into the Japanese *minzoku* (see Chapter 3) and their language varieties have been treated as local variations within the overarching monolingual and monoethnic Japanese nation. From the Meiji period, the development of mass education in Japan involved processes of dialect levelling and the promotion of middle-class Tokyo Japanese as the standard language (Calvetti, 1992), and the Ryukyuan languages were subject to the same dialect levelling as other varieties. The equation between Ryukyuan and Japanese implied by the dialect status of the former emphasised the Japanese claim to the Ryukyu Islands (affirmed by their relatively recent acquisition by the Japanese nation),[6] a claim furthered through the purposeful conflation of linguistic and ethnic with national characteristics (Rabson, 1999). Because Ryukyuan varieties were identified as dialects of Japanese, no specific language-in-education planning was undertaken at national level for the Ryukyu Islands. The local language varieties were viewed negatively and the imposition of standard Japanese was accompanied by a move to eradicate dialects as inferior forms of the language. In the Ryukyu Islands, the prefectural government in 1907 issued the Dialect Control Ordinance (方言取締令, *Hougen Torishimari-rei*), which banned the use of Ryukyuan languages in the school system and stipulated the punishment of children who spoke them (Calvetti, 1992; Heinrich, 2004).

The process of dialect levelling was disrupted at a policy level during the United States' control of the islands from 1945 to 1952. The American administration's education policy documents do not specifically discuss language as an issue in education. For example, Military Government Directive 86 of 2 January 1946 ('Okinawa Education System'), which established education in the Ryukyu Islands under US control, stated simply that 'the minimum curriculum amounts to three hours of instruction per day six days per week in reading, writing and arithmetic' (Gekkan Okinawa-sha, 1983: vol. 3, p. 162), without specifying the language in which this was to be done. In practice, education was provided in Japanese, continuing the pre-war practice.

Although education in Japanese persisted during the occupation, the US military government's policy emphasised the differences between the Ryukyuan languages and Japanese and sought to promote education in Ryukyuan and English (Heinrich, 2004). This focus on Ryukyuan and English was intended to emphasise the separateness of the Ryukyu Islands from Japan and to create a non-Japanese identification of the islands. The policy to promote Ryukyuan identity is reflected mostly in government documents relating to culture. Military Government Directive 153 of 17 April 1946 (Okinawan Department of Cultural Affairs) states 'The Department of Cultural Affairs shall endeavour to preserve the cultural traditions of Okinawan [*sic*] and actively promote all aspects of native Okinawan culture' (Gekkan Okinawa-sha, 1983: vol. 3, p. 306). The US administration in its policy sought to construct an identity which was distinct from that of Japan and in so doing reversed the policy position that had been introduced during the Meiji period. This change was also reflected in the use of the term 'Ryukyu' rather than 'Okinawa' to designate the area in later US documents (Rabson, 1999). This was the name of the quasi-independent kingdom which preceded the absorption of the area into Japan and its renaming as the Okinawa prefecture. Thus the choice of Ryukyu as a name emphasised a pre-Meiji non-Japanese identity and marked a form of reversion to an earlier, pre-occupation state.

The US occupation administration mandated English language study in Ryukyu schools in 1946 (Okinawa-ken Kyouikuiinkai, 1995) and the aim of education was to create a form of relationship between the Ryukyuan people and America in which English would be the vehicular language. In 1963, the US High Commissioner, Paul Caraway, stated:

> In a small area where thousands of Americans reside, where English is not an academic discipline but a vocational tool, a functional English program is a must. (Ishihara, 2004: 20)

The purpose of English education was therefore to establish a form of inter-cultural relationship between the Ryukyuans and the Americans resident in the Islands. It was a process of educating the local population to deal with foreign occupying forces in which the local people were constructed as needing to adapt to the Americans, but such adaptation was not required of the Americans. It was therefore a form of intercultural relationship which emphasised the dominating role of the United States as a military occupier of the Islands and the subordination of the locals.

The US policy in effect legitimised the separation of Ryukyu from Japan as a US trusteeship through a process of differentiation of the territories – a differentiation which was marked linguistically through an emphasis on Ryukyuan languages and on the teaching of English. However, this policy was resisted by local institutions, which promoted the use of standard Japanese and supported reunification with Japan. The US policy supporting the Ryukyuan languages was therefore understood locally within a framework of resistance to the US occupation and this resistance was constructed in terms of Japanese identity and thus with the Japanese language. The discursive recognition of the difference between Ryukyuan and Japanese therefore became identified as a discourse relating to enemy occupation and subjugation to a foreign power. When the US military began to reassign administration to the Ryukyuans themselves, they implemented educational policies focused exclusively on Japanese.

The discourse of reunification was the predominant political discourse of the period of trusteeship and alternative discourses, such as those of independence or integration with the United States, do not seem to have been influential (Heinrich, 2004). When the idea of return to Japan began to emerge as a political focus in the 1950s, it was associated with a focus on Japanese as the normal language of both public and private communication. The US policy was perceived as a discourse of occupation and colonialism and the way of resisting such discourses was constructed in terms of a return to Japan. The imperialist discourse of Japan which assigned the status of dialect to Ryukyuan languages in order to assimilate Ryukyu into Japan and to integrate the Ryukyuans within the Japanese monoethnic ideology served as a resource for resistance to US occupation. Indeed, the imperialist discourses of Japan were adopted by the Ryukyuans themselves in a new context as the basis for legitimising reunification with Japan (Heinrich, 2004). This discourse was made manifest in the 1957 Okinawa Fundamental Education Law, which introduced the concept of 'education for Japanese citizenship', in which the Japanese identity of Okinawans was framed as a key educational goal (Noiri, 2011) and standard Japanese was legitimised as the language of education.

When the Ryukyu Islands were returned to Japan in 1972, they were reincorporated as a Japanese prefecture and the language-in-education policies of the Japanese government were applied there as elsewhere. This meant that, at national level, Ryukyuan languages were again considered as dialects of Japanese and no specific educational provisions have been made for these languages in national policy.

Language planning for the people of the Ryukyu Islands has not been an example in which any form of intercultural relationship was perceived as relevant, except during the period of the American administration of the islands. By discursively constructing Ryukyuan identity as Japanese, the Japanese government removed the notion of diversity from communication between Ryukyuans and the mainstream. Instead, the focus of education was to remove some 'defects' which existed in their knowledge of Japan and Japanese in order to bring the people into greater conformity with the mainstream, in which local differences were reduced to local 'colour' within a common and otherwise undifferentiated culture. The discursive mechanism which allowed for such a policy was the identification of the language varieties spoken on the Ryukyu Islands as dialects, which then became stigmatised as faulty versions of the standard, to be removed through education.

The Ainu of Hokkaido were also subject to the assimilating processes of Meiji Japan. The Ainu have posed a greater challenge to the Japanese monoethnic ideology than that posed by the Ryukyuan Islanders, as their language and culture are not as easily identified with those of the dominant group. In fact, in pre-Meiji times, these linguistic and cultural differences were emphasised for political purposes. Prior to the Meiji period, Hokkaido was known as Ezochi (蝦夷地, 'Barbarian Land') – that is, the inhabitants of the island, as barbarians, were positioned as being outside the Japanese nation, society and culture. The Meiji administration sought to bring Ezochi more closely into the Japanese state and in 1869 renamed the island Hokkaido (北海道, 'North Sea Road'). This renaming symbolically and linguistically removed the 'foreign' designation and in so doing integrated the island more closely within the ethnic Japanese state.

This integration of the island into Japan also required an integration of the Ainu into the Japanese people, in conformity with the Japanese discourses of unity and uniformity. This is represented in academic work (for example, by Torii, 1903) that sought to demonstrate the commonality of Japanese and Ainu cultures at an earlier point in history. This idea of commonality was accompanied by a view that Yamato[7] Japanese culture had since evolved, while Ainu culture had not (for overviews see Jacobson, 2008; Siddle, 1996). The Ainu culture therefore represented an earlier stage of a common culture, and one which was degenerate compared with that of the dominant group. Such a view allowed the Ainu to be incorporated into the ideology of the monoethnic state, because the Ainu were not separated ethnically from the Japanese. That is, their difference was simply a manifestation of regional variety within a common Japanese frame of reference.

In 1899, the Japanese government passed the 北海道旧土人保護法 (Hokkaidou Kyuudojin Hogohou, 'Hokkaido Former Aborigines Protection Act' (Japanese government, 1899), which included educational provisions. The term used to identify the Ainu was not an ethnonym but rather a geographical term – the term translated as 'aborigine' 土人 (*dojin*) refers to a person of the land – that is, it refers to the fact of their geographical location, while 旧 (*kyuu*, 'old/former') locates that association as a fact of the past. The designation of the Ainu as 'Former Aborigines' effectively removed any ethnic distinctiveness of the Ainu and located their difference from the Japanese mainstream as a feature of the past. Instead, it substituted a geographical understanding of these people, as inhabitants of Hokkaido, for an ethnic identity, Ainu. The ideological construction of the Ainu at this period was as remnants of a more primitive stage of cultural evolution (Jacobson, 2008; Siddle, 1996): something which could be overcome by cultural assimilation to the more evolved mainstream – hence the term *former* aborigines, a state which was now past. The difference between the Ainu and the Japanese was no longer one of geography or ethnicity but of historical development (Morris-Suzuki, 1998). One of the provisions of the Act was to introduce mandatory education for Ainu children:

北海道旧土人ノ貧困ナル者ノ子弟ニシテ就学スル者ニハ授業料ヲ給スルコトヲ得
To give free tuition to the children of the impoverished Hokkaido former aborigines.
(Japanese government, 1899: provision 7)

The framing here of the Ainu as 'impoverished ... former Aborigines' constructs the community in terms of economic dimensions which are addressed in the Act by a paternalistic state. The policy, however, was not simply one of improving economic status; instead, compulsory education in standard Japanese was a mechanism for assimilation of the Ainu into the Japanese mainstream. This Act remained in place, albeit with modifications, until it was formally repealed in 1997 as part of the new Ainu Cultural Protection Act.

The Ainu Cultural Protection Act (アイヌ文化の振興並びにアイヌの伝統等に関する知識の普及及び啓発に関する法律; *Ainu Bunka no Shikou Narabi ni Dentou nado ni Kansuru Chishiki no Fukyuu Obyobi Haihatsu ni Kansuru Houritsu*) (Diet of Japan, 1997) is significant in that it acknowledged for the first time diversity within the Japanese state. Siddle (2003: 449) calls it 'the first "multicultural" legislation in Japan'. The Act recognises the distinctness of Ainu culture and acknowledges a state responsibility for the protection and promotion of that culture, but it does not recognise the Ainu people as a distinct ethnic group. This means that even though the Act may be 'multicultural' it constructs this multiculturalism as one that exists within monoethnic Japan and without disrupting this ideological construction of the society. Thus, it appears to recognise diversity *within* the Japanese people rather than diversity *of* the Japanese people. In this way, previous attitudes towards Japanese homogeneity and the management of minorities that results are not significantly changed by the Act (Siddle, 2002).

Although the Act is framed in terms of cultural protection, it defines culture in such a way that language is present as an aspect of culture:

第二条: この法律において「アイヌ文化」とは、アイヌ語並びアイヌにおいて継承されてきた音楽、舞踊、工芸その他の文化的所産及びこれらから発展した文化的所産をいう。

Article 2: In this Act, 'Ainu Culture' includes the Ainu language, and also music, dance, crafts and other cultural products which have been developed by the Ainu people or which are developed from these.
(Diet of Japan, 1997)

The language is listed alongside a number of traditional activities as features of Ainu culture. The construction of Ainu culture here is a traditionalising and archaising one. It focuses on the preservation of something from the past and omits reference to the existing and developing practices of the Ainu. The language is constructed therefore as a form of cultural relic, alongside other such relics. In this way the Act does not envisage that the different language and culture of the Ainu mean that there is a form of intercultural relationship between the Ainu and the dominant Japanese but rather that, in contemporary terms at least, the relationship already exists as one between *Japanese*, within a common cultural context in which some ancient traditions of one group of Japanese need special protection as a form of cultural heritage.

The dissemination element of the Act is even more strongly focused on traditional versions:

Article 5
2　基本方針においては、次の事項について定めるものとする。…
三　アイヌの伝統等に関する国民に対する知識の普及及び啓発を図るための施策に関する事項
2　The basic policy shall make decisions concerning the following...
iii　Provisions relating to the dissemination of knowledge of Ainu traditions and the like to the people as well as measures to educate the people.

Article 6
2　基本計画においては、次に掲げる事項について定めるものとする。…
三　アイヌの伝統等に関する住民に対する知識の普及及び啓発を図るための施策の実施内容に関する事項
2　The basic policy will establish the following: …
iii　Provisions relating to the dissemination of knowledge of Ainu traditions to the local people as well as measures to carry out their education. (Diet of Japan, 1997)

The focus of these two paragraphs of the Act is essentially educative in its focus – it aims to promote knowledge of Ainu culture, including language. Article 5 concerns developing a wider knowledge of Ainu culture among the Japanese people as a whole (国民 *kokumin*, people of the country). In article 6, the audience for this dissemination is local people (住民*juumin*, people living in a particular place). A similar term is also used in policy documents to refer to those who would benefit from developing intercultural abilities as a result of interaction with immigrants (see Chapter 3). The use of this term focuses the recipients of enactive work of the policy in geographic rather than ethnic terms. The Act is not therefore a measure to preserve Ainu culture for the Ainu but rather to protect it and promote it to an undifferentiated local people and for the nation as a whole. This framing therefore enables Ainu culture to be protected and promoted not as an activity focused on an Ainu cultural group but rather on a Japanese one, in which the Ainu are included as a subset.

The majority of provisions of the Act apply only in a geographically restricted area, in that the Ainu Cultural Protection Act pertains to Hokkaido, not to Japan as a whole. Thus, the local people who are the audience of this policy are to be understood as a regional subset of the Japanese people and the Japanese people as a whole are included only to the extent that they may be in Hokkaido. The focus on Hokkaido here recalls the Hokkaido Former Aborigines Protection Act, in which a geographical designation was used to replace a possible ethnic association. The Culture Protection Act, moreover, does not recognise those Ainu who live outside Hokkaido and they are therefore not recognised as a minority group in any way within Japan as a whole. This, too, would seem to be commensurate with a focus on Ainu as a regional group within Japan.

The Act also focuses on traditional constructions of Ainu culture in the limited dissemination activities it proposes. The Japanese term referring to culture in articles 5 and 6 of this document – 伝統等 (*dentou nado*, 'traditions') – provides a definition of what constitutes Ainu culture for the purposes of protection. It is not the modern lives of the Ainu and their present lived culture which are to be protected but that which comes from the past. The Act therefore constructs authentic Ainu culture as a traditional set of practices, which isolates the protected Ainu culture from the contemporary lived experience of the Ainu people. In a sense, this framing of Ainu culture harks back to the Meiji-era construction of the Ainu language and culture as primitive forms of Japanese language and culture. In both framings, the value of the Ainu language and culture has been pushed back into the past – as a remnant or relic. In the Hokkaido Former Aborigines Protection Act, this relic was seen as flawed and valueless and needed to be replaced by the more developed Japanese versions, while in the Ainu Cultural Protection Act it becomes a valued part of Japanese heritage. In this way, the Ainu culture can be differentiated and protected without addressing any underlying sense of Japan's ethnic identity.

The policies adopted in Japan to deal with internal linguistic and cultural diversity have been framed within a dominant ideology of ethnic unity and the diversity is normalised as part of an overarching national culture rather than being represented as different from this culture. As a result, Japanese language policies for indigenous groups do not construct a form of intercultural relationship between the indigenous group and the mainstream; rather, they work to deny that such a relationship is relevant. By representing indigenous minorities as manifesting local variation within Japanese culture, they construct such variation as a minor departure from a unifying norm. These differences have been conceived as defects in cultural development that need to be remedied, not as points of difference with which people can engage. These policies therefore represent discursive attempts to deny intercultural differences and which have, nonetheless, at various times, required those who were different to assimilate. That is, they have expected cultural adjustment of minorities to the mainstream. Although the Ainu Cultural Protection Act now recognises the difference as having value as part of Japanese heritage, it does not fully acknowledge Ainu language and culture as different, or as something which needs to be engaged with, beyond developing knowledge of these differences.

Indigenous Language-in-education Policy in Colombia

Indigenous education in Colombia and other parts of Latin America dates to the early days of the arrival of Europeans. The initial programmes of education were largely developed as part of missionary work and the main language-in-education policy agents were religious organisations.[8] The initial focus of educational work was on the learning of indigenous languages by missionaries. For example, the Council of Lima in 1567 recommended that missionaries learn Quechua and the Spanish government required missionaries to have an adequate command of indigenous languages for preaching and teaching work (Sánchez & Dueñas, 2002). By 1578, chairs of Quechua had been set up in Lima by the local Catholic diocese and by the Jesuits and another was established in Potosí (Bolivia) in 1582. At the same time, church organisations began to teach Spanish to indigenous people. In 1516, the 'plan Ximenes' made provisions for the teaching of Spanish in the American colonies, although they had little impact in practice, and in 1545 the Bishop of Lima required the teaching of Spanish to children in church schools. Government policies were also issued in favour of Spanish in schools, although they were somewhat ambivalent about the place of indigenous languages in schools. In 1550, the Spanish king, Charles V, ordered that Spanish must be taught to the indigenous population and that the indigenous languages were not to be taught, while in 1596 Phillip II favoured maintaining them. The aims of these programmes were to convert indigenous people to the Catholic religion and thus to assimilate them more closely to the culture of Spain (Sánchez, 1996).

By the time of the liberation of the Latin American colonies from Spain, Spanish had come to predominate as the language of the local elites, especially the mestizos. The newly liberated colonies adopted the Spanish of the elites as their national languages and implemented mass education through Spanish. Thus, from the mid-19th century, Spanish dominated education in Latin American countries and indigenous languages were excluded in most countries.

Colombia began to recognise the place of indigenous languages in education in the 1970s and a number of documents have since dealt with this issue. The most significant is the 1991 constitution; however, a number of decrees and laws have been issued both before and after the development of the new constitution, including:

- Decree 88 of 22 January 1976 (Presidente de la República Colombiana, 1976);
- Decree 1142 of 19 June 1978 (Presidente de la República Colombiana, 1978);
- Law 115 of 8 February 1994 (República de Colombia, 1994);
- Decree 804 of 18 May 1995 (Presidente de la República Colombiana, 1995a);
- Decree 3020 of 10 December 2002 (Presidente de la República Colombiana, 2002); and
- Decree 2406 of 26 June 2007 (Presidente de la República Colombiana, 2007).

The inclusion of indigenous languages in education policy first began with a recognition of the special educational needs of indigenous people in 1974 (Liddicoat & Curnow, 2007). Decree 88/1976 stated that cultural maintenance was to be one of the goals of the education of indigenous people:

Artículo 11. Los programas regulares para la educación de las comunidades indígenas tendrán en cuenta su realidad antropología y fomentarán la conservación y la divulgación de sus culturas autóctonas.
Article 11. The normal programmes for the education of indigenous communities will take into account their anthropological reality and foster the conservation and dissemination of their indigenous cultures.
(Presidente de la República Colombiana, 1976)

Two years later, Decree 1142/1978 developed a specific linguistic dimension for indigenous language education by giving prominence to the acquisition of literacy in the first languages of indigenous children:

Artículo 9° La alfabetización para las comunidades indígenas se hará en la lengua materna, facilitando la adquisición progresiva de la lengua nacional sin detrimento de la primera.
Article 9: Literacy teaching for indigenous communities will be done in the mother tongue, facilitating the progressive acquisition of the national language without detriment to the first.
(Presidente de la República Colombiana, 1978)

Literacy in the indigenous language is therefore closely tied to the development of literacy in Spanish and indigenous languages are thus subordinated to it. The decree frames the acquisition of Spanish as unproblematic for the maintenance of the first language but does not consider the questions of power and marginalisation that are at play in the relationship between the indigenous languages and the language of the majority. The underlying assumption appears to be that the provision of education in indigenous languages is adequate to address the problems of language maintenance for linguistic minorities.

The development of Spanish in mentioned twice in the same decree, including in the listing of initial assumptions for the decree:

> Que el Ministerio de Educación Nacional debe asegurar la conservación y el desarrollo de las lenguas maternas de las comunidades indígenas y proporcionarles a dichas comunidades el dominio progresivo de la lengua nacional sin detrimento de las lenguas maternas.
> That the Ministry of Education should ensure the conservation and development of the mother tongues of the indigenous communities and give the said indigenous communities the progressive mastery of the national language without detriment to the mother tongues.
> (Presidente de la República Colombiana, 1978)

The decree therefore has a focus on the preservation of indigenous languages but always in tandem with a concern for the development of Spanish. The framing of indigenous language development is thus understood in a context where acquiring Spanish is a necessary element of language maintenance. Spanish is therefore understood as the normal and normative language of the society. The document makes provision for learning by non-indigenous Colombians, although in this case there is not an expectation of language acquisition but rather of the development of declarative knowledge about languages and cultures:

> Articulo 12. En el currículo de la educación formal que se diseñe para todo el país deberá incluirse, dentro de las ciencias sociales, conocimientos relativos a la historia y cultura de las comunidades indígenas colombianas, insistiendo en aquellas que aún subsisten en el territorio nacional como un medio más de proporcionar una verdadera comprensión de estas comunidades.
> Article 12. In the curriculum of formal education which is designed for the whole country there must be included, within social sciences,

knowledge relative to the history and culture of Colombian indigenous communities, emphasising those that still survive in the national territory as a means to give a true understanding of those communities. (Presidente de la República Colombiana, 1978)

Thus the decree sees the understanding to be developed by the mainstream as one which remains external to the communities: they are represented as an object of study, not as people with whom the mainstream will necessarily engage.

These laws can be seen as a starting point for a developing focus on indigenous languages, both in education and in society more generally, which culminated in the specific recognition of indigenous languages in the constitution of 1991 (República de Colombia, 1991). The constitution officially recognised and undertook to protect the cultural diversity of Colombia (articles 7 and 70). These provisions are general statements of intent:

Article 7. El estado reconoce y protege la diversidad étnica y cultural de la Nación Colombiana.
The state recognises and protects the ethnic and cultural diversity of the Colombian Nation.

Article 70. La cultura en sus diversas manifestaciones es fundamento de la nacionalidad. El Estado reconoce la igualdad y dignidad de todas las que conviven en el país. El Estado promoverá la investigación, la ciencia, el desarrollo y la difusión de los valores culturales de la Nación.
Culture in its various manifestations is fundamental to nationality. The State recognises the equality and dignity of all [cultures] which cohabit in the country. The State will promote research, knowledge, development and dissemination of the cultural values of the Nation.
(República de Colombia, 1991)

These statements do not specifically include references to language, and language is recognised and protected only to the extent that it is considered an aspect of culture. Moreover, the focus of these statements is not on the indigenous people of the country but rather on cultural diversity as a more general concept, of which the language and cultures of indigenous people are only one manifestation.

Indigenous languages are, though, recognised specifically in article 10 of the constitution, which recognises that education in indigenous areas is to be bilingual (that is, in the indigenous language and Spanish):

Las lenguas y dialectos de los grupos étnicos son también oficiales en sus territorios. La enseñanza que se imparta en comunidades con tradiciones lingüísticas propias será bilingüe.

The languages and dialects of ethnic groups are also official in their territories. Teaching in communities with their own linguistic traditions will be bilingual.

(República de Colombia, 1991)

Article 10 focuses primarily on status planning – it states that Spanish is the official language of the country but also gives territorial recognition to other language varieties. The constitution does not state what is entailed in the recognition of languages as official, except insofar as it accepts that minority languages will be used in education. Article 68 of the constitution also addresses the issue of culturally appropriate education:

Los integrantes de los grupos étnicos tendrán derecho a una formación que respete y desarrolle su identidad cultural.

Members of ethnic groups will have a right to an education which respects and develops their cultural identity.

(República de Colombia, 1991)

Articles 10 and 68 of the Colombian constitution therefore recognise a role for indigenous languages in education, but without specification of what exactly is involved. Words such as 'bilingual', 'respect' and 'develop' are all subject to interpretation and these interpretations rest on legislation developed to enact these texts.

The language of these articles is also interesting, in that in no place does the constitution refer explicitly to indigenous groups, using instead the term *'etnicos'* (ethnic) to name the groups being considered. This use of *etnicos* may be an attempt to avoid words which have strong negative connotations in the Colombian context (such as *indigenas* or *indios*) or it may be intended to capture other forms of diversity, such as communities descended from African slaves brought to South America. The focus on territory in article 10 suggests that the definition of ethnic group in the constitution presupposes that such groups are territorial linguistic minorities, not immigrant groups; however, such a territorial definition would also include groups of African descent, who do have territorial concentrations (for example in Chocó).[9] Moreover, article 10 recognises that ethnicity does not necessarily equate with having a separate language. This may represent an attempt to reflect the actual conditions of language shift in Colombia prior to the development of the constitution or a recognition that some ethnic groups, again those of African descent, use a variety of Spanish as they do not have a collective traditional language. In reality, the formulation 'comunidades con tradiciones lingüísticas propias' (communities with their own linguistic traditions) is problematic and subject to interpretation. A linguistic tradition may mean that, in the community, a local language is currently in use, or it may mean a community in which a local language has been lost, as it is interpreted by at least some indigenous groups (see, for example, Liddicoat & Curnow, 2007, for the Awa).

The provisions of the constitution are therefore complex, in that the terminologies used are open to wide interpretation. However, it does make a clear symbolic statement of the value attached to linguistic and cultural diversity and it projects a particular form of educational provision involving the languages of Colombia. The forms of this educational provision have been worked through in subsequent legislation, most notably Law 115 of 1994, the 'General Law on Education' (República de Colombia, 1994). This law established the general educational provisions for all pre-tertiary education in Colombia but includes special provision for ethnic languages, to bring educational legislation in line with the policy statements of the 1991 constitution. The law integrates the provisions of the constitution with regard to the education of ethnic minorities, mainly in a section consisting of several articles focusing on *etnoeducation* (ethnoeducation). The law defines ethnoeducation as education for groups or communities who possess a culture, a language, traditions and a code of laws of their own (article 55 of Law 115/1994). Here the working through of the scope of 'ethnic group' involves further specification beyond the idea of a territorial linguistic tradition found in the constitution.

The law introduces a national ethnoeducation programme, with a vernacular language component, for ethnolinguistic minority groups. It also provides some definition of the nature of bilingual education in indigenous contexts in the general provisions for primary schooling in article 21:

> c) El desarrollo de las habilidades comunicativas básicas para leer, comprender, escribir, escuchar, hablar y expresarse correctamente en lengua castellana y también en la lengua materna, en el caso de los grupos étnicos con tradición lingüística propia, así como el fomento de la afición por la lectura;
>
> c) The development of basic communicative abilities for reading, understanding, writing, listening, speaking and expressing oneself correctly in Spanish and also in their mother tongue, in the case of ethnic groups with their own linguistic tradition, and also fostering a liking for reading;
>
> (República de Colombia, 1994)

Article 21, therefore, allocates a place for indigenous languages in primary school, for those groups who have access to an indigenous language: that is, the law seems to exclude those groups which, as the result of considerable language loss due to Spanish colonisation, have not maintained their languages. Article 21(c) seems, in fact, to go no further than the provisions for first language literacy which already existed under Decree 1142 of 1978. The text projects bilingualism and constructs this bilingualism in a particular way. The emphasis is given to the acquisition of Spanish, with the development of another language framed in second position. This text constructs bilingualism as involving the development of Spanish, which allows for relationships between ethnolinguistic minorities and the mainstream, and, as an additional provision, the development of the individual's own language. That is, the maintenance of an ethnic language has as a prerequisite integration into the mainstream language and culture. The provision made for indigenous languages in education therefore is articulated within the context of the hegemony of the Spanish language and culture, and this language maintains its pre-eminent position in the society.

In the law's next statement, article 21(d), the respective roles of Spanish and indigenous languages are made problematic by a vague formulation of what is being planned:

    d) El desarrollo de la capacidad para apreciar y utilizar la lengua como medio de expresión estética;

    d) The development of the ability to appreciate and use the language as a medium for aesthetic expression;

In this text the focus is uncertain because *la lengua* could refer to either Spanish if taken as a subsection of article 21 as a whole or it could refer to the indigenous language if it continues the bilingualism of article 21(c). The text does, however, clearly refer to *lengua* in the singular and does not in itself frame a multilingual reality for education. Depending on how the text is read, it is uncertain whether the indigenous languages are intended for more than developing basic skills or whether they are intended for use in developing more elaborated codes. The policy clearly constructs Spanish as the language that allows for indigenous people to become intercultural and participate in the mainstream. That is, Spanish is normalised as the language of all Colombians, while indigenous languages have a peripheral, additional place for those who identify with them. The status of indigenous languages is therefore understood within an ideology of Spanish as a necessary language for society. The indigenous languages are understood as having a limited role in the educated lives of indigenous people and as being of lesser importance than Spanish as the normalised language. Their ideological positioning does not therefore challenge the hegemonic position of Spanish.

The respective roles of the languages are taken up again in article 57 of the same law, which defines the nature of bilingual delivery in ethnoeducation:

> En sus respectivos territorios, la enseñanza de los grupos étnicos con tradición lingüística propia será bilingüe, tomando como fundamento escolar la lengua materna del respectivo grupo, sin detrimento de lo dispuesto en el literal c. del artículo 21 de la presente ley.
>
> In their respective territories, the teaching of ethnic groups with their own linguistic tradition will be bilingual, taking the mother tongue of the relevant group as a basis for schooling, without detriment to the provisions of section (c) of Article 21 of the present law.
>
> (República de Colombia, 1994)

Article 57, when read (as intended) in conjunction with article 21, frames ethnoeducation as education for indigenous groups who continue to use an indigenous language, but the principal purpose of that language education is in fact ultimately the development of literacy in Spanish. This means that indigenous languages and hence the identities with which they are associated are placed in a lesser position to Spanish and that the main focus of education remains the language of the dominant group. Such an analysis is further borne out by the lack of mention of indigenous languages in secondary education in article 22. It appears that under the policy, the linguistic aim of ethnoeducation is to develop competence in Spanish by the end of primary school and the law provides only a limited space for indigenous people and languages within the ideological space projected by the policy text. The texts therefore appear to co-opt indigenous languages into the ideology of Spanish dominance at the same time as they allocate them a place in Colombian society.

There are several more recent decrees, such as Decree 804/1995 (Presidente de la República Colombiana, 1995a), Decree 3020/2002 (Presidente de la República Colombiana, 2002) and Decree 2406/2007 (Presidente de la República Colombiana, 2007), which relate to the application of Law 115/1994, particularly given the readjustments required to move from the previous administrative system of municipalities to the constitutionally required concept of *Entidades Territoriales* (Territorial Entities) including *Entidades Territoriales Indígenas* (Indigenous Territorial Entities). However, these decrees add little of substance to Law 115/1994 and the constitutional provisions for ethnoeducation. This means that the dominating position of Spanish and the subordinated position of indigenous languages have remained in the ways in which ethnoeducation is understood in policy terms.

Decree 804/1995 specifically defines ethnoeducation as being inter-cultural in its focus:

> Interculturalidad, entendida como la capacidad de conocer la cultura propia y otras culturas que interactúan y se enriquecen de manera dinámica y recíproca, contribuyendo a plasmar en la realidad social, una coexistencia en igualdad de condiciones y respeto mutuo.
>
> Interculturality, understood as the capacity to know one's own culture and other cultures that interact and are enriched in a dynamic and reciprocal way, contributing to forming in social reality a coexistence in equality of conditions and mutual respect.
>
> (Presidente de la República Colombiana, 1995a)

The phrasing in this decree expresses mutuality and reciprocity as the funda-mental aims of ethnoeducation and this focus suggests that interculturality is something broader than the practices of indigenous groups. However, as ethnoeducation is aimed solely at indigenous people, the mutuality and reciprocity expressed are very one-sided, developed through the education of indigenous people as adjustment to the mainstream, but not through the education of the rest of the society. The dominant group therefore retains its hegemonic position as the group to which others adjust and are expected to adjust.

This lack of reciprocity is also found in the ways in which the word *bilingüismo* (bilingualism) is understood in different policy texts: in texts relating to indigenous people the term refers to the acquisition of Spanish in addition to an indigenous language spoken as a first language; in contrast, in language-in-education policies for the mainstream it means the acquisition of English – for example, the Programa Nacional de Bilingüismo 2004–19 (MEN, 2005, 2009) deals only with the teaching and learning of English. This means that bilingualism for the mainstream orients outwards, to intercultural relationships outside Colombia, not to the development of capabilities in indigenous languages. As a result, the intercultural relation-ships that language education is intended to develop for the dominant Spanish speakers is not oriented to internal linguistic and cultural differ-ences but to external ones. Internal relationships are mediated through the language of the majority and the indigenous language component of the bilingualism of indigenous people is removed from the national scope.

In Colombia, those policies which seek to recognise indigenous people and to act upon that recognition reveal the ways in which the social constructs of the two languages and the power relationships between them are ideologically entrenched. The place of indigenous languages is understood within an ideology of Spanish as the normal, natural and obvious language of the society. From the perspective of this ideology, indigenous people using indigenous languages remain in a subordinated position in their relationships with the mainstream. Bilingualism in such policies is framed as the acquisition of Spanish as a precondition for the maintenance of the indigenous language, as it must not be to the detriment of the acquisition of Spanish. Spanish in this way is represented as the vehicular language for intercultural relationships within Colombia and it is not projected in the policies that such relationships could be developed through the acquisition of indigenous languages for the mainstream.

Conclusion

These three polities show quite different responses to the place of indigenous languages in education and society, although all of them maintain a dominance of the national language over indigenous languages in the ways they articulate linguistic and cultural pluralism. Japan is the most extreme case of this, as its policies effectively deny the linguistic and cultural distinctiveness of indigenous minorities. Japanese language-in-education policy deals exclusively with the development of the national language through the educational system and makes no place for indigenous languages. Colombia, on the other hand, recognises indigenous languages explicitly in its constitution and allocates some rights to indigenous communities in the context of education. Australia lies between the two, recognising the presence of indigenous languages and including them in education policy as an aspect of language learning, but without other forms of explicit recognition.

In all three polities, the main language education focus is on the dominant language of the polity; equally, there appears to be greater emphasis on the national language than on indigenous languages in formulating educational objects, regardless of other aspects of the recognition of indigenous languages, and the discourses of the policy presume and preserve the hegemonic position of the dominant language. One of the main roles allocated to the indigenous language, where it is included in language-in-education policies, is the ability of education in the indigenous language to contribute to the educational goals of the mainstream society, including acquisition of the dominant language. For this reason, most attention is given to the teaching of indigenous languages in communities which have maintained their languages rather than in communities which have lost their languages as the result of earlier language-in-education policies and other social pressures. This means that the role of language as a marker of identity and as an element of cultural distinctiveness for indigenous people seems to have been backgrounded in policy texts.

Most of the policy texts construct the learning of indigenous languages as an educational matter for indigenous people and there is little provision for the learning of indigenous languages by people outside indigenous communities. This position is less strongly articulated in Australia because of the conflation of all forms of language learning under the umbrella of foreign language learning. Thus, Australian policy rarely states that the acquisition of indigenous languages by non-indigenous people is a policy objective, but neither does it preclude it. The construction of the learner of an indigenous language as an indigenous person represents an understanding of the place and value of indigenous languages as being within indigenous communities only. That is, they are languages for carrying out intracultural relationships and not languages for intercultural relationships. Intercultural relationships, as they are represented in policy texts, are established between indigenous people and others through the dominant language of the society. This means that an intercultural relationship involves the adjustment of the indigenous person to the language and culture of the mainstream, an adjustment which is constructed as monodirectional and requiring little if any adjustment of the non-indigenous person to the indigenous person, and which replicates the power relations between the hegemonic group and indigenous groups. The possibilities for indigenous languages to be seen as languages of intercultural relationship are eclipsed by the lack of policy expectation that these languages will be learnt outside indigenous communities.

To the extent that education prepares non-indigenous people to relate to indigenous people, it does so largely through processes of linguistic and cultural awareness. This constructs the non-indigenous person as an observer of indigenous linguistic and cultural particularities, who uses knowledge to accept and tolerate difference. That is, the non-indigenous person as an intercultural subject is not a participant in the society and culture of the indigenous person, but remains external to them. The indigenous person as an intercultural subject, however, is projected as being a person who is actively involved in, and shares the concerns of, the mainstream society. There are therefore two different constructions of the intercultural subject, and these parallel the constructions found in policies for immigrants discussed in Chapter 3: the intercultural subject as an observer of diversity and the intercultural subject as a participant in diversity. The positioning which requires the most adjustment to the other is that of participant and this positioning is allocated to the indigenous person. In this way, language-in-education policies preserve the dominated status of indigenous people, even where they make provision for indigenous languages, by requiring a differential adjustment by members of each group. The position of intercultural subject as participant therefore becomes an additional requirement placed on indigenous people as a consequence of their maintenance of linguistic and cultural difference, in order for that difference to be acceptable to the dominant group. It is an additional requirement because it is not represented as a reciprocal accommodation between groups but as an integration of the minority person into the majority group.

Notes

1. The terminology used to refer to indigenous people in Australia varies and is often the subject of dispute. Terms include 'Aborigines', 'Aborigines and Torres Strait Islanders' and 'Indigenous Australians' and their languages may be known as 'Aboriginal languages', 'Australian languages' or 'indigenous languages'. In this discussion the term 'indigenous' is used throughout for consistency with other case studies, although the terms used in policy documents are also maintained.
2. The number of speakers of creoles is not easily recoverable from available census data for the 1980s and 1990s as there was no breakdown presented of the languages which were identified as 'Australian'. Schmidt (1990) estimated that there were about 15,000 speakers of creoles, but many of these would also have spoken other indigenous languages. The 2006 census identified Torres Strait Creole as being the most widely spoken indigenous language, with 10.6% of indigenous people who used a language other than English reporting using it at home, while Kriol was spoken by 7.9% at home.
3. A similar observation was made in the context of immigrant languages in Australia in Chapter 3.
4. Luke *et al.* (1993) note that Torres Strait Islanders as a group are usually elided in the document itself and are treated as Aborigines, rather than acknowledging the specific linguistic and cultural identity of these people. In fact, they argue that there is a consistent silence in Australian policy about the internal linguistic and cultural diversity of indigenous people in Australia.
5. More completely, this legislation is called アイヌ文化の振興並びにアイヌの伝統等に 関する知識の普及及び啓発に関する法律 (Ainu bunka no shinkou narabi ni Ainu no dentou nado ni kansuru chishiki no fukyuu oyobi keihatsu ni kansuru houritsu, 'Law for the Promotion of the Ainu Culture and for the Dissemination of Knowledge of Ainu Traditions').
6. The Ryuku Islands had become a vassal state in 1609, but were not formally annexed to Japan until 1872 and were made into a prefecture in 1879, thus being territorially integrated into Japan at the same level as all other areas within the Japanese nation-state (Heinrich, 2004).
7. Yamato was an ancient name for Japan and has become extended to refer to the Japanese people as an ethnic group.

8. See Sanchéz (1996) and Sanchéz and Dueñas (2002) for an overview of Spanish language planning and policy in Latin America.
9. Ethnoeducation was officially extended to Afro-Colombian groups by Decree 2249/1995 (Presidente de la República Colombiana, 1995b).

5 External Language Spread Policies

Introduction

Ammon (1997: 51) defines language spread policy as 'a policy which has as its objective the spread of a specific language, or sometimes a set of languages, either to new speakers or to new domains'. This definition frames language spread in very broad terms and for the purposes of this chapter it needs some refining. Ammon establishes the possibility that language spread policy may be either internal – promoting the spread of a language within a polity – or external – promoting the spread of a language in other polities. In this chapter, the focus is on external language spread policies. Such policies are in many ways different from other forms of language policy, as they represent attempts to influence the language use of people outside the administrative control of those designing the policy. In addition, not all language spread policies are related to education.[1] As Ammon notes, language spread policies may seek to extend the use of a language into new domains. An external language spread policy may therefore seek to increase the use of a language in international organisations – an issue relating to status planning – or it may seek to influence how the language is perceived by others – an issue relating to prestige planning. In fact, even those language spread policies which are specifically educational may include aspects of other types of language planning and policy activity, especially those relating to prestige planning (Ager, 2005b).

Language planning and policy work is typically undertaken by governments, or governmental bodies. In external language spread policy, this is, however, often not the case and language spread policy work is delegated to various types of non-government bodies. The devolution of language spread policy to bodies which are to some extent independent of the apparatus of government appears to be a result of the nature of external language spread.

As external language spread policy involves intervention in societies controlled by other governments, direct government intervention in education by a foreign power could be difficult. A non-government organisation may appear to be less intrusive as an agent of language policy than a government body. This does not mean that direct involvement in education in another polity is not possible – the example of the Brazilian government accrediting schools in Japan to teach Portuguese, discussed in Chapter 3, is a case in point. Such activities do, however, require the consent of the recipient polity, typically expressed through agreements between governments or institutions. One advantage of exercising language spread policy through non-government bodies is that the operations of such bodies do not have to be closely aligned to a government's foreign policy and may operate in places with which there is limited or no diplomatic contact.

Non-government organisations responsible for language spread policy are not necessarily always separate from government. Many language spread policy bodies have been established directly by governments and receive government funding (e.g. the British Council, the Japan Foundation, the Cervantes Institute, the Instituto Camões) while others have been established as private institutions but receive government funding (e.g. the Alliance Française). Organisations of both types may be subject to some direct or indirect government control. This government control is often exercised through a Ministry of Foreign Affairs rather than a Ministry of Education, indicating that the perceived function of such bodies is typically to develop international relations rather than being strictly educational.

If we consider language policy as an attempt to address a perceived language problem, the articulation of a language spread policy would imply a perceived problem in the (inadequate) use of one's own language by others. Thus the problem identified for language spread policy is not usually a strictly linguistic one, but relates more to questions of international status and prestige. Ammon (1997) notes that language spread policies are often defensive – they respond to a perception that the use of a particular language is declining in favour of another, and consequently that the prestige, or symbolic capital (Bourdieu, 1982), of the polity is being reduced. Language spread policy can therefore be seen as an attempt through language to claim or reclaim national prestige through the diffusion of a language. In such attempts, language spread is usually conceived as part of a broader policy of cultural diffusion, in which the spread of the language is associated with efforts to enhance appreciation of the linguistic and non-linguistic cultural products of the polity. In such a context, language is represented both as in itself one of the valued cultural products of the polity and also as a vehicle for accessing other valued products. The focus of such policy clearly overlaps with issues relating to prestige and image planning and in some cases language-in-education work cannot clearly be distinguished from prestige planning, as the teaching of the language is undertaken to enhance the prestige of the language and its associated culture and society rather than for purely educational objectives. The preservation of a language in the education system of other polities is associated with the maintenance of national pride and national self-image.

The concerns for symbolic capital that underlie language spread policy mean that such policies have been identified as significant elements in linguistic imperialism (Phillipson, 1992, 1997, 2010). External language spread policies, because they frame the dissemination of the official language of one polity to people in another polity who do not speak that language as a first or official language, seek to entrench the use of the language being diffused as a vehicle for intercultural contact. Phillipson (1992) argues that this reinforces a linguistic asymmetry in which one partner in the communication, the speaker of the diffused language, preserves an advantage in being able to use this language rather than acquiring an additional language for such communication. This means that the speaker of the diffused language is able to enjoy significant communicative advantages over those who do not speak the language well (see also Ammon, 1997). In addition, the diffusion of a particular language becomes a channel for the dissemination of the ideology of the community that speaks that particular language. The teaching of a particular language may be constructed as the development of a resource for the language learner to access something of value (technology, modernity, high culture, etc.). Implicitly, therefore, the information and cultural products available in the diffused language are deemed to have some objective, universal value, which others will necessarily want to access. This allocates value asymmetrically to one culture. Phillipson (1992) also argues that language spread policy may be associated with economic asymmetries and dependencies – the diffusion of a particular language facilitates trade between polities which learn that language and the polity responsible for the diffusion of the language. In addition, the teaching and learning of a language with high symbolic capital may become a source of revenue for polities identified as native speakers of that language. In this way, foreign education can be seen as a form of language spread in which the linguistic and non-linguistic resources of the educator become economic capital.

Both language spread and linguistic imperialism are processes which involve much more than policy documents. Languages can spread whether or not there are policies and institutions to support their spread and linguistic imperialism emerges as much, if not more, from the practices of language education than it does from particular texts. Nonetheless, policy documents can be significant sources for discursive understandings of language spread. The evolution of language spread policies reveals, as the three case studies in this chapter will show, a discursive move away from constructions of language spread as the one-way dissemination of culture to a greater focus on reciprocity. This discursive emphasis on reciprocity appears to be a reaction to the increasingly negative view of imperialist notions and rhetoric, while at the same time opening a discursive space in which external language spread can be continued.

British Language Spread Policy

British language spread policy grew from a colonial perspective in which English was spread through education within colonised countries. It gained its emphasis on external language spread in part through processes of decolonisation as an attempt to support the acquisition of English in former colonies and more broadly in the world (Phillipson, 1992, 1994). The first appearance of external language spread policy outside zones of British control, however, pre-dated decolonisation and was a response to the cultural propaganda of pre-war fascist governments in Germany and Italy.

The first activity by the government began in 1934 with the establishment of the British Committee for Relations with Other Countries, which became the British Council for Relations with Other Countries in 1935. In November 1934, the British government brought together a group of businessmen and educational experts who formed a committee to consider 'a scheme for furthering the teaching of English abroad and to promote thereby a wider knowledge and understanding of British culture generally' (Nicolson, 1955: 10). The British Council was established with a broad agenda of cultural promotion, of which English language spread was only one component. This policy emphasised external language spread as a way to enhance the international prestige of Britain and used language education as a way of elevating the symbolic capital of English. The aim of the policy was therefore that, through language learning, people in targeted countries would develop their capacity to communicate with and appreciate the British. Although the structure of the British Council was designed to allow it significant autonomy, it is funded through the Foreign Office budget and the Foreign Office maintains a supervisory role.

Donaldson (1984) argues that the British began work in cultural diplomacy, and thus in language spread, because the government of the time believed that the Germans and Italians were creating an atmosphere of hostility towards Britain in Asia and Latin America. Language spread work was therefore conceived as a form of 'image planning' (Ager, 2005a, 2005b), to influence attitudes towards both the polity and the language. The aim of the work was to deal with issues of prestige, in this case the damage to prestige that resulted from the competition of other polities. The focus on maintaining the image and prestige of Britain was expressed in documents presented to Cabinet prior to the outbreak of the Second World War. While these documents were not publically available, they represent ideologies about language and the value of language education being articulated more widely. A 1939 survey of foreign publicity argued that:

> the best answer to the hostile propaganda of the totalitarian States is to educate foreigners in the British point of view, to explain the British way of life, as shown in our institutions, our education, art, science, and literature, and to give facts about our industrial strength and the way it is being adapted for purposes of defence. (Foreign Office, 1939: 1)

Education about Britain was seen as being a response to the propaganda of enemies and was an aspect of a competition for the esteem of others. The survey acknowledges a central role in this task for the British Council and its English language programme. The discourse grows out of a jockeying for position before the outbreak of hostilities, in which language and intercultural relationship are manipulated for the goals of defence and/or aggression. Cultural diplomacy thus began as an aspect of international competition for influence throughout the world. This diplomatic agenda was further supported by an economic agenda promoted by the Department of Trade, which argued that 'cultural projection was inseparable from successful commerce and diplomacy' (Coombs, 1988: 2). In this way, policies involving cultural and linguistic spread were seen as contributing to Britain by achieving objectives in international relations, trade and the enhancement of British cultural and symbolic capital.

The English language teaching work of the British Council was viewed as having a central role in fostering British interests overseas:

> [The British Council] adopted as its primary task the spreading of a knowledge of the English language abroad, on the ground that with a knowledge of the language there would come a desire to learn more about the British point of view and the British way of life. (Foreign Office, 1939: 1)

Here, the teaching of English is understood in terms of establishing a desire to move beyond language. The development of language abilities is seen as engendering a desire to engage with Britain. In this way, language education creates both the possibility of and desire for developing an intercultural relationship with Britain, which will be for the benefit of Britain. The British point of view and way of life are represented as objects of value, which are currently unknown to others because of their lack of language, and the value of which, once the language has been acquired, will automatically be seen. The intercultural relationship is therefore one in which English is seen as both vehicular – it allows for engagement – and productive – it establishes engagement as a response – with the engagement always being from the other to the self and for the ultimate benefit of the self.

This view that English is both vehicular in that it allows for communication and productive in that it creates desire for British language and culture persists in discourses about language education in British policy documents. The 1954 Drogheda report, for example, states: 'A knowledge of English gives rise in its turn to a desire to read English books, talk to British people and learn about British life or some particular aspect of it' (Drogheda *et al.*, 1954: 47). In its discussion of the role of the British Council in Asia, the report makes an association between language and an induction into westernised practices:

> [The Professor of English or the British Council educational officer's] real function is to be a sort of missionary who uses the English language as a key to open the door, so that the Asian student, if he wishes, can enter into the life of the West.... [The activities of the British Council] form part of a single process designed to condition the thinking of a selected number of educated Asians in such a way that a great deal of goodwill towards the United Kingdom will be created among the people who may be expected to play a leading part as politicians or industrialists in the new Asia. (Drogheda *et al.*, 1954: 63)

That is, English provides a way to access the west, which is constructed as an undisputable good. The religious vocabulary used here places the language educator as one who brings enlightenment to others through the teaching of English and at the same time predisposes those who acquire it to think well of Britain. The focus of interaction therefore remains between the Asian other and the British self, with the other adopting the practices of the self for the benefit of both.

Within this environment, the focus on the British Council's work was primarily on cultural diplomacy for Britain, and Britain represented the main point of engagement between cultures, through English. Although English was acknowledged to be a pluricentric language, the focus of the British Council's work was not on the teaching of English as a pluricentric language but rather on securing the place of Britain internationally, with English as a mechanism allowing others to connect with Britain. The agenda is a foreign affairs one, which necessarily focuses on a particular nation-state, rather than an educational one, promoting language capabilities to achieve learners' own goals.

The foreign affairs agenda of the British Council is well documented. The Royal Charter for the British Council, which was issued in 1940, stated the purpose of the British Council as:

> Promoting a wider knowledge of the United Kingdom of Great Britain and Ireland and the English Language abroad, and developing closer cultural relations between the United Kingdom and other countries, for the purposes of benefiting the British Commonwealth of Nations. (British Council, 1941: 10)

The aims of the British Council were to promote engagement with Britain, and to a lesser extent the British Commonwealth, and this was in competition with the cultural emphasis of the United States. The Commonwealth was at this time, as Phillipson (1996) notes, the white, English-speaking dominions: Australia, Canada, New Zealand and South Africa. In this way, the work of the British Council was articulated in a way which emphasised the British zone of control and the disseminated British culture within that zone. The reference to the Commonwealth is, however, deleted in the text of the Supplemental Charter of 1993, which states the British Council's goals as:

> (a) promote a wider knowledge of Our United Kingdom;
> (b) develop a wider knowledge of the English language;
> (c) encourage cultural, scientific, technological and other educational co-operation between Our United Kingdom and other countries; or
> (d) otherwise promote the advancement of education.
> (British Council, 2002)

The objectives here are framed in terms of dissemination – of knowledge and language – and of the development of capacity through engagement with the United Kingdom, and with possible benefits for it. The aims, from the perspective of language spread policy, are specific to English and to engagement through English between Britain and other countries.

Similar aims have been articulated in a variety of ways in British Council documents, but have focused always on developing relationships with Britain. For example, the *Annual Report* of 1941 states:

> The Council's aim is to create in a country overseas a basis of friendly knowledge and understanding of the people of this country, our philosophy and way of life, which will lead to a sympathetic appreciation of British foreign policy. (British Council, 1941: 15)

This excerpt constructs the intercultural relationship between Britain and others as a friendly and sympathetic one. That is, the aim of the British Council is to develop among others a liking of Britain (i.e. Anglophilia). This relationship is manifested through knowledge about Britain and understanding of the country. The discourse in the British Council's early documents therefore presents a monodirectional relationship in which Britain works to promote others' understanding of the self, but understanding of others is not presented as an objective. That is, the place of Britain in the world depends on the development of engagement with Britain by others, rather than on the engagement of Britain with others.

> The aim of the British Council is to promote an enduring understanding of Britain in other countries through cultural, educational, and technical co-operation. (British Council, 1985: cover page)

The focus of these formulations remains on the development of others' knowledge of Britain. The use of 'co-operation' in the 1985 text implies that the development of understanding of Britain is a desirable outcome not only of British action but of the actions of other governments and agencies and that others can be expected to cooperate in order to achieve such an outcome. Understanding Britain is therefore presented not simply as an objective of value and benefit to Britain but also as of value to others. That is, the dissemination of the English language is a dissemination of a preferred value system about English that recognises the prestige of the language and develops a positive image for it (see Ager 2005a, 2005b). In this way, the monodirectional construction of intercultural relationships between Britain and others is represented as the result of cooperation – that is, a collaborative, bilateral achievement. In understanding language spread, then, the acquisition of English becomes a vehicle for engagement with Britain – an engagement which is presented ideologically as being of value to those who acquire the language.

More recent framings of the British Council's objects have focused on engagement and the building of trust. For example, the *Annual Report* for 2008–09 states that 'The British Council builds engagement and trust for the UK through the exchange of knowledge and ideas between people worldwide' (British Council, 2009: 2). Here, the discourse introduces the idea of exchange, which develops the idea of cooperation present in the 1985 quote above. Exchange implies an act of mutual giving – there is thus an implied bidirectionality in the relationship that is envisaged. This bidirectionality is at the same time constrained – it is framed as an exchange for the benefit of Britain, rather than mutual benefit. It is also constrained when the work is viewed in the context of the language spread goals of the British Council, because the exchange is one which results from the diffusion of English. The bidirectionality of relationships is also present in the formulation of the work of the British Council in terms of 'intercultural dialogue':

> Intercultural dialogue: our aims are to strengthen understanding and trust between and within different cultures and to encourage people to play an active, constructive part in their societies. (British Council, 2009: 2)

The phrase 'intercultural dialogue' seeks to cast the work of the organisation in terms of mutual engagement. The framing of intercultural dialogue implies a multidirectional relationship between groups and individuals within groups which benefits the societies from which individuals come. There is a tension in the ideological framings of engagement in the British Council's documents, between the discourses of benefit for Britain from the work of the British Council and those of more general benefit, which may potentially exclude direct benefit to Britain. The tension relates to the ways in which participants are understood to be engaged with each other. The discourses of benefit to Britain imply an engagement with the British as the normal partners for communication in English, while the engagement of individuals within their own societies potentially excludes the British, as external to these societies.

These forms of engagement need to be understood within the English language spread functions of the British Council, which are represented as core work for the organisation:

> English and examinations are a growing part of the British Council's work. We aim to reach one million learners through our own centres and three million people who wish to take UK qualifications. We also plan to reach a higher proportion of the estimated eight million teachers of English and two billion learners of English worldwide with new products and services that help them to achieve their goals. In doing this we provide access to skills and qualifications that open up opportunities and build an appreciation of the UK. (British Council, 2009: 3)

The focus on English given in the text above represents a version of the discourses of engagement with Britain. The British Council's aim is to examine large numbers of language learners who wish to engage with Britain through education and also to develop teachers who will support this engagement. Moreover, the capabilities that the British Council's work is to develop are not represented as language capabilities for their own sake, but rather as vehicles for developing greater attachment to Britain – that is, Britain is the targeted interlocutor for both learners and teachers of English. The role of English, therefore, is represented very strongly in terms of a British focus and this stands in contrast to the more pluralistic discourses relating to intercultural dialogue.

In the 2008–09 *Annual Report*, intercultural dialogue and English language education have been separated out. This allows them to develop as parallel and potentially contradictory discourses. However, in the 2010–11 *Annual Report* they seem to have been brought together more closely, under the umbrella of 'cultural relations':

> The cultural relations work of the British Council focuses on the following key areas:
>
> • English
> • Arts
> • Education and Society
>
> The British Council's strength lies in our understanding of what the UK has to offer, combined with our on-the-ground knowledge of people, partners and other countries' goals and priorities. Through our work we increase our participants' and partners' awareness and understanding of the UK and share and learn from each other. We forge links, create opportunities and establish relationships which build trust.
> (British Council, 2011: 14)

In this formulation, English is presented as a core element of the work of cultural relations – that is, cultural relations for the British Council are relations carried out through English and thus English is to be understood as immediately salient for intercultural engagement. The work of cultural relations is further associated with Britain and what Britain has to offer others – that is, it returns to a more monodirectional ideology of engagement, in which Britain provides its cultural capital to others. The selection and application of this cultural capital can be targeted through awareness of the goals and priorities of others. The monodirectional ideology is countered by an assertion of learning from each other, which re-establishes reciprocity, although, again, this is located in relationship to awareness and understanding of Britain.

The British Council has a continued discourse of cultural work for the benefit of Britain which implies a one-way form of engagement with others. This monodirectionality has been modified over time, with greater emphasis being given to forms of reciprocity in the discourse of relevant documents. However, this movement to reciprocity is in tension with the expressed agenda of benefit for Britain. The tension appears to be resolved through an assumption that what Britain has to offer, both linguistically and more generally, is a valued commodity, the value of which is unproblematically recognised by all.

The idea of British language and culture as valued commodities is the basis on which an ideology of intercultural relationship is established in British language spread policies. The primary form of intercultural relationship articulated throughout the history of such policies is one in which others use English in order to access British culture, knowledge and so on. Over time, this relationship moves from one constructed in almost exclusively monodirectional terms to one which is framed more reciprocally, in terms of collaboration, cooperation and exchange. The dimensions of that exchange, included in later policy texts, are, however, restricted, at least implicitly, to the use of the English language as the normal vehicular language of intercultural relationship, the dissemination of British language and culture as objects of unproblematised value and those aspects of others' cultures which may be of value to Britain. The intercultural subject is constructed as a speaker of English and interculturality itself becomes incorporated into the objects of value associated with British language and culture.

Japanese Language Spread Policy

Japan's initial work in language spread began like that for Britain and France (discussed below) – within the context of imperialism. The first activities involved the extension of Japanese schooling to Taiwan after the territory had been acquired from China, and later to Korea and Manchuria (Hirataka, 1992). The activities are essentially forms of internal language spread designed to develop the Japanese presence, and attachment to Japan, in the regions annexed (Rhee, 1992).

Japan's policies relating specifically to external language spread began with the establishment of the Kokusai Bunka Shinkōkai (KBS) (国際文化振興会, International Culture Organisation), a Japanese government agency set up by the military government in 1934 to help promote Japanese culture. The KBS began to play an increasingly nationalistic role from the end of the

1930s, eventually becoming part of the cultural propaganda of the Japanese military government and the implementation of Japanese political, linguistic and cultural dominance in the Greater East Asia Prosperity Sphere (Shibasaki, 1999). The focus of the KBS was primarily on culture rather than language: the KBS was to promote a correct understanding of Japan in the west through identifying correct representations of Japan and exporting the approved version of Japanese culture. The work of the KBS included the development of materials for the teaching and learning of Japanese in areas under Japanese occupation at the time. The language work of the KBS was integrated into the project for Japanese to become the dominant language in East Asia as part of Japanese hegemony in the region (Hirataka, 1992). In addition to the work of the KBS, the Japanese government supported the establishment of schools for Japanese emigrants, especially in Hawaii and Brazil, both financially and by providing teachers (Hirataka, 1992). These schools functioned alongside the national educational system, that is, as a form of complementary education. This was not directed at foreign nationals but was rather focused on the maintenance of the Japanese language and culture by Japanese communities outside Japan. Following the end of the Second World War, the work of the KBS was curtailed (Takahashi, 1998). The organisation was relaunched in 1954 as a private foundation sponsored by the government, and conducted some work in promoting Japanese culture, although on a limited scale.

Japanese effort in external language spread policy was relaunched as a major activity of the Japanese government when the Japan Foundation (国際交流基金, Kokusai Kōryū Kikin, Foundation for International Exchange) was established in 1972 to replace the KBS. The Japan Foundation was established as a quasi-independent body funded by, and to some extent directed by, the Ministry of Foreign Affairs. The work of the Japan Foundation has strongly focused on language spread, although it also took on the cultural dissemination work of the KBS. The purpose of the Foundation is described in article 1 of its establishment law as being twofold: the promotion of knowledge of Japan and the development of international understanding:

第一条　国際交流基金は、わが国に対する諸外国の理解を深め、国際相互理解を増進するとともに、国際友好親善を促進するため、国際文化交流事業を効率的に行ない、もつて世界の文化の向上及び人類の福祉に貢献することを目的とする。

Article 1 The purpose of the Japan Foundation is to deepen foreign countries' understanding of our country, increase international mutual understanding, promote international friendship and carry out

international exchanges efficiently, thereby improving world culture and contributing to the welfare of humanity.
(Diet of Japan, 1972)

The text emphasises dissemination of knowledge about Japan and also a reciprocal involvement between Japan and other countries. In the text, others' understanding of Japan is problematised, and this problematising reflects the discursive construction of Japan as different and therefore difficult for others to comprehend, as is found in the ideology of *Nihonjinron*. Within the overarching aims of the Japan Foundation, language spread is articulated as one of the key elements of its work, in article 23:

二 海外における日本研究に対する援助及びあつせん並びに日本語の普及
2. Spread Japanese language by aid and mediation for Japanese studies in foreign countries.
(Diet of Japan, 1972)

The mission of the Japan Foundation can be understood as one of dissemination of the Japanese language and culture and promotion of understanding of Japan. This focus relates to the development of the cultural and symbolic capital of Japan in the international sphere and the development of relationships between the Japanese and others. In this way, the fostering of learning about Japan and the Japanese language aims to influence others' image of Japan and to bolster the prestige of Japan in the world (see Ager, 2005a, 2005b). That is, the mission involves an attempt by Japan to manage a particular type of interaction with others. The inclusion of an exchange dimension appears to be a reaction to the nationalistic ideology of pre-war cultural policy, in which the focus was placed on a monodirectional representation of Japan to others, emphasising the superiority of Japanese culture (Hirano, 2002).

The language spread policy of the Japanese government has not focused solely on the work of the Japan Foundation. The teaching of Japanese for fostering understanding of Japan was one of the themes of a 2004 appeal to the Japanese Prime Minister about the international study of Japanese (Ogoura, 2004). The appeal document argued that communicating about Japan in English is inadequate for representing Japan on the world stage and that communication in Japanese is necessary and strategic in disseminating Japanese culture and ideas:

にもかかわらず、いまだに国際社会での日本の対外発信は、英語に代表される国際流通性の高い外国語に頼っているのが現状です．今、私たちの思想や文化を育んできた言語文化を戦略的に発信する努力を怠れば、世界の人々の日本に対する関心や興味を引き止めておくことは難しいでしょう

Nevertheless, when communicating with the international community, Japan still relies on English or another widely used foreign language. If now Japan neglects efforts to disseminate the language in which our ideas and culture are cultivated strategically, it will probably be difficult to keep the rest of the world interested in Japan.
(Ogoura, 2004)

This document problematises an understanding of foreign language education policy as the main mechanism for communicating the Japanese worldview to others (see Chapter 2) and argues that Japan's need is not only to disseminate its ideas to the world but also to do so in its own language. This text links to the idea of the *kotodama* of the Japanese language – the unique spirit of the language that shapes communication in the language as special and specific to Japanese realities (see Chapter 3). The use of Japanese as a language of intercultural relationship between Japan and others is framed in part in terms of maintaining the cultural and symbolic capital of Japan and maintaining the world's interest. In addition, the appeal argues for 'aggressive promotion' of Japanese as a way of increasing Japan's international role:

私たち一同は、そのために有効な方策として、日本語教育をこれまでの受動的な支援から積極的な推進へと転換することにより、国際社会における日本の役割を一層強化することが可能であると考えます。

We think that converting from the former policy of passive support to aggressive promotion of Japanese language education would be an effective plan to strengthen Japan's role in the international community.
(Ogoura, 2004)

Again, there is evidence of an association between the dissemination of Japanese and the maintenance of Japanese cultural and symbolic capital in the international arena.

In this document, Japanese language spread has a dual function: (1) it is a vehicle for disseminating understanding of Japan; and (2) it is strategically important for enhancing Japan's international presence. The document does not, however, restrict itself to issues framed as relevant to Japan's interests: it also argues that access to Japanese is beneficial for the learner, in that it gives access to one of the world's great cultural assets, in the form of the accumulated literature in Japanese, Japan's 'charming' culture (魅力ある日本文化, *miryoku aru nihon bunka*) and Japan's culture of 'craftsmanship' (「ものずくり」文化, *'monozukuri' bunka*).[2] In all of these constructions, access to Japanese culture is represented as enhancing for the learner, as an object of self-evident value to be transmitted to others.

The document does not emphasise Japanese distinctiveness and is even at pains to set aside perceptions that the language is 'too unique'. That is, it addresses an older ideology within *Nihonjinron* that claims that Japanese is too difficult for non-Japanese people to learn (see Chapter 3) – an argument which is inherently counter-productive for an external language spread policy. Nonetheless, the document does to a certain extent articulate with ideologies relating to *kokusaikakyouiku* ('international education') in foreign language teaching (see Chapter 2) through its desire to foster understanding of Japan. In particular, there is a sense in which the maintenance of distinctiveness is found in the discourse about Japan as an international player. For example: 'Considering itself a distinct civilization, Japan has therefore no other choice but to fight to preserve its uniqueness while tuning its interests to the global pulse' (Costescu, 2000: 18). In this conceptualisation, international engagement is opposed to the preservation of distinctiveness and the inherent conflict is the preservation of distinctiveness during engagement. Ogoura's (2004) quote above, seen in relation to this discourse, can be interpreted as an argument for maintaining distinctiveness by increasing communication in and through the Japanese language, the source of Japanese culture and ideas.

The emphasis on the strategic deployment of Japanese reflects other discourses relating to strategy and distinctiveness found in the *Nihonjinron* ideology and to the unique *kotodama* of the language. In particular, it links with Suzuki's (1978) argument that the Japanese language represents a weapon for the defence of Japan, in the sense that once Japanese has been taught more widely, it will enable the Japanese to 'communicate to foreign countries, what Japan is thinking about, what Japan is hoping for, and what Japan wishes to accomplish. Then the Japanese language will have become an extremely powerful tool' (Suzuki, 1978, cited in Miller, 1982: 288). The underlying idea here is that Japanese ideas and aspirations cannot adequately be communicated through other languages, but only through Japanese. Suzuki argues that, if Japan is to be a significant international power, it must be able to articulate its particular Japanese worldview through its language. An external language spread policy therefore is needed to create an audience for the dissemination of Japanese ideas and values through the Japanese language. If Japanese is the ideal way to communicate about Japan, that is, if it is to be a vehicle for international relationships, there is a need to create interlocutors. Japanese language spread policy faces a different agenda from the language spread policies for English, French or Spanish, among others, in that there is neither widespread use of the language resulting from colonialism or other economic and social processes, nor is there a long-established tradition of Japanese teaching in countries which would be considered to be relevant interlocutors. This means that rather than being a defence against the erosion of language learning, which Ammon (1997) suggests is the usual focus of language spread policies, Japanese policies need to address a situation of limited learning of the language.

The Japan Foundation is not the only language spread activity undertaken by the Japanese government. In addition, the government has established programmes in which teachers of Japanese are sent to teach in other countries, most notably the Regional and Educational Exchanges for Mutual Understanding (REX) programme. These programmes for language spread have a focus on the teaching of both language and culture, as can be seen from the following description from the REX programme:

> 派遣先では、中学校・高等学校の生徒に日本語を教えるほか、日本の社会や歴史、文化を紹介する活動などを行います。
>
> After being dispatched, they will teach pupils at junior high school and high school not only Japanese language but will also introduce Japanese society and history and culture.
>
> (MEXT, 2004a)

The ways in which Japanese culture is conceptualised for dissemination among the non-Japanese is seen most clearly in the study of *Nihonjijou* (日本事情, Japanese way of life). *Nihonjijou* was established officially by the Ministry of Education in 1962 and covers a syllabus of a general introduction to Japan, Japanese history, culture, politics, economics, nature, science and technology:

> 日本事情に関する科目としては、一般日本事情、日本の歴史及び文化、日本の政治、経済、日本の自然、日本の科学　技術といったものが考えられる
>
> the subjects for *Nihonjijou* may be considered to include a general introduction to Japanese way of life, Japanese history and culture, Japanese politics, the economy, Japanese nature, Japanese science and technology.
>
> (Ministerial order 21/1962, cited in Toyota, 1988)

The nature of culture taught under a *Nihonjijou* approach is exemplified by the following extract from a description of the REX pre-departure training programme:

日本の文化・社会の紹介に備え、日本の政治・近代史などを振り返るとともに、華道・茶道・武道などを学びます。また、異文化間コミュニケーションの視野も取り入れながら、現地の生活・教育事情について学びます。

Trainees will learn how to introduce Japanese culture and society, Japanese politics, modern history including flower arranging, the tea ceremony, martial arts etc.

(MEXT, 2004b)

The themes represented here are traditionalising themes which privilege distinctly Japanese practices that may have limited applicability for the lived experiences of Japanese people. While the scope of *Nihonjijou* is not restricted to such practices, the approach is criticised for presenting an ethnocentric and stereotypical view of Japan which reinforces a view of the society as monoethnic, monocultural and monolingual (Nagata, 1995). In this way, the dissemination of the Japanese language and culture links with the monoethnic ideology of the Japanese state and seeks to disseminate this view of the country. The teaching of Japanese culture for overseas learners of Japanese focuses on an essentialised version of the culture and is conducted in a way which emphasises the distinctiveness of Japanese culture in conformity with the Japanese ideologies of cultural distinctiveness (*Ninhonjinron*).

The language spread policies of contemporary Japan structure a form of intercultural relationship in which others will be brought knowledge of Japan through the learning of Japanese. Policies construct a relationship between Japan and the other which is essentially monodirectional and the flow of knowledge is from Japan to the other. At the same time, policies construct an authorised version of what this knowledge should be – that is, the interaction is with an idealised Japan and the purpose of the interaction is to transmit this idealised view outside Japan. This means that the discourses which exist in language spread policy mirror those in foreign language policy, with only the language being used differing between the two policy contexts. The focus of intercultural relationships in both types of policy is on the dissemination of a particular image of Japan and a particular understanding of a Japanese worldview – one which the Japanese themselves may need to learn in order to disseminate it. In language spread policies, the vehicular language for intercultural relationships is Japanese, but its effectiveness for such purposes is rendered problematic by the comparatively low levels of language use internationally.

French Language Spread Policy

The language spread policy of the French government has been operationalised through both government and non-government organisations which have received some government support and have worked in close relationship with governments and their policies.[3] One of the most longlasting activities for the spread of French has been the work of the Alliance Française. The Alliance Française was founded in 1883 as a private organisation but received various forms of support from the French government from its inception (Salon, 1985), including government funding under the budget of the Ministry for Foreign Affairs from 1886 (Frank, 2003). The use of private organisations was the main mechanism to further the language spread agenda of the French government prior to the early 20th century and Chaubet (2004) argues that, until the French government took charge of policy for linguistic and cultural spread following the First World War, the Alliance Française provided the main policy and action in this area. The government provided funding for the Alliance Française, and for other similar but smaller organisations,[4] and also influenced the direction and activities of these organisations.

The forms of support became more formalised and in 1900 the French Ministry of Foreign Affairs established a special section to provide funding for French schools and organisations abroad, and funding of the Alliance Française has continued as part of foreign affairs funding (Deibel & Roberts, 1976). In addition, it has attracted powerful patrons: for example, Poincaré served two terms as president in the 1920s and 1930s, while de Gaulle was honorary president during the Alliance Française's exile in London during the Second World War (Bruézière, 1983). Thus, although the Alliance Française is not a government agency, its work can be considered a form of government action in language planning and policy work (Salon, 1981).[5]

The Alliance Française was originally established with a brief to spread the French language in the colonies and elsewhere in the world ('la propagation de la langue française dans les colonies et à l'ètranger' – The propagation of the French language in the colonies and in foreign countries) (*Bulletin de l'Alliance Française*, 1884: 6); that is, it is specifically a language spread organisation. The early focus was on language spread in colonial contexts as a way of strengthening France:

> Puisque [la France] manque d'enfants, qui l'empêche de franciser les fils de ses sujets et protégés coloniaux ?... Le premier fait de cette annexion morale doit être l'enseignement de notre langue
> Since France lacks children, what is to stop it from making the sons

of its colonial subjects and protégés French? The first act of this moral annexation should be the teaching of our language.

(*Bulletin de l'Alliance Française*, 1888, cited in Barko, 1999: 3)

The mission of the Alliance Française was therefore understood as a moral dimension of colonialism in which colonised people would be assimilated (*franciser* – 'to make French') into the moral system of French civilisation. The dissemination of language is therefore an element of the French hegemony over its subject populations and a dissemination of the ideological system that support the hegemony. This is an overtly assimilationist activity which represents French civilisation as an objective good to be conferred on others, the local identities of colonised people being less relevant than their identities as French subjects. The dissemination of language and culture is also understood in terms of the strengthening of France, which at the time had been weakened nationally and internationally in the wake of the Franco-Prussian War and the rise of Germany.

The spread of French was seen as operating at a number of levels: as part of colonial conquest, as a way of establishing social relationships and as an economic tool:

faire connaître et aimer notre langue, car c'est là peut-être le meilleur moyen de conquérir les indigènes, de faciliter avec eux des relations sociales et les rapports commerciaux.

to make our language known and loved, since that is perhaps the best means to conquer the indigenous people, to facilitate social and commercial relations.

(*Bulletin de l'Alliance Française*, 1884, cited in Barko, 199: 64)

The assimilationist project was constructed by the Alliance Française in terms of the development of a relationship between the indigenous people of the colonies and France, which would be conducted through French. That is, the coming together of the coloniser and the colonised would be done through the French language and through assimilation to French norms. These relationships are understood primarily as results of colonial conquest, and discussion of conquest is frequent in the early discourse of the Alliance Française. Foncin, the first general secretary (1883–97) and sixth president (1899–1914) of the Alliance Française, in fact, constructed the process of colonialism as one in which military conquest (*conquête militaire*) should be followed by cultural assimilation (*conquête morale*) realised through the teaching of the French language (Bruézière, 1983). Language was therefore closely connected with the articulation of the *mission civilisatrice* (civilising mission) of French colonialism (Costantini, 2008) and it is the movement to civilise which underlies the beginnings of French language spread policy. Language is thus constructed as the instrument of both conquest and civilisation:

> L'Alliance française s'avance en conquérant, mais en conquérant pacifiquement. Seule conquête qu'elle ambitionne, c'est celle des âmes et des intelligences; ses armes ce sont des livres, ses champs de combat, l'école... étendre la limite de la langue, c'est étendre les limites de la patrie.
> The Alliance Française goes forth conquering, but conquering peacefully. The only conquest that she desires is that of souls and intellects; her arms are books, her battlefield, the school ... to spread the limits of the language is to spread the limits of the motherland.
> (*Bulletin de l'Alliance Française*, 1884, cited in Spaëth, 2010: 64)

The attention of the Alliance Française was soon moved from the dissemination of French language in French colonies to the broader dissemination of the language and French culture to the wider world. In 1893, the Alliance Française proposed:

> Que notre Association [... reporte] toute l'énergie de son action dans les pays étrangers proprement dits.
> That our Association bring all the energy of its action to bear on foreign countries, properly so-called.
> (*Bulletin de l'Alliance Française*, 1884, cited in Barko, 1999: 5)

Bruézière (1983) argues that this change in emphasis resulted from a perception that the role of diffusing French in the colonies had become a government responsibility, which was operated through the establishment of French language schools. The role of the Alliance Française in the colonies had therefore become less important and, as a result, the focus of its work moved to language spread beyond those parts of the world under the political control of France. The decision to work in foreign countries meant a movement beyond the French sphere, bringing the activities of language spread into contact with new linguistic and cultural realities, in areas which were not subordinated to French political and cultural control.

This change in focus meant that the assimilationist discourse was later moderated by an emerging discourse of interest in other civilisations and cultures, which has subsequently been labelled *dialogue des cultures* (dialogue between cultures) (Barko, 1999). The *dialogue des cultures* parallels the British

Council's discourse of intercultural relationships, although this emerged much later in the discourse of the British Council than in the Alliance Française. De Bellescize (1986) credits the organisation's post-Second World War president Georges Duhamel with the formulation of the objectives of respect for civilisation and *dialogue des cultures* in 1949, by which time the Alliance Française's mission in external language spread was well established. The discursive favouring of dialogue recognises that the assimilationist ideology of the Alliance Française in the French colonialist sphere is less applicable to language spread activities in other countries and that the languages and cultures of the new audience for the Alliance Française needed to be respected as a part of language spread policy. The ideological construction of a dialogue between cultures locates the expansion of French within an articulation of an intercultural relationship which positions cultures and their speakers as having equality. At the same time, it constructs French as the language which enables such dialogues to be realised. The teaching of French brings benefits to France in the form of access to the cultures of others, while at the same time enabling access to French culture for others.

The Alliance Française has adopted a decentralised model of provision of the French language in which local communities become the operators of French language spread policy:

L'Alliance Française, au fond, est née d'une idée simple: laisser les étrangers eux-mêmes propager la culture française, céder partiellement la responsabilité de l'action culturelle de la France.
The Alliance Française is essentially born from a simple idea: let foreigners themselves propagate the French culture to hand over partially the cultural action of France.
(Dubosclard, 1998: 143)

The social actors of language spread are therefore constructed as those to whom language spread policy is targeted – the learners of the language themselves. In this way, the Alliance Française constructs itself as being outside the possibilities of linguistic and cultural imperialism by denying itself the sole responsibility for language spread and allocating it to others. This giving up of responsibility is in part a statement of the symbolic capital which the Alliance Française claims for the French language and culture. It is not asserted by claims of the benefits of learning French but is enacted by the desire of others to speak French. It is therefore the desire to communicate with France and the French which becomes the driving force for the establishment of the Alliance Française in particular localities (Dubosclard, 1998). That is, the work of the Alliance Française is part of French hegemony that relies on the spontaneous consent of others to its project because of a shared perception of the prestige of the language and culture (see Gramsci, 1975). It can thus be seen as a form of prestige and image planning that starts first from the prestige that exists for the language in other polities and the Alliance Française deploys this to maintain and further the image and prestige of the language (see Ager, 2005a, 2005b).

While the Alliance Française is the largest element of French language spread policy, other specifically government organisations have worked in parallel with it since the end of the First World War. In the early 20th century, language spread policy became part of the work of the government, largely operated through the Ministry for Foreign Affairs. It began on a small scale with the Bureau des écoles et des œuvres françaises à l'étranger, which focused primarily on the diffusion of French culture through education. The Bureau operated to coordinate the various cultural agencies operating abroad, and the establishment of an international network of cultural institutes began in 1910 (Balous, 1970).

In 1920, the Bureau des écoles et des œuvres became the Service des œuvres françaises à l'étranger (SOFE). The SOFE operated through three programmes:

- the Section universitaire et des écoles, which focused on establishing French schools and institutes in foreign countries, contributing to university-level teaching of French and funding scholarships for foreign students to study in France;
- the Section littéraire et artistique, which disseminated French cultural products; and
- the Section des œuvres, which worked with other associations, including the Alliance Française.

The SOFE and its predecessor treated language as an element of culture, but the discourse of culture itself was often framed in linguistics terms. In fact, although the span of activities was large, the main goal of the SOFE programmes was the teaching of the French language – the language being conceived as the vehicle through which French culture would be accessed (Lebovics, 1999). The work of the SOFE in schools and universities represents a direct involvement by the French government in the teaching of language in foreign educational institutions. It can be seen as an attempt to allocate to French the role of a language of communication between cultures and also to promote the diffusion of French cultural products as valued objects of consumption. The principal conceptualisation of the intercultural relationship in these activities is one in which others come into relationship with France, using French, and through that relationship receive the benefits of French culture.

In 1945, the SOFE was transformed into the Direction générale des relations culturelles et des œuvres françaises à l'étranger. The Direction générale continued the strong educational aims of the SOFE and established institutes for the teaching of French language and culture and provided French teaching staff for foreign universities. The Direction générale signalled the development of a new ideology about the promotion of French; this presented the position of French as endangered by the spread of English and the language as therefore in need of support to maintain its international position (Allain et al., 1984). That is, the work of disseminating French increasingly is shaped by an ideology of threat and the image and prestige of the language are constructed as a problem that needs to be resolved through language spread policy. The focus of language spread policy is therefore specifically on the planning of image and prestige (Ager, 2005a, 2005b).

The emphasis on the defence of French as an international language was seen in the development within the Direction générale of a sub-directory, the Direction du français, in 1984, with a focus specifically on the French language. The development of the Direction du français was associated with a more strongly articulated programme of restoring the eroded value of French and promoting the acquisition of the language. The bureaux pédagogiques of the Direction génerale were turned into *bureaux d'action linguistique (les BAL)*, underlining the movement away from a focus in language spread policy on strictly educational approaches to one related to prestige planning. Essentially, the Direction générale and the Direction du français continued to articulate a vision of intercultural relationships of the SOFE – interactions with the French through French to access the cultural products of France – but rather than asserting this as a self-evident good, this construction of intercultural relationship was seen as needing to be defended. The change was not in the policy's articulation of intercultural relationship but rather in the perception of how this was understood by others. The policy discourse grows out of the view that the symbolic capital of French had been eroded, in particular by the growth of English, and that this capital needed to be preserved and extended (Boulanger & Daniel, 1984). The spread of French outside France was therefore constructed as an index of French symbolic capital and a desire on the part of others to establish intercultural connections with France became the basis for asserting the value of this capital. This essentially has remained the focus of French language spread policy since, albeit with small adjustments being made to the organisation and implementation of the policy.

In 1990, the Agence pour l'enseignement français à l'étranger (AEFE) replaced the Direction du français. The AEFE was established within the Ministry for Foreign Affairs with the aims of supporting the maintenance of French by French emigrants and also fostering the learning of French by foreign students. The AEFE was given the power to establish schools in other polities (Assemblée nationale, 1990) and so marks a direct intervention into language education in other education jurisdictions. In 1994, the Direction générale was replaced by the Direction de la coopération culturelle et linguistique. The change in title emphasises a more collaborative framing of French work in language and culture and brings the linguistic dimension into the name of the overarching organisation. The emphasis on cooperation parallels the emergence of the discourse around the *dialogue des cultures* in the work of the Alliance Française. It represents a form of cooperation in which France is the focus of the cooperation and the French language is the ideal vehicle through which cooperation will occur.

French language spread policy began in the context of colonialism and the conceptualisation of colonialism as a *mission civilisatrice* in which French language and culture were constructed as an objective good and their dissemination as a moral enterprise for the betterment of others. In many ways, this ideological construction of the place and value of French and France has persisted as an element of language spread policy, although it has become less overtly articulated. The language spread policy texts discussed have been oriented towards the French language as a valued commodity which others would wish to acquire, and have seen intercultural relationships in terms of accessing the language and culture of France. This has been offset by a discursive construction of language spread policy as an element of cultural collaboration and cooperation – the *dialogue des cultures*. This framing of dialogue is, however, restricted, in that it presupposes that the language of dialogue will be French and that French is a natural vehicle for such dialogue. This is an assertion in policy discourse of the symbolic capital relating to French as a legitimate medium through which interculturality can be established and precludes other languages from such a role. The place of French is problematised only by the emergence of a competitor language for this role, and this emergence leads to a discourse of the need to defend the status of French in the face of competition.

Conclusion

In the cases examined here, external language spread policies have been typically an element of foreign policy and constitute a response through education to foreign policy needs. In this way, national priorities and national self-interest are inevitably a core element of the ideologies which inform and are communicated by such policies. These language spread policies have not specifically pertained to the diffusion of a language but rather have been elements within a broader policy of cultural diffusion. Within these policies, the culture of the polity creating the policy is positioned and represented as an object of value, the value of which is inherent and self-evident. Cultural policy works to make this culture available to others for the benefit of others and uses language education as a mechanism to achieve this.

In associating language with cultural diffusion, language spread policies construct language as a medium through which tangible and intangible cultural products can be accessed by others. Language therefore is represented as the conduit through which cultures can be accessed. The cultural products provide the language with a basis for developing the image and prestige of the language itself and in turn the acquisition of the language enhances the prestige of the culture and nation to which it is attached. Language spread therefore directly addresses issues of image and prestige (Ager, 2005a, 2005b). In the policy discourses around English and French, this vehicular role of the language usually remains tacit; however, in Japanese discourses it emerges as a more explicit focus. This difference in emphasis appears to relate to differences in the place and role of Japanese in the international sphere and also to the relationship between the objectives of language spread policies and foreign language education policies. Japanese, unlike English and French, has never had a role as a language of wider communication beyond Japan and its territories, and Japanese colonialism did not succeed in establishing Japanese as a viable language for official use in its former colonies after their independence. Therefore Japanese language spread policy could never be conceptualised as one in which existing linguistic practices could be preserved or defended. In addition, in all three polities, language spread policy has been conceived as a mechanism to communicate the cultural perspectives and products of the polity; however, in Japan this is also seen as the role of foreign language education. This means that there are two languages which are constructed in policy as being vehicles for the dissemination of the Japanese worldview – English and Japanese – and these languages are unequal in their share of international communication. Therefore, there is a need in Japanese policies to create a discursive space in which an international role for Japanese can be projected as a future possibility, while in the other two national contexts such a space pre-dated the policies.

The dissemination of language is an element of hegemony for the nation that is diffusing the language, in that it is a non-coercive exercise of the cultural power of the polity involved (Mumby, 1997). It is non-coercive in that any attempt at language spread requires a desire on the part of others to learn the language, and this can be generated only indirectly, through the promotion or creation of perceptions of the image and prestige of the language. This means that the success of such programmes requires the active consent of those it seeks to influence. The assent of others to acquisition of the language is an instantiation of the power of the language on the international stage and the promotion of learning of the language is a promotion of the symbolic capital that attaches to that language.

In addition to its role as a vehicle for disseminating culture, the language itself is represented as an object of value for language learners. It becomes a vehicle for participation in international communication. This role appears most prominently in the policy texts in the ways in which they construct exchanges and cooperation. These policies either assume or state that the language for the conduct of intercultural relationships will be the language of the country developing the policy. This means that discourses around exchange, cooperation and forms of reciprocity construct these in an asymmetric way. Speakers of the language being diffused do not need to develop additional capabilities in order to participate in international collaborations, while speakers of other languages need to acquire the diffused language to establish their place in such relationships. There is also an implication, because the language spread policies are embedded within policies for cultural diffusion which emphasise the value of the diffused culture, that the practices and expectations of speakers of the diffused language will be normative.

Language spread policies may be articulated in cultural policies which have reciprocity as a discursive focus but language itself seems to be separated from this reciprocity. While cultures may be represented as things to be exchanged, languages are not. They are to be disseminated to others in order that exchange of other things may occur. Thus, while policies may project a reciprocal valuing of cultures, they do not reflect a reciprocal valuing of languages. In the case of Japan, this asymmetry is tempered somewhat by the parallel focus of foreign language education policies which depict a Japanese intercultural subject who disseminates Japanese worldviews in English or in Japanese, and so is constructed as being bilingual. This bilingualism is, however, not alluded to in documents for either type of policy.

There are therefore two different types of intercultural subject being articulated in these policies. The first is the intercultural subject within the home polity – this person will use existing knowledge of language and culture in order to become a consumer of the cultural products of others. The second is the culturally diverse other – this person will develop a knowledge of a new language and its associated culture in order to engage with speakers of this language to access their cultural products and to exchange their own cultural products if they are wanted by others.

The linguistic inequality discussed above relates to the perceived and asserted symbolic capital of the languages concerned. Symbolic capital can be conceived in terms of the perceptions of others that the acquisition of a particular language brings benefits for an individual in the international linguistic marketplace (Bourdieu, 1982). A language which is learnt by many is perceived as having much symbolic capital, one which is learnt by few as having little. In policies relating to English, symbolic capital is assumed. In those relating to French, it is defended and this defence is constructed in terms of a lack of realisation by others of the value that French holds. In the case of Japanese, this symbolic capital is presented as something which needs to be established through policy work. The assertion that a language becomes the normal vehicle of intercultural relationships is a claim for the social and cultural capital of that language – it obtains some part of its value because of the relationships it enables with others. In this way, questions of language education become closely aligned with questions of language image and prestige. As Ammon (1992: 6) notes: 'Any kind of language-spread policy is typically justified, upon questioning, by some noble motives, which however, upon close examination prove to camouflage more earthly interests'. These interests are frequently related to the hegemony of the language being diffused and the discourses of benefit represent ideological devices to maintain or develop hegemony.

Notes

1. In this chapter, I will use the term 'language spread policy' to refer to policies designed to spread a language through education, rather than adopting a more cumbersome term to designate this specific area of work.
2. *Monozukuri* (literally, the way of making things) is a recent coining in Japanese which expresses a specifically Japanese style manufacturing process. It contrasts with two older Japanese words, 製造, *seizou* (manufacture, production) and 生残, *seizan* (production), which express manufacturing more generally and which do not connote anything specifically Japanese. It refers to a way of manufacture which is perceived to be uniquely Japanese and in so doing locates the act of production within the framework of the *Nihonjinron* ideology.
3. The language-in-education dimensions of French language spread policy have been strongly supported since the mid-20th century by other aspects of language planning and policy work to maintain and enhance the place of French. The establishment of *la Francophonie* as a political and institutional international sphere for the French language and the work supporting the role of French in official use in the European Union and in international organisations represent

significant attempts in French language policy to maintain and spread French (see Calvet, 1994; Kasuya, 2001; Kleineidam, 1992).

4. Other organisations responsible for language spread included religious congregations, Catholic and Protestant missions, the Alliance Israélite Universelle and the Mission Laïque Française. While these organisations did contribute to language spread, they were largely concerned with other agendas, of which language was only a part (Salon, 1981, 1985; Spaëth, 2010).

5. Salon (1981, 1985) makes a distinction between *politique* (policy/politics) and *action* in discussing French cultural policy, in which the former is understood as specifically government work while the latter refers to national effort to achieve similar goals outside direct government control. In language spread policy, the two dimensions have been closely intermeshed.

6 Language-in-education Policies and Intercultural Relationships

Introduction

Language-in-education policies are manifestly statements of provision for language learning in which the selection of languages for educational purposes and the details of the delivery, focus and goals of language programmes are articulated. However, this book has attempted to show that such policies cannot be considered only in terms of their structuring of education but must also been seen as ways of structuring the social realities that result from the teaching and learning of languages. That is, policy texts are not simply texts which enact the provision for language education in a polity but are also projections of future ways of communicating through the languages (Gee, 1994a, 1994b; Gee & Lankshear, 1995). Language-in-education policies for the acquisition of additional languages by learners, by framing provisions for the creation of individuals who speak more than one language, discursively construct images of this individual. Seeing policy texts as projections opens the possibility of examining what is projected – the plurilingual individual and the ways in which language, culture and interculturality will be developed through education and employed after education. Because language is ultimately a means of communication and interaction, the projections of language-in-education policies can be seen in terms of the sorts of relationships they construct between interlocutors and ways in which participants in projected interactions are positioned in relation to each other.

Such relationships are not developed in isolation from other relationships which exist between potential interlocutors but rather they embody other understandings of such relationships created through historical and social processes. The intercultural relationships represented in policies, and the intercultural subjects who will engage in these relationships, are thus located in broader belief systems in which ideas and attitudes exist about the social world in which language is used. Language-in-education policies, then, have a place in the production and reproduction of ideologies of relationship between members of different language groups. The understanding of the forms of intercultural relationship presented in policy texts is the result of an ideological framing through which languages and their speakers are understood. These ideologies represent a set of discursive concerns about linguistic realities that influence what can be done in educational contexts to develop language capabilities.

Language-in-education Policies and Ideology

Van Dijk (2000) argues that ideologies are fundamentally discursive – that is, they are constructed and disseminated through processes of discourse. The focus of this book has been to examine how language-in-education policies function as discourses that represent and disseminate ideologies about language as it is manifested in education. Language-in-education policies as linguistic productions are parts of the discourse about the things they treat and as such are ideological products articulating the values and worldviews of those who produce them (Voloshinov, 1929). They are therefore constituent parts of the realities they articulate, in particular the realities of language and intergroup relationships. They do not constitute the entire discourse about these realities and coexist with other discourses, accomplished through speech and writing, that also form a part of these realities (Lo Bianco, 2005). While these discourses have not been discussed in this book, it is nonetheless important to acknowledge that they may play a significant role in shaping the production, reception and implementation of language policy and may in turn be shaped by language policies. In addition, the ideologies of language-in-education policies are not self-contained. Rather, they interact with other ideologies and other discourses that exist in society. This means that language-in-education policy documents are not independent ideological productions but rather exist within complex webs of signification.

Each of the policy contexts examined in this book involved the articulation of ideologies, and different ideological constructions can be seen in different contexts, although there are also similarities between the ideological framings of language issues across contexts. In each context, ideologies functioned to shape the ways in which language education was understood and achieved.

In foreign language education, ideologies primarily relate to the ways of allocating value to the acquisition of particular languages. In the three polities examined (Australia, Japan and the European Union), economic ideologies were a common element in the construction of value. That is, languages were seen as skills that were deployable for economic purposes related to the interests of the polity concerned. In this way, the three polities demonstrated a similar underlying ideology of the nature and purpose of education as developing the required human capital resources of the polity (Gee & Lankshear, 1995; Hursh, 2007). In the European Union, this economic rationale was related to questions of mobility and European integration, in which the economic needs and possibilities were understood not in national terms but in supranational terms. Languages therefore were understood within a context of European commonality, not only of European diversity.

In immigrant language education, the common ideological themes across the three polities (Australia, Japan and Italy) relate to ways of understanding diversity and so structuring responses to it. In the polities, there are two possible constructions of diversity. The first is diversity as a problem for national cohesion. In this ideological framing the presence of diverse others is understood as a threat to national unity, which is represented by the domination of the hegemonic group. Diversity is therefore understood through an ideology of threat to the status quo. The response to diversity understood in this way is essentially assimilatory and involves the induction of the immigrant into the dominant language and culture. This approach was seen in each of the three polities, although manifested in different ways. The second possible construction of diversity is that it is a source of enrichment or other positive benefit. This construction sees diversity as a resource to be retained and developed and was seen in texts from Italy and Australia, but less so in those from Japan. This view of diversity leads to responses that include immigrant languages in educational provision in some way. This is done in a way that subordinates the immigrant languages to the dominant language and reinforces the hegemony of the dominant language group. The subordination of immigrant languages to the dominant language takes a number of forms: the construction of the dominant language as self-evidently useful and of the immigrant language as having only private or in-group usefulness; the framing of the acquisition of the immigrant language as a necessary step in the acquisition of the dominant language; and the understanding of the maintenance of the immigrant language as always being accompanied by full command of the dominant language. The hegemony of the dominant group is also maintained by expectations of accommodation of the immigrant group to the majority, with expectations of lesser or no accommodation of the majority to the minority.

The situation of indigenous groups in the polities examined (Australia, Japan and Colombia) is similar to that of immigrant groups, although there seems to be a different recognition of the place of indigenous languages in the polity. These languages are seen as being a part of national heritage and so are recognised by the dominant group as nationally relevant, but as lying outside the dominant linguistic and cultural norms. In Japan, the heritage dimension is strongly articulated and results in the indigenous group being subsumed into the mainstream. In Colombia and Australia, the distinctiveness of the indigenous group is recognised and policy responds to this by allocating some place in education to these languages. As with immigrant languages, however, the inclusion of indigenous languages in education positions these languages in a subordinated position to the dominant language and reinforces the utility of the dominant language. The policies also presupposed the same patterns of accommodation between the minority and the majority as was discussed for immigrants.

In language spread policy, the polities involved (Britain, Japan and France) developed educational responses that were constructed largely in terms of the prestige and image of their language. In each case, the need for dissemination was constructed as a response to a threat to that prestige. The various polities constructed the threat differently. For Britain, the threat was initially from enemy propaganda prior to the Second World War and language spread policy continued after the war not so much because of a perceived threat to the status of English but rather as a strategy to maintain British prestige in a changing world environment following decolonisation. For France, the threat was understood in terms of the erosion of prestige of French with the rise of English and so the aim was to re-establish the image and prestige of French and France as a defence of symbolic capital (Bourdieu, 1982). For Japan, the discourse of threat was characterised as a lack of understanding of Japan and its perspective that compromised Japan's role and influence in the world. The perception was not one of eroded or changed prestige but the need to establish prestige. In all three cases, the language being diffused was understood as an objective good that is of value to others and that image and prestige planning (Ager, 2005a, 2005b) were needed in order for the value of that good to be recognised.

Each area of policy is therefore framed within a particular ideology or set of ideologies that shapes both how the language problem is understood and how the problem is resolved through policy actions. The provisions of a language-in-education policy text are therefore meaningful not just in terms of what they propose for enactment but also in terms of the ways they construct languages as phenomena to be planned. Each area of planning entails particular engagements within ideologically constructed realities that may be specific to the particular domain or may overlap a number of different domains.

Ideologies in Specific Polities

The case studies in this book examine language-in-education policies in two polities – Australia and Japan – across multiple policy contexts. While this allows a focus on policy types, it fragments an analysis of how ideologies work across types within each polity. This section will attempt a synthesis of some of the issues that arise within each of these two polities to examine the ways in which ideologies function across policy contexts.

Australia

Australia was chosen for case studies across a number of domains because it is a polity that explicitly holds a multicultural social policy. This means that linguistic and cultural diversity is seen as an inherent part of the Australian social landscape and that, at official levels at least, this diversity is given value. Australia's ideological construction of diversity is, however, much more complex than the official adoption of multiculturalism suggests and this complexity is reflected in the various policy contexts studied.

In Australia, there have been a number of ideological framings of the value of foreign language education that range from the significance of language learning in personal development to the importance of language for achieving economic goals. The first of these is a justification of language for the development of the individual's cultural capital (Bourdieu, 1981; Bourdieu & Passeron, 1970) and presupposes a humanistic understanding of learning. That is, it is framed with reference not only to ideologies of language but also to ideologies relating to the function and purpose of education and understandings of what it means to be educated. This is also true of the economic framing of language learning; however, the ideologies that underlie this framing are different. The economic justification of language learning is one that focuses on the development of human capital and constructs education as a utilitarian activity resulting in economically deployable skills. Although both these ideologies have existed in the discourses of language-in-education policy in Australia, they have not been equal and instead there has been a progressive erosion of the idea of language learning as personal development and a corresponding increase in economically focused rationales. This process in Australia reflects a larger ideology of education that responds to neoliberal understandings of the role of education (Gee & Lankshear, 1995; Hursh, 2007). The economic rationale for language learning sees language as a skill that is deployable in a globalised marketplace to achieve economic national interests.

These ideologies overlay a broader ideological issue that relates to Australia's own internal multilingualism and reflects ideologies of diversity in Australia, primarily in relation to languages of immigrant communities and the construction of distinct ethnic identities. In this context, too, it is possible to observe two different ideological framings. One is a set of beliefs about ethnic particularism, the maintenance of ethnic separateness, as a threat to national cohesion and a force to create social divisions. This ideology constructs diversity as a threat to the hegemony of the dominant group because it undermines the national unity represented by that hegemony. This contrasts with the ideological construction of multiculturalism as a source of cultural enrichment and as an alternative construction of national identity. The purpose of language education in such a context is assimilatory, although overt discourses of assimilation are problematic in an officially multicultural society and instead the ideology makes use of discourses of deficit. Viewing linguistic diversity as divisive leads to its construction as a problem characterised by a lack of knowledge of the dominant language and culture – that is, knowledge of another language is seen as a deficit in knowledge of English and therefore as a deficit in being able to participate in the hegemonic culture. In contrast, the ideology of diversity as enrichment constructs diversity as a resource to be developed and language education does this through fostering language maintenance among immigrant groups, together with the acquisition of English to produce bilingualism. This discourse, which emerged with official multiculturalism in the 1970s, received its strongest articulation in the National Policy on Languages (NPL), in the 1980s, but afterwards began to decline. At all points in the documents studied in this book, these two ideological constructs have been in tension and coexist in the documents in complex ways that require negotiation and resolution (Eagleton, 2007).

The resolution of the internal complexity of Australia's ideologies of diversity has been to conflate the learning of immigrant languages with the learning of foreign languages to create an undifferentiated construction of language learning (often termed 'languages other than English'). This conflation removes from language policy discourses the idea that language learning constitutes special provision for minorities and thereby increases risk to social cohesion. By signalling that language education is equally applicable to all learners, it makes language maintenance only a special case of general educational practice. The conflation of different types of language learning means that the learning of immigrant languages comes to be shaped by the ideologies of foreign language education (personal development and the development of economically useful skills). In discourses of personal development, the maintenance of immigrant languages articulates with language maintenance as a form of cultural capital, and this is evidenced strongly in the NPL. The maintenance of immigrant languages articulates less strongly with economic rationales for language learning, as many of these languages are not classified as economically useful. One consequence of this is that, in strongly economically focused documents – such as those relating to the National Asian Languages and Studies in Australian Schools (NALSAS) strategy and the National Asian Languages and Studies in Schools Program (NALSSP) – language maintenance is largely ignored. The language education of immigrants then becomes specifically education in English and this articulates unproblematically with the project of national unity.

Indigenous languages do not seem to be included in the ideological construction of diversity as threat, possibly because of the smaller contribution that indigenous languages make to Australia's linguistic and cultural diversity. Indigenous Australians constitute around 2% of the population, while immigrants constitute around 30%, although some of these are from English-speaking countries (Australian Bureau of Statistics, 2008). In addition, the presence of an indigenous minority in Australia cannot be constructed as a choice, in the same way as it can for immigrants, and so their status as minorities is less amenable to being treated as the consequence of a decision made by the individual but, rather, is a consequence of colonisation by the majority. The discursive construction of the language needs of indigenous Australians tends to give more recognition to the need for language maintenance as part of the maintenance of cultural identity. At the same time, most emphasis is given to the need to develop English and in this context the ideologies of deficit that apply to the speaking of immigrant languages are also applied to understanding speakers of indigenous languages. The deficit is similarly understood as a deficit in the capacity to participate in mainstream Australia and in particular as a deficit in economically useful language and literacy skills.

One common feature of all the policy texts is that they seek to maintain the hegemonic position of English while at the same time allocating a place in education to other languages. This is least strongly articulated in the policies on foreign language learning and this would appear to be because the target audience for such learning is typically constructed as the monolingual, monocultural dominant group. The addition of another language to the linguistic repertoire of this group does not destabilise the normalisation of English and its hegemonic role. Nonetheless, one rationalisation for the learning of foreign languages is that it facilitates the development of English language literacy skills and, to this extent, foreign language learning is subordinated to the hegemonic role of English. The hegemony of English is more overt in policies dealing with immigrant and indigenous languages and is manifested through discourses of deficit in which speaking another language is understood as a lack of capacity in English. The maintenance of immigrant and indigenous languages is always set alongside the acquisition of English and is ideologically feasible only in the context of developing a full capability in English. English is represented as the self-evidently useful language and the utility of a language is understood in terms of the ideologies of national interest, which construct utility largely in economic terms. Indigenous languages, and many immigrant languages, have no place within this construction of utility. The maintenance of immigrant and indigenous languages is therefore constructed as the maintenance of something in addition to the strictly useful. Usefulness in this context is understood as the ability to participate in the agenda of the dominant group. It is therefore often relegated to the private sphere and to group organisation rather than being a specific focus of normal educational provision. Where language maintenance exists within the public sphere of education, it is given some utility as a support for the acquisition of English by those who do not speak English – that is, it gets its utility from its contribution to the development of the self-evidently useful dominant language.

The hegemony of speakers of English is also seen in the expectation that speakers of immigrant and indigenous languages will adapt in some way to the language and culture of the mainstream, while members of the mainstream are not expected to adapt to others in the same way. That is, the construction of the intercultural subject is one that sustains the hegemony of English – and this will be discussed further below.

Japan

Japan represents a polar opposite to Australia in that it is a society in which linguistic and cultural diversity has a much lower profile and the ideological construction of national identity is a monoethnic one. This monoethnic identity largely ignores internal linguistic and cultural differences, or seeks to fit them into a monoethnic mould. The nature of the purportedly single ethnic group in Japan is also constructed in particular ways through the ideologies associated with *Nihonjinron* to emphasise the uniqueness of Japan and its language and culture. These ideologies pervade all of the language policies considered here.

In foreign language learning, the emphasis in Japanese educational policy documents is on the development of language capabilities that will allow Japanese people to express Japanese ideas and the Japanese worldview to non-Japanese people. That is, the additional language becomes a way to articulate Japanese distinctiveness internationally. The articulation of Japanese distinctiveness is problematised in policy texts not only in terms of the lack of understanding of this by outsiders but also by a lack of clarity about it among Japanese people learning a foreign language (principally English). Learning to articulate Japanese ideas in Japanese therefore forms a necessary basis for the learning of foreign languages. Language learners need to learn to articulate Japanese ideas because Japanese distinctiveness is understood as a manifestation of traditional Japanese culture and this culture has been eroded by modernisation and western influence (Yoshimi & Buist, 2003). The international audience for the dissemination of Japanese distinctive is constructed as an English-speaking one and foreign language education in Japan means English language education. The selection of English itself rests on a number of ideologies. A principal focus is the ideological construction of English as a world language – as one that allows communication not only with English-speaking countries but with others. Thus, it is the lingua franca function of English that makes it an effective language in which to communicate Japanese distinctiveness. There is also an ideology of the west that supports the selection of English, which dates from the period of the Meiji restoration in the 19th century and which, with some modifications, persists. This is a view of the west as a source of technology, culture and development that constructs the west as an object of consumption (Yoshimi & Buist, 2003). This view of the west has been, from the beginning, one in which English-speaking societies dominated, but this domination has increased since the end of the Second World War, since when the view has become increasingly focused on America.

The ideology of Japanese distinctiveness also underlies Japan's language spread policy, which has similar objectives to its foreign language education policy. The dissemination of Japanese as an international language aims to communicate Japanese distinctiveness internationally through the Japanese language. Language spread policy adds a further dimension of the ideology of *Nihonjinron*, in that it introduces the idea of needing to communicate Japanese ideas and the Japanese worldview in the language in which they were originally conceptualised. This connects with the idea that Japanese has a unique spirit (*kotodama*) and that this unique spirit pervades all communication and thought in Japanese. Thus, to communicate Japanese realities fully can be done only in the Japanese language.

While the ideology of Japanese distinctiveness pervades policies for teaching additional languages, it is most strongly articulated in policies relating to minorities. In these cases, the Japanese ideology of monoethnicity renders the presence of linguistic and cultural diversity within Japan highly problematic. Policies relating to distinct groups therefore need to manage the existence of diversity within the context of the monoethnic state. Largely this has been done by ignoring the diversity itself and asserting the hegemony of the dominant language and culture. This has been done most strongly in the case of indigenous groups. The Ryukyuan Islanders have been assimilated into the Japanese ethnic group (*minzoku*) and their distinctiveness has been constructed as diversity that is internal to the Japanese language and culture. This has been facilitated by the genetic relatedness of Japanese and Ryukyuan language varieties. The differences between Japanese and Ryukyuan varieties have not, however, been tolerated in education policies and explicit processes of dialect levelling – of correcting the non-standard Japanese of Ryukyu – have been in place from the beginning of education in the Meiji period. The US occupation of the Islands following the Second World War involved an attempt to accentuate the differences between Ryukyu and Japan; however, with little success. The ideological construction of Ryukyu as distinct was seen as an attempt by the occupying power to establish its own control over the Islands and ideologies of Japaneseness became a strategy for resisting US domination. Thus, the hegemony of Japanese in the Islands provided the discursive possibility of resistance, and the eventual return of the Islands to Japan perpetuated the Japanese hegemony.

The situation of the Ainu is more complex, as the language does not fit neatly into a genetic relationship with Japanese – that is, the difference between Ainu and Japanese languages and cultures is much greater than that between Ryukyuan and Japanese. In fact, the starting point for Japanese interaction with the Ainu was to reject their Japaneseness and to designate them 'barbarian'. The polity-building project of the Meiji era required greater integration of Hokkaido into the Japanese nation-state and so the distinctiveness of the Ainu came into conflict with the monoethnic construction of the Japanese people. The solution to this was to reclassify the Ainu culture as a variant form of Japanese culture, characterised by arrested development, which could be overcome through education. That is, Ainu language and culture were deficient forms of Japanese language and culture that needed to be brought up to date. In this way, the Ainu could be included into the Japanese *minzoku* and their distinctiveness minimised. The Ainu Cultural Protection Act gave greater recognition to Ainu diversity within Japan but without fully recognising the Ainu as a distinct ethnic group. Rather, they were constructed as a part of Japanese heritage in Hokkaido. In this way, diversity could be recognised without destabilising the monoethnic ideology of Japan.

Immigrants pose a great problem, as immigrants from other countries cannot be as easily absorbed into the Japanese *minzoku*. The discursive strategy used to deal with this problem has been to consider immigrants not as Japanese but as resident foreigners (定住外国人, *teijū gaikokujin*, or 在日外国人, *zainichi gokokujin*); that is, they are in Japan but not of Japan. As a result, Japanese language-in-education policy obviates the need to engage with their languages and cultures. The situation is more complex in the case of Japanese returned emigrants whose heritage is Japanese, but who do not speak Japanese. In this case, they belong to the Japanese *jinshu* (race), but they are not fully a part of the Japanese *minzoku*. For these groups there is greater recognition of the first language needs of the students, but again there is no specific education provision for them. Instead, their learning needs are catered for through schools that are accredited by the Brazilian government, for example, through an arrangement supported by the Japanese government. The policy provision of the Japanese government for both these groups involves the teaching of the Japanese language to integrate immigrants better into Japanese society and to make their presence less visible, and so to challenge less the dominant monoethnic ideology.

The role of policies in maintaining the hegemony of the majority group in Japan resides in the discursive accomplishment of the monoethnic nature of Japan. That is, hegemony is maintained by not recognising alternatives to it, or by seeking to disguise the presence of such alternatives. Hegemony is also maintained by the assimilationist nature of provisions that do exist for the education of outsiders and in the expectation that those who are outside the mainstream will accommodate to that mainstream without any reciprocal accommodation. In fact, because diversity is rendered invisible, there is no need for the mainstream to engage with it inside Japan. Any engagement with internal diversity is understood therefore as preparation for engagement with external (that is, international) diversity.

Language-in-education Policies, Intercultural Relationships and Power

The policies discussed here all project some future possibility of interaction with another linguistic/cultural group as the outcome of language learning. The ideological construction of such interculturality typically shows a significant influence of power on the nature of the relationships projected. Where the imagined interlocutor is a member of another polity – that is, in the context of policy on foreign language education and language spread – there is a greater equality of power between the groups of interlocutors represented in the texts and this seems to correlate with a more reciprocal form of intercultural relationship. Equality in intercultural relationships is especially a feature of the foreign language education policies of the European Union, in which the intercultural relationship is constructed in terms of the development of a European identity through the learning of the languages of other member states. The intercultural relationships envisaged in these texts are ones in which there is mutual accommodation between interlocutors and a movement away from positionings associated with pre-established group identities. Intercultural subjects are constructed as those who, through their knowledge of language and culture, move beyond their own cultural positioning to develop a new positioning related to a plurilingual and pluricultural European identity. This equality and reciprocity in intercultural relationships parallels a wider European discourse of equality among members and so language-in-education policies reflect broader ideologies (Shohamy, 2007).

Such equality is also present in the foreign language policies of Japan and Australia but in different ways and with different ideological positioning of the participants. In Australia, the primary focus envisaged for intercultural relationships is economic and the accommodation made to others is constructed in terms of those which are economically useful. This is often in terms of knowledge about the other and the possibilities to communicate with them for national economic advantage. The project is a less mutual one than that proposed for the European Union and is constructed in terms which allow Australians to maintain their own cultural positioning while deploying linguistic and cultural capabilities for their own advantage in the global marketplace. In Japan, similarly, the relationship between interlocutors is presented as one of equality; however, the national purpose of the policy is more strongly articulated than in Australia. The locus of the intercultural relationships is Japan itself and the nature of engagement is not framed in terms of accommodation to others but as the articulation of essentialised versions of Japanese realities. The Japanese intercultural subject is therefore not constructed in terms of being able to accommodate to others but rather as one who maintains a Japanese identity at all times and can communicate about this identity to others who do not share this identity. Neither of these policies envisages changes in the cultural positioning of the intercultural speaker, as each is constructed in terms of national group membership and communicates from this positioning.

In language spread policy, there is also a framing of relationships in terms of equality, but the situation is more complex, as ideologies of cultural equality have emerged over time and displaced older, less egalitarian constructions. Many of the discourses about external language spread are framed in terms of reciprocity (exchange, collaboration, cooperation); however, this discourse overlies an ongoing privileging of the national language being spread, which constructs asymmetries (see the linguistic imperialism critique of Phillipson, 1992, 1997, 2010). The predominant asymmetry lies in the projected patterns of language use, in which the language being promoted is assumed to be the normal language of intercultural contact. This means that language spread policies are implicit (or sometimes explicit) statements about the utility of particular languages as languages for international communication and therefore for establishing intercultural relationships with others. This creates a linguistic asymmetry between participants in interaction and reciprocity as involving two different kinds of action: the native speakers' action involves engagement in a first language, within the cultural context of that language, with others for the purposes of cultural consumption (Jordan & Weedon, 1995), largely according to their own taste; the non-native-speakers' action involves acquiring the language of the other in order to engage with and to accommodate to the other. The asymmetry here supports the symbolic capital of the language being used and reinforces its value in the global linguistic marketplace. In this asymmetry, the national and cultural positions of the source country of the language to be spread remain intact, while there is an expectation of repositioning of others.

In contexts relating to internal linguistic diversity – language education for indigenous and immigrant communities – intercultural relationships are marked by more clearly defined power asymmetries that preserve the hegemony of the majority over the minority. In such contexts, the official language of the polity is privileged in educational policy over the language of the indigenous and immigrant groups. In fact, in some contexts, education in the official language is the only real provision made in language-in-education policy. This is the case for Japan, but was also true in Australia for part of the post-Second World War period of mass immigration. An emphasis on the language of the dominant group and neglect of minority languages construct the only possible intercultural relationship to be achieved through language education: assimilation of minorities to the majority.

Where indigenous and immigrant languages are included in language-in-education policies, they are usually subordinated to the language of the dominant group. In particular, their inclusion is often articulated as a mechanism to facilitate education in general and particularly for the acquisition of the dominant language. This means that community agendas of language maintenance may be subordinated to external agendas of integration into mainstream society. The recognition of the languages of minority groups in educational contexts may be oriented to the need to create social and linguistic spaces for minority groups within a polity but, at the same time, they arise in contexts of social and linguistic inequality (Fuentes & Nieto, 2011; Wroblenski, 2011).

Such policies can construct intercultural relationships in terms of asymmetries between majority and minority, even when the overt rationales may be inclusivity and recognition of minorities. Through their rationales, the texts recognise some minority aspirations but rearticulate these through the lens of majority concerns. The recognition of aspirations can be understood as a practical strategy through which the dominant group secures consent from those dominated (Condit, 1989; Eagleton, 2007). The policies reproduce asymmetries by embodying an expectation that members of a minority group will accommodate to mainstream linguistic and cultural practices to a greater degree than the majority will accommodate to the minority. Interculturality is therefore constructed as a consequence of the maintenance of diversity in a society – those who persist in being different are expected to integrate into the mainstream. Thus the minority intercultural subject is one who can participate in two cultures, the culture of his or her own ethnolinguistic community and that of the mainstream, while the majority intercultural subject participates only in one culture, but is expected to know about and tolerate the diversity of others. Diversity is therefore something that members of the majority observe externally and the culture of the minority becomes an object of appropriation by the majority (Wroblenski, 2011), as does its language, to a lesser extent. Members of minorities are therefore expected to reposition themselves linguistically and culturally to adjust to the mainstream, but there is no reciprocal accommodation of the mainstream to the minority.

In some cases, language-in-education policies leave open other possibilities for members of the mainstream to develop intercultural relationships with others. For example, the blurring of the focus of foreign language policy in Australia means that languages of indigenous and immigrant communities may be made available to members of the mainstream. This means that a majority intercultural subject could be a person who accommodates to the language and culture of the minority and participates in a minority culture. This possibility is not, however, emphasised in most policy texts, which instead focus on the languages of foreign polities. The blurring of boundaries therefore tends to favour members of immigrant communities whose languages represent a form of symbolic capital in the global linguistic marketplace, and which by virtue of their external role have a place in education. For indigenous groups, the possibilities of inclusion are much lower, as there may be no external polity to provide symbolic capital to support the language and so they are less likely to benefit from blurred distinctions about the purpose of language learning.

Across the four types of language-in-education policy examined in this book, there is a discernible pattern of concern for particular types of intercultural relationships. The focus for majority groups is on relationships which are external to the polity: language learning is targeted at the languages of other polities. Thus, the value of language education is constructed in terms of the development of intercultural relationships with interlocutors from other societies, who are also typically members of the dominant group in their own polities. The focus of intercultural relationships for members of minorities is, in the first instance, the establishment of relationships with the dominant group in the polity in which they live. That is, it is an internally oriented relationship and the educative focus of language learning is primarily related to participation in the mainstream. In addition, the policy expectation may be that members of minority groups will develop the intercultural capabilities expected of the mainstream. That is, for members of minorities, there is an expectation of intercultural adaptation to the mainstream and also to those (external) others with whom the mainstream seeks to develop intercultural relationships.

Language-in-education Policies and the Intercultural Subject

The forms of intercultural relationship discussed above presuppose particular roles for social actors who will participate in those relationships. The policies examined in this book essentially show four main constructions of the intercultural subject: as participant, as ambassador, as observer and as non-participant.

The intercultural subject as participant is one who engages actively with interlocutors from another culture using knowledge of language, culture and intercultural processes. This individual is an intercultural mediator who interprets different cultural realities and adopts both internal and external perspectives in exploring diversity. That is, the intercultural subject as participant is a social actor engaged in diversity and is typically a plurilingual individual. Such an actor is actually very commonly presented in the literature on intercultural language teaching and learning (see, for example, Byram, 2008; Kramsch, 1993; Zarate *et al.*, 2004), but is less well attested in the policy documents examined here. This construction of the intercultural subject was found in the European Union's foreign language policy and made a brief appearance in Australian policy in the Statement and Plan for Languages Education in Australian Schools (MCEETYA, 2005). Otherwise, it is found mainly in policy texts relating to the education in official languages for indigenous people and immigrants. This is the case in policies in Australia, Japan, Italy and Colombia.

The intercultural subject as ambassador is one who uses knowledge of the language and culture of others in order to communicate to them a particular worldview. This person is an intercultural mediator in the sense that he/she can interpret his/her own cultural perspective in a way which is comprehensible to those who do not share the same perspective. Such an individual does not, however, accommodate in other ways to the linguistic and cultural practices, views and values of others. The intercultural subject as ambassador involves an expectation that such individuals will represent to others a definitive version of their society (Dlaska, 2000) and this definitive version is itself an ideological construct. This version of the intercultural subject is not usually explicitly articulated in policy documents, although Japanese foreign language policies do seem to understand the intercultural subject in this way. There do, however, appear to be echoes of such a view of the intercultural subject in the ways in which native speakers are represented in language spread policies. Further, the economic focus in Australian policy texts can be thought of as a variant of the intercultural subject as ambassador, as the motivation for communication with others is the presentation of Australia as a source for goods and services. As the Japanese policies construct the intercultural subject as representing Japanese culture to others, Australian policies construct intercultural subjects as representing Australia's economy. The features of this interlocutor are largely implied by policy and would seem to differ from the more explicit articulation of the intercultural subject as ambassador in Japanese foreign language policy in that no real mediation of culture is required of such individuals in presenting their culture to others. Such an intercultural subject may be plurilingual but the representations in language spread policy would seem to indicate that they could also possibly be monolingual.

The intercultural subject as observer is one who is able to see and understand the difference of others but who remains positioned in his/her own original culture. For such a subject, diversity is an object of study and the response is one of understanding and tolerance of the diversity of others, a diversity in which he/she has no active role, other than as a consumer of difference and otherness (Jordan & Weedon, 1995). In the policies studied, this seems to be the most common construction of the intercultural subject. It occurs in foreign language education policies at some periods in Australia and Japan. It is the usual construction of the relationship between the mainstream group and linguistically and culturally diverse minorities in Australian, Italian, Colombian and Japanese texts. Such an individual is not inherently constructed as plurilingual and language capabilities seem to have little role in the forms of observation that the policy documents envisage. It is also the typical role found in language spread policies in constructing the home polity participant in intercultural dialogue or *dialogue des cultures* in texts relating to the British Council and the Alliance Française.

The intercultural subject as non-participant is an individual for whom linguistic and cultural diversity is not a feature of lived experience. Such an individual makes no accommodation to the linguistic and cultural diversity of others. This construction was rare in the policy documents examined but can be seen as the way in which the mainstream was imagined to interact with minorities in early Japanese responses to indigenous and immigrant groups. It could also been seen as the normal construction of the mainstream intercultural subject in contexts in which there is no policy provision for the recognition of linguistic and cultural diversity.

These four possible constructions interrelate with the issues of power discussed above. Groups with more power are more likely to be positioned either as observers or non-participants in relationships with those who have less power, while groups of roughly equal power will be more likely to have participatory relationships. This means that, where a group exercises hegemony over another, intercultural subjects are constructed as acting within that hegemony and the nature of their action serves to maintain the existing linguistic and cultural hegemony.

It must be stressed that these four characterisations of intercultural relationships do not exhaust the possibilities for intercultural interactions. They represent an analysis of the ways these relationships are constructed in policy texts. Even in these texts these ways of thinking about the intercultural subject are not clearly delimited and it is possible for multiple understandings of the intercultural subject to be present in a single text. In part, this is because the intercultural subject is rarely addressed directly in policy texts but rather is implied by the goals and purposes of language education, the languages identified for teaching and learning and the projected language capabilities to be developed through education. What do appear to be missing from such texts, however, are ideas of hybridity and fluidity in intercultural relationships. This means that policy texts tend to construct the intercultural subject in rather unidimensional ways – typically, ways which meet issues of national interest.

Language-in-education policies for the acquisition of additional languages introduce into the goals and purposes of education the capacity to communicate with others in their language. In so doing, they insert intercultural relationships, and thus intercultural subjects, into other social relationships, which may have been constructed in terms of asymmetries (Abdallah-Pretceille, 1986; Holliday, 2010). They also construct this relationship in terms of idealised actors – the intercultural subject is ultimately a generic, essentialised actor from whom aspects of the individual's self-identity have been erased and for whom particular group identity categories are made salient – mainstream/minority, self/other, and so on. This is, on the one hand, an inevitability of the processes of policy formation which lead to the development of generic, global and inherently monological solutions to address real-world complexities. Policy involves activities of standardisation and normalisation which remove difference and diversity in order to render complex realities amenable to institutional action (Escobar, 1992; Spiegel *et al.*, 1999). Thus, the intercultural subject as represented in policy, like the literate subject, is ultimately a rather two-dimensional construct, from which individuality has been removed. On the other hand, the erasure of the individual can be seen in constructions of the intercultural itself. Lavanchy *et al.* (2011) argue that when interculturality is described as an encounter with others, it inevitably reduces the identity of the other to a single element – the cultural, often the national. It is an engagement between types, rather than between individuals. In this way, the idea of the intercultural subject used here differs from Kramsch's (2009) understanding of the multilingual subject, who is a complex, multivalent social actor acting and interacting at the interstices of languages, cultures and identities. The complexity, hybridity and liquidity (see Dervin, 2008, 2010; Kraidy, 2002) found in intercultural encounters is thus absent from the policy framings of intercultural actors examined in this book.

Concluding Comments

This book has analysed one element of the constellation of discourses around constructions of intercultural relationships and intercultural subjects – language-in-education policy texts. It has shown that such texts construct the nature and purpose of language education in particular ways and project relationships which both produce and are influenced by systems of belief about languages and their speakers. In so doing, such texts produce and reproduce ideologies of the intercultural. Such ideologies can be seen as an element of a *politics of otherness* (Lavanchy *et al.*, 2011) in which representations of language practices are conveyed as solutions to ideologically created language problems. Neither the problem nor its solution is therefore conceived or articulated outside a system of beliefs.

This book has analysed language-in-education policy texts in a small number of polities. Although these polities are quite diverse, it would be impossible to claim on the basis of these that they allow for an exhaustive account of the constructions of intercultural relationships and the intercultural subject. This study is therefore indicative of the ways in which policy texts represent ideologies of the intercultural, and much work is needed to understand these processes as they apply in other contexts. There is also a need to examine how intercultural relationships and the intercultural subject are constructed in other discourses. Language-in-education policy texts represent official, authorised discourses about intercultural relationships but they are only one element of policy and of the discourses about language and language use which exist in any society. They are therefore only one element of the discursive construction of intercultural relations and the intercultural subject, and are supplemented by other discourses, which may develop, extend, restrict or challenge the constructions present in policy texts.

As argued above, language-in-education policies exist with and interact with other forms of discourse – academic discourses, media discourses, popular discourses, educational practices and so on – and each area of discourse may have its own particular ideological constructions of intercultural relationships and the intercultural subject. This means that while language-in-education policy texts may influence how interculturality is understood within a polity, they do not determine this. Rather, interculturality is constructed through competing and complementary discourses, and the study of broader discursive constructions of intercultural relationships and the intercultural subject may reveal cleavages and tensions in the language policy context.

Examining language policies as discursive representations of ideologies opens the possibility of critical analyses that go beyond accounts of provision to examine the role of deeper issues in the encounters between languages and cultures. It helps to reveal the starting points for understanding how language problems are identified and resolved within polities, and how the frameworks for actions are developed and implemented. It recognises that policy discourses and the actions they project have signification that goes beyond the instrumental level and relates to the power structures and relations that exist within a society. Recognising this means that policies which, in terms of their enactment, appear to address inequalities and asymmetries can be seen in terms of the realities they project to maintain and reinforce the existing hegemony.

References

Abdallah-Pretceille, M. (1986) *Vers une pédagogie interculturelle* [*Towards an Intercultural Pedagogy*]. Paris: Economica.

Abdallah-Pretceille, M. (2003) *Former et éduquer en contexte hétérogène*. Paris: Economica.

Ager, D.E. (2005a) Prestige and image planning. In E. Hinkel (ed.) *Handbook of Research in Second Language Teaching and Learning* (pp. 1035–1054). Mahwah, NJ: Lawrence Erlbaum.

Ager, D.E. (2005b) Image and prestige planning. *Current Issues in Language Planning* 6 (1), 1–43.

Allain, J-C., Coste, D. and Catalan, R. (1984) *Aspects d'une politique de diffusion du français langue étrangère depuis 1945: Matériaux pour une histoire* [*Aspects of a Policy for the Diffusion of French as a Foreign Language Since 1945: Materials for a History*]. Paris: Hatier.

Althusser, L. (1965) *Pour Marx* [*For Marx*]. Paris: François Maspero.

Althusser, L. (1976) Idéologie et appareils idéologiques d'état [Ideology and state ideological apparatus]. In L. Althusser (ed.) *Positions (1964–1975)* (pp. 67–125). Paris: Éditions sociales.

Amano, I. (1990) *Education and Examination in Modern Japan*. Tokyo: University of Tokyo Press.

Ambrosini, M. (2001) *La fatica di integrarsi. Immigrati e lavoro in Italia* [*The Effort to Integrate. Immigrants and Work in Italy*]. Bologna: Il Mulino.

Ammon, U. (1992) Editor's preface. *International Journal for the Sociology of Language* 95 (1), 5–9.

Ammon, U. (1997) Language-spread policy. *Language Problems and Language Planning* 21 (1), 51–57.

Anderson, B. (1991) *Imagined Communities: Reflections on the Origin and Spread of Nationalism*. London: Verso.

Ang, I. and Stratton, J. (1998) Multiculturalism in crisis: The new politics of race and national identity in Australia. *Topia: Canadian Journal of Cultural Studies* 1 (2), 22–41.

Assemblée nationale (1990) Loi n° 90-588 du 6 juillet 1990 portant création de l'Agence pour l'enseignement français à l'étranger [Law No. 90-588 of 6 July, 1990 Relating to the creation of the Agence pour l'enseignement français à l'étranger]. Retrieved 24 August 2011 from http://www.legifrance.gouv.fr/affichTexte.do?cidTexte=LEGITEXT000006071201&dateTexte=20000621

Australian Bureau of Statistics (2008) *2006 Census QuickStats: Australia*. Retrieved 6 October 2011 from http://www.multiculturalaustralia.edu.au/doc/2006census-quickstats-australia.pdf

Australian Bureau of Statistics (2012) *Cultural Diversity in Australia*. Retrieved 3 August 2012 from http://www.abs.gov.au/ausstats/abs@.nsf/Lookup/2071.0main+featu res902012-2013

Australian Education Council (1992) *National Report on Schooling in Australia, 1991*. Melbourne: Curriculum Corporation.

Bakhtin, M.M. (1981) *The Dialogic Imagination: Four Essays* (C. Emerson and M. Holquist, trans.). Austin, TX: University of Texas Press.

Bakhtin, M.M. (1994) Проблемы Творчества Достоевского [*Problems of Dostoevsky's Poetics*]. Kiev: Next (original work published 1929).

Baldauf, R.B., Jr (2005a) Coordinating government and community support for community language teaching in Australia: Overview with special attention to New South Wales. *International Journal of Bilingual Education and Bilingualism* 8 (2–3), 132–144.

Baldauf, R.B., Jr (2005b) Micro language planning. In P. Bruthiaux, D. Atkinson, W.G. Eggington, W. Grabe and V. Ramanathan (eds) *Perspectives on Applied Linguistics: Essays in Honor of Robert B. Kaplan* (pp. 227–239). Clevedon: Multilingual Matters.

Baldauf, R.B., Jr (2006) Rearticulating the case for micro language planning in a language ecology context. *Current Issues in Language Planning* 7 (2,3), 147–170.

Baldauf, R.B., Jr (2008) Rearticulating the case for micro language planning in a language ecology context. In A.J. Liddicoat and R.B. Baldauf (eds) *Language Planning in Local Contexts*. Clevedon: Multilingual Matters.

Baldauf, R.B., Jr and Kaplan, R.B. (2005) Language-in-education policy and planning. In E. Hinkel (ed.) *Handbook of Research in Second Language Teaching and Learning* (pp. 1013–1034). Mahwah, NJ: Lawrence Erlbaum.

Ball, S.J. (1990) *Politics and Policy Making in Education: Explorations in Policy Sociology*. New York: Routledge.

Ball, S.J. (1993) What is policy? Texts, trajectories and toolboxes. *Discourse* 13 (2), 10–17.

Ball, S.J. (1997) Policy sociology and critical social research: A personal review of recent education policy and policy research. *British Education Research Journal* 23 (3), 257–274.

Balous, S. (1970) *L'action culturelle de la France dans le monde* [*France's Cultural Action in the World*]. Paris: Presses Universitaires de France.

Barko, I. (1999) The foundation and early history of the Alliance Française of Sydney. *Explorations: A Journal of French-Australian Connections* 26, 3–42.

Bayart, J-F. (2002) *The Illusion of Cultural Identity*. Chicago, IL: University of Chicago Press.

Befu, H. (1993) Nationalism and Nihonjinron. In H. Befu (ed.) *Cultural Nationalism in East Asia: Representation and Identity* (pp. 107–135). Berkeley, CA: Institute of East Asian Studies.

Befu, H. (2001) *Hegemony of Homogeneity: An Anthropological Analysis of Nihonjinron*. Melbourne: Trans Pacific Press.

Berry, J.W. (1997) Immigration, acculturation, and adaptation. *Applied Psychology: An International Review* 46 (1), 5–34.

Berry, J.W. (2005) Acculturation: Living successfully in two cultures. *International Journal of Intercultural Relations* 29, 697–712.

Béteille, A. (1998) The idea of indigenous people. *Current Anthropology* 39 (2), 187–192.

Betts, K. (1988) *Ideology and Immigration: Australia 1976 to 1987*. Melbourne: Melbourne University Press.

Boulanger, L. and Daniel, P. (1984) Vingt-cinq ans dans l'evolution d'une politique de diffusion du français [Twenty-five years in the evolution of a diffusion policy for French]. *Français dans le Monde* 182, 71–76.

Bourdieu, P. (1972) *Esquisse d'une théorie de la pratique* [*Outline of a Theory of Practice*]. Geneva: Droz.

Bourdieu, P. (1980) *Le sens practique* [*Logic of Practice*]. Paris: Éditions de Minuit.

Bourdieu, P. (1981) *Questions de sociologie* [*Sociology Questions*]. Paris: Éditions de Minuit.

Bourdieu, P. (1982) *Langage et pouvoir symbolique* [*Language and Symbolic Power*]. Paris: Arthème-Fayard.

Bourdieu, P. and Passeron, J-C. (1970) *La réproduction: Eléments pour une théorie du système d'enseignement* [*Reproduction: Elements for a Theory of Educational Systems*]. Paris: Éditions de Minuit.

British Council (1941) *Annual Report 1940–41.* London: British Council.

British Council (1985) *Annual Report 1984–85.* London: British Council.

British Council (2002) *Royal Charter and Bye-laws 1993.* London: British Council.

British Council (2009) *Annual Report 2008–09.* London: British Council.

British Council (2011) *Annual Report 2010–11.* London: British Council.

Brock, P. (2001) Australia's language. In J. Lo Bianco and R. Wickert (eds) *Australian Policy Activism in Language and Literacy* (pp. 47–74). Melbourne: Language Australia.

Bruézière, M. (1983) *L'Alliance Française: Histoire d'une institution* [*The Alliance Française: History of an Institution*]. Paris: Hachette.

Burns, A. and De Silva Joyce, H. (2007) Adult ESL programs in Australia. *Prospect* 22 (3), 5–17.

Buruma, I. and Margalit, A. (2004) *Occidentalism: The West in the Eyes of Its Enemies.* New York: Penguin.

Butler, Y.G. (2007) Foreign language education at elementary schools in Japan: Searching for solutions amidst growing diversification. *Current Issues in Language Planning* 18 (2), 129–147.

Butler, Y.G. and Iino, M. (2005) Current Japanese reforms in English language education: The 2003 'Action Plan'. *Language Policy* 4 (1), 25–45.

Byram, M. (2008) *From Foreign Language Education to Education for Intercultural Citizenship.* Clevedon: Multilingual Matters.

Calvet, L-J. (1994) Les politiques de diffusion des langues en Afrique francophone [The policies of language spread in French-speaking Africa]. *International Journal of the Sociology of Language* 107, 67–76.

Calvetti, P. (1992) Language education and standardisation in the formation of the modern state: A comparison of Italy and Japan. *Senri Ethnological Studies* 34, 109–121.

Cameron, D. (2006) Language ideologies. *Journal of Political Ideologies* 11 (2), 141–152.

Campbell, L. (1994) Language death. In R.E. Asher and J.M.Y. Simpson (eds) *The Encyclopedia of Language and Linguistics* (vol. 4, pp. 1960–1968). Oxford: Pergamon Press.

Chapman, D. (2006) Discourses of multicultural coexistence (*tabunka kyōsei*) and the 'old-comer' Korean residents of Japan. *Asian Ethnicity* 7 (1), 89–102.

Chaubet, F. (2004) L'Alliance Française ou la diplomatie de la langue (1883–1914) [The Alliance Française or language diplomacy (1883–1914)]. *Revue historique* 632, 763–785.

Cignatta, T. (2007) Le lingue comunitarie [Community languages]. In G. Cerini, C. Fiorentini and E. Testa (eds) *Indicazioni per il curricolo: Analisi, proposte, percorsi possibili* [*Pointers for the Curriculum: Analyses, Proposals and Possible Pathways*] (pp. 84–92). Rome: Editoriale CIID.

Clyne, M. (1991) Australia's language policies: Are we going backwards? In A.J. Liddicoat (ed.) *Language Planning and Language Policy in Australia* (pp. 3–22). Melbourne: Applied Linguistics Association of Australia.

Clyne, M. (2011) Three is too many in Australia. In C. Hélot and M. Ó Laoire (eds) *Language Policy for the Multilingual Classroom: Pedagogy of the Possible* (pp. 174–187). Clevedon: Multilingual Matters.

COAG [Council of Australian Governments] (1994) *Asian Languages and Australia's Economic Future*. Canberra: Australian Government Publishing Service.

Codd, J.A. (1988) The construction and deconstruction of educational policy documents. *Journal of Education Policy* 3 (3), 235–247.

Commission of the European Communities (2003) *Promoting Language Learning and Linguistic Diversity: An Action Plan 2004–2006*. Retrieved 14 November 2011 from http://eur-lex.europa.eu/LexUriServ/LexUriServ.do?uri=COM:2003:0449:FIN:EN:PDF

Commission of the European Communities (2005) *A New Framework Strategy for Multilingualism*. Retrieved 14 November 2011 from http://ec.europa.eu/education/languages/archive/doc/com596_en.pdf

Committee on Multicultural Education (1979) *Education for a Multicultural Society*. Canberra: Schools Commission.

Commonwealth of Australia (1999) *A New Agenda for Multicultural Australia*. Canberra: Australian Government Publishing Service.

Condit, C.M. (1989) The rhetorical limits of polysemy. *Critical Studies in Mass Communication* 6, 103–122.

Considine, M. (1994) *Public Policy. A Critical Approach*. Melbourne: Macmillan.

Coombs, D. (1988) *Spreading the Word: The Library Work of the British Council*. London: Mansell.

Costantini, D. (2008) *Mission civilisatrice: Le rôle de l'histoire coloniale dans la construction de l'identité politique française [Civilising Mission: The Role of Colonial History in the Construction of French Political Identity]*. Paris: Éditions La Découverte.

Costescu, A.S. (2000) Building new foundations for Japanese foreign policy and rapprochement with Europe. *Japan Foundation Newsletter* 27 (3–4), 16–18, 24.

Coulmas, F. (2002) Language policy in modern Japanese education. In J.W. Tollefson (ed.) *Language Policies in Education: Critical Issues* (pp. 203–224). Mahwah, NJ: Lawrence Erlbaum.

Council for the Promotion of Measures for Foreign Residents of Japanese Descent (2011) 日系定住外国人施策に関する行動計画 *[Action Plan on Measures for Foreign Residents of Japanese Descent]*. Retrieved 19 February 2012 from http://www8.cao.go.jp/teiju/guideline/pdf/fulltext-koudo.pdf

Council of Europe (1992) European Charter for Regional or Minority Languages. Retrieved 12 October 2011 from http://conventions.coe.int/treaty/en/Treaties/Html/148.htm

Council of the European Communities (1977) Council Directive 77/486/EEC of 25 July 1977 on the education of the children of migrant workers. Retrieved 12 July 2008 from http://eur-lex.europa.eu/smartapi/cgi/sga_doc?smartapi!celexapi!prod!CELEX numdoc&lg=EN&numdoc=31977L0486&model=guichett

Crawford, J. (1995) Endangered native American languages: What is to be done, and why? *Bilingual Research Journal* 19 (1), 17–38.

Crichton, J. (2007) Doing battle with a noun: Notes on the grammar of 'terror'. *Australian Review of Applied Linguistics* 30 (2), 19.11–19.18.

Croft, K. and Macpherson, R.J.S. (1991a) Client demand, policy research and lobbying: Major sources of languages administrative policies in NSW 1980–1986. In A.J. Liddicoat (ed.) *Language Planning and Language Policy in Australia*. Melbourne: Applied Linguistics Association of Australia.

Croft, K. and Macpherson, R.J.S. (1991b) The evolution of languages administrative policies in New South Wales: 1962–1979. *Australian Review of Applied Linguistics* 14 (1), 35–58.

Cryle, P., Freadman, A. and Hannah, B. (1994) *Unlocking Australia's Language Potential: Profiles of 9 Key Languages in Australia* (Vol. 3, French). Canberra: National Languages and Literacy Institute of Australia.

Crystal, D. (2000) *Language Death*. Cambridge: Cambridge University Press.

Dale, P.N. (1986) *The Myth of Japanese Uniqueness*. London: Routledge.

Dandy, J. and Pe-Pua, R. (2010) Attitudes to multiculturalism, immigration and cultural diversity: Comparison of dominant and non-dominant groups in three Australian states. *International Journal of Intercultural Relations* 34 (1), 34–46.

De Bellescize, G. (1986) Editorial. *Notre Librairie* 83, 1–4.

Deaux, K. and Bikmen, N. (2010) Immigration and power. In A. Guinote and T.K. Vescio (eds) *The Social Psychology of Power* (pp. 381–407). New York: Guilford Press.

DEET (Department of Employment, Education and Training) (1989a) *National Aboriginal and Torres Strait Islander Education Policy: Joint Policy Statement*. Canberra: Commonwealth of Australia.

DEET (Department of Employment, Education and Training) (1989b) *National Survey of Language Learning in Australian Schools: 1988*. Canberra: Australian Government Publishing Service.

DEET (Department of Employment, Education and Training) (1990) *The Language of Australia. Discussion Paper on Australian Literacy and Language Policy in the 1990s*. Canberra: Australian Government Publishing Service.

DEET (Department of Employment, Education and Training) (1991a) *Australia's Language: An Australian Language and Literacy Policy, Vol. 1*. Canberra: Australian Government Publishing Service.

DEET (Department of Employment, Education and Training) (1991b) *Australia's Language: An Australian Language and Literacy Policy, Vol. 2*. Canberra: Australian Government Publishing Service.

DEETV (Department of Employment, Education and Training, Victoria) (2000) *Linking Languages Other Than English to the Early Years Literacy Program*. Melbourne: State of Victoria.

DEETYA (Department of Employment, Education, Training and Youth Affairs) (1998) *Literacy for All: The Challenge for Australian Schools. Commonwealth Literacy Policies for Australian Schools*. Canberra: Australian Government.

DEEWR (Department of Education, Employment and Workplace Relations) (2009a) *National Asian Languages and Studies in Schools Program – Overview*. Retrieved 14 July 2011 from http://www.deewr.gov.au/schooling/NALSSP/Pages/default.aspx

DEEWR (Department of Education, Employment and Workplace Relations) (2009b) *National Asian Languages and Studies in Schools Program: Program Guidelines 2009–2012*. Retrieved 20 July 2009 from http://www.deewr.gov.au/Schooling/NALSSP/Documents/NALSSP_ProgramGuidelines_June2009.pdf

Deibel, T.L. and Roberts, W.R. (1976) *Culture and Information: Two Foreign Policy Functions*. Beverly Hills, CA: Sage.

Dervin, F. (2008) Pour un interculturel en devenir [Towards a constantly evolving intercultural]. *Écarts d'identité* [*Identity Differences*] 113, 76–82.

Dervin, F. (2010) Pistes pour renouveler l'interculturel en éducation [Avenues for renewing intercultural education]. *Recherches en éducation* [*Research in Education*] 9, 32–41.

Dervin, F. (2011) A plea for change in research on intercultural discourses: A 'liquid' approach to the study of the acculturation of Chinese students. *Journal of Multicultural Discourses* 6 (1), 37–51.

DIAC (Department of Immigration and Citizenship) (2008) *The People of Australia: Statistics from the 2006 Census*. Retrieved 16 July 2011 from http://www.immi.gov.au/media/publications/research/_pdf/poa-2008.pdf

DIAC (Department of Immigration and Citizenship) (2011) *People of Australia: Australia's Multicultural Policy*. Retrieved 12 June 2011 from http://www.immi.gov.au/media/publications/multicultural/pdf_doc/people-of-australia-multicultural-policy-booklet.pdf.

Diallo, I. (2010) *The Politics of National Languages in Post-colonial Senegal*. New York: Cambria Press.

Diet of Japan (1972) 昭和47年法律第48号　国際交流基金法 [Showa 47 (1972) Law No. 48: Japan Foundation Law]. Retrieved 25 September 2011 from http://hourei.hounavi.jp/seitei/hou/S47/S47HO048.php

Diet of Japan (1997) アイヌ文化の振興並びにアイヌの伝統等に関する知識の普及及び啓発に関する法律 [Law for the Promotion of the Ainu Culture and for the Dissemination of Knowledge of Ainu Traditions]. Retrieved 8 November 2012 from http://law.e-gov.go.jp/htmldata/H09/H09HO052.html.

Djité, P. (1994) *From Language Policy to Language Planning*. Canberra: National Languages and Literacy Institute of Australia.

Dlaska, A. (2000) Integrating culture and language learning in institution-wide language programmes. *Language, Culture and Curriculum* 13 (3), 247–263.

Donaldson, F.L. (1984) *The British Council: The First Fifty Years*. London: J. Cape.

Dressler, W. (1988) Language death. In F.J. Newmwyer (ed.) *Linguistics: The Cambridge Survey, Vol. 4. Language: The Sociocultural Context* (pp. 184–192). Cambridge: Cambridge University Press.

Drogheda, Earl of, Heyworth, J.L., Feather, V., Stocks, M., Platt, J.W., McLachlan, D. and Huxley, G. (1954) *Report of the Independent Committee of Enquiry into the Overseas Information Services*. London: HMSO.

Dubosclard, A. (1998) *Histoire de la Fédération des Alliances Françaises aux États-Unis. L'Alliance au coeur* [History of the Federation Alliances Françaises in the United States. The Alliance at the Heart]. Paris: L'Harmattan.

Eagleton, T. (2007) *Ideology: An Introduction* (2nd edn). London: Verso.

Early, M. (2008) Second and foreign language education in Canada. In N.H. Hornberger (ed.) *Encyclopedia of Language and Education* (pp. 1293–1304). New York: Springer.

Ehara, T. (1992) The internationalization of education. In G.D. Hook and M.A. Weiner (eds) *The Internationalization of Japan* (pp. 269–283). London: Routledge.

Emerson, C. (1981) The outer world and inner speech: Bakhtin, Vygotsky, and the internalization of language. *Critical Enquiry* 10 (2), 245–264.

Escobar, A. (1992) Planning. In W. Sachs (ed.) *The Development Dictionary: A Guide to Knowledge as Power* (pp. 132–145). London: Zed Books.

European Commission (1995) *Teaching and Learning: Towards the Learning Society, White Paper on Education and Training*. Retrieved 14 September 2011 from http://europa.eu/documents/comm/white_papers/pdf/com95_590_en.pdf

European Council (1995) Council Resolution of 31 March 1995 on improving and diversifying language learning and teaching within the education systems of the European Union. Retrieved 9 November 2011 from http://eur-lex.europa.eu/LexUriServ/LexUriServ.do?uri=CELEX:31995Y0812(01):EN:HTML

European Council (2000) Decision No. 1934/2000/EC of the European Parliament and of the Council of 17 July 2000 on the European Year of Languages 2001. *Official Journal of the European Communities* (L232), 1–5. Retrieved 9 November 2011 from http://eur-lex.europa.eu/LexUriServ/LexUriServ.do?uri=OJ:L:2000:232:0001:0005:EN:PDF

European Council (2002) Council Resolution of 14 February 2002 on the promotion of linguistic diversity and language learning in the framework of the implementation of the objectives of the European Year of Languages 2001. *Official Journal of the European Communities* C50, 1–2. Retrieved 9 November 2011 from http://eur-lex.europa.eu/LexUriServ/LexUriServ.do?uri=OJ:C:2002:050:0001:0002:EN:PDF

European Council (2008a) Council Conclusions of 22 May 2008 on multilingualism. *Official Journal of the European Communities* C140, 10–13. Retrieved 9 November 2011 from http://eur-lex.europa.eu/LexUriServ/LexUriServ.do?uri=OJ:C:2008:140:0010:0013:EN:PDF

European Council (2008b) Council Resolution of 21 November 2008 on a European strategy for multilingualism. *Official Journal of the European Communities* C20, 1–3. Retrieved 9 November 2011 from http://eur-lex.europa.eu/LexUriServ/LexUriServ.do?uri=OJ:C:2008:320:0001:0003:EN:PDF

Fiala, R. and Lanford, A.G. (1987) Educational ideology and the world educational revolution, 1950–1970. *Comparative Education Review* 31 (3), 315–332.

Finch, J. and Nynäs, P. (2011) *Transforming Otherness*. New York: Transactions.

Foreign Office (1939) *A Survey of Our Foreign Publicity*. London: HMSO.

Foster, L.E. and Stockley, D. (1988) *Australian Multiculturalism: A Documentary History and Critique*. Clevedon: Multilingual Matters.

Foucault, M. (1969) *L'archéologie du savoir* [*Archaeology of Knowledge*]. Paris: Gallimard.

Foucault, M. (1994) Entretien avec Michel Foucault [Interview with Michel Foucault]. In D. Defert and F. Ewald (eds), *Dits et écrits, 1954–1988* [*Sayings and Writings, 1954–1988*] (Vol. 3, pp. 140–160). Paris: Gallimard.

Fox, W. and Meyer, I.H. (1995) *Public Administration Dictionary*. Cape Town: Juta.

Frank, R. (2003) La machine diplomatique culturelle française après 1945 [The French cultural diplomacy machinery after 1945]. *Relations internationales* 115, 325–348.

Fuentes, R. and Nieto, R. (2011) The discourse of interculturality in indigenous education in Mexico. In F. Dervin, A. Gajardo and A. Lavanchy (eds) *Politics of Interculturality* (pp. 99–126). Newcastle upon Tyne: Cambridge Scholars.

Fujimoto-Adamson, N. (2006) Globalization and history of English education in Japan. *Asian EFL Journal* 8 (3), 259–282.

Gal, S. (2009) Migration, minorities and multilingualism: Language ideologies in Europe. In C. Mar-Molinero and P. Stevenson (eds) *Language Ideologies, Policies and Practices: Language and the Future of Europe* (pp. 13–27). Houndmills: Palgrave Macmillan.

Gee, J.P. (1990) *Social Linguistics and Literacies: Ideology in Discourse*. London: Falmer.

Gee, J.P. (1994a) New alignments and old literacies: Critical literacy, post-modernism and fast capitalism. In P. O'Connor (ed.) *Thinking Work* (pp. 82–104). Sydney: Albsac.

Gee, J.P. (1994b) New alignments and old literacies: From fast capitalism to the canon. In B. Shortland-Jones, B. Bosich and J. Rivalland (eds) *Living Literacy* (pp. 1–35). Carlton South: Australian Reading Association.

Gee, J.P. (1999) *An Introduction to Discourse Analysis: Theory and Method*. London: Routledge.

Gee, J.P. and Lankshear, C. (1995) The new work order: Critical language awareness and 'fast capitalism' texts. *Discourse: The Australian Journal of Educational Studies* 16 (1), 5–19.

Gekkan Okinawa-sha (1983) *Laws and Regulations During the U.S. Administration of Okinawa, 1945–1972*. Naha: Ikemiya Shokai & Co.

Gjerde, P.F. and Onishi, M. (2000) Selves, cultures, and nations: The psychological imagination of 'the Japanese' in the era of globalization. *Human Development* 43, 216–226.

Gramsci, A. (1975) *Quaderni del carcere* [*Prison Notebooks*]. Turin: Instituto Gramsci.

Grant, A.N. (1997) A multi-storied approach to the analysis: Narrative, literacy and discourse. *Melbourne Studies in Education* 38 (1), 31–71.

Haarmann, H. (1990) Language planning in the light of a general theory of language: A methodological framework. *International Journal of the Sociology of Language* 86, 103–126.

Hashimoto, K. (2000) 'Internationalization' is 'Japanisation': Japan's foreign language education and national identity. *Journal of Intercultural Studies* 21 (1), 39–51.

Hattori, R. (2005) A policy on language education in Japan: Beyond nationalism and linguicism. *Second Language Studies* 23 (2), 45–69.

Haugen, E. (1972) *The Ecology of Language*. Stanford, CA: Stanford University Press.

Haugen, E. (1983) The implementation of corpus planning: Theory and practice. In J. Cobarrubias and J.A. Fishman (eds) *Progress in Language Planning: International Perspectives* (pp. 269–289). Berlin: Mouton.

Hawkes, D. (1996) *Ideology*. London: Routledge.

Heinrich, P. (2004) Language planning and language policy in the Ryūkyūan Islands. *Language Policy* 3, 153–179.

Heinrich, P. (2011) Heritage language education in Uchinaa. In P. Heinrich and C. Galan (eds) *Language Life in Japan: Transformations and Prospects* (pp. 34–49). London: Routledge.

Hirano, K. (2002) 国際文化交流しの中の国際交流基金 [The Japan Foundation in international exchange]. 国際文化交流 [*International Exchange*] 97, 119–124.

Hirataka, F. (1992) The language spread policy of Japan. *International Journal for the Sociology of Language* 95 (1), 93–108.

Holliday, A. (2010) *Intercultural Communication and Ideology*. London: Sage.

Hornberger, N.H. (1998) Language policy, language education, language rights: Indigenous, immigrant, and international perspectives. *Language in Society* 27 (4), 439–458.

Howatt, A.P.R. (1984) *A History of English Language Teaching*. Oxford: Oxford University Press.

Hugo, G. (2002) Australia's changing non-metropolitan population. In D. Wilkinson and I. Blue (eds) *The New Rural Health* (pp. 12–43). Melbourne: Oxford University Press.

Hursh, D. (2007) Assessing No Child Left Behind and the rise of neoliberal education policies. *American Educational Research Journal* 44 (3), 493–518.

Ikenberry, G.J. (2004) American hegemony and East Asian order. *Australian Journal of International Affairs* 58 (3), 353–367.

Ishihara, M. (2004) USCAR's language policy and English education in Okinawa. *Okinawan Journal of American Studies* 1, 19–27.

Ivy, M. (1995) *Discourses of the Vanishing: Modernity, Phantasm, Japan*. Chicago, IL: University of Chicago Press.

Jacobson, J.P. (2008) Time and the Ainu: Japanese nation-building and the conceptualization of difference. *Historical Geography* 36, 163–181.

Japanese government (1899) 北海道旧土人保護法 [Hokkaido Former Aborigines Protection Act]. Retrieved 8 November 2012 from http://www.city.asahikawa.hokkaido. jp/files/bunkashinko/bunkashinko/ainu-plan/ap-data.html.

Johnson, C. (1983) The internationalization of the Japanese economy. In H. Mannari and H. Befu (eds) *The Challenge of Japan's Internationalization: Organization and Culture* (pp. 31–58). New York and Hyōgo: Kodansha International Ltd and Kwansei Gakuin University.

Jordan, G. and Weedon, C. (1995) The celebration of difference and the cultural politics of racism. In B. Adam and S. Allan (eds) *Theorizing Culture: An Interdisciplinary Critique After Postmodernism* (pp. 149–164). London: UCL Press.

Jupp, J. (1995) From 'White Australia' to 'part of Asia': Recent shifts in Australian immigration policy towards the region. *International Migration Review* 29 (1), 207–228.

Kachru, B. (1985) Standards, codification and sociolinguistic realism: The English language in the outer circle. In R. Quirk and H. G. Widdowson (eds) *English in the World: Teaching and Learning the Language and Literatures* (pp. 11–30). Cambridge: Cambridge University Press.

Kalantzis, M. and Cope, B. (1988) Why we need multicultural education: A review of the 'ethnic disadvantage' debate. *Journal of Intercultural Studies* 9(1), 39–57.

Kaplan, R.B. (1991) Applied linguistics and language policy and planning. In W. Grabe and R.B. Kaplan (eds) *Introduction to Applied Linguistics* (pp. 143–165). Reading, MA: Addison-Wesley.

Kaplan, R.B. and Baldauf, R.B., Jr (1997) *Language Planning: From Practice to Theory*. Clevedon: Multilingual Matters.

Kaplan, R.B. and Baldauf, R.B., Jr (2003) *Language and Language-in-Education Planning in the Pacific Basin*. Dordrecht: Kluwer.

Kasuya, K. (2001) Discourses of linguistic dominance: A historical consideration of French language ideology. *International Review of Education – Internationale Zeitschrift für Erziehungswissenschaft – Revue Internationale de l'Education* 47(3–4), 235–251.

Kitao, K. and Kitao, K.S. (1995) *English Teaching: Theory, Research, Practice*. Tokyo: Eichosha.

Kleineidam, H. (1992) Politique de diffusion linguistique et francophonie: L'action linguistique menée par la France [Language spread policy and Francophonie: The linguistic action undertaken by France]. *International Journal for the Sociology of Language* 95 (1), 11–31.

Kosaku, Y. (1992) *Cultural Nationalism in Contemporary Japan: A Sociological Enquiry*. New York: Routledge.

Kosaku, Y. (2002) English and nationalism in Japan: The role of the intercultural communications industry. In S. Wilson (ed.) *Nation and Nationalism in Japan* (pp. 135–145). New York: Routledge Curzon.

Kotoo, A. (1992) ジャンル別英文読解以前　基礎知識充溢編 [*Foundations of English Reading Comprehension by Genre: Building Basic Knowledge*]. Tokyo: Kenkyuusha.

Kraidy, M.M. (2002) Hybridity in cultural globalization. *Communication Theory* 12 (3), 316–339.

Kramsch, C. (1993) *Context and Culture in Language Education*. Oxford: Oxford University Press.

Kramsch, C. (2009) *The Multilingual Subject*. Oxford: Oxford University Press.

Kubota, R. (2002) The impact of globalization on language teaching in Japan. In D. Block and D. Cameron (eds) *Globalization and Language Teaching* (pp. 13–28). London: Routledge.

Lavanchy, A., Gajardo, A. and Dervin, F. (2011) Interculturality at stake. In F. Dervin, A. Gajardo and A. Lavanchy (eds) *Politics of Interculturality* (pp. 1–25). Newcastle upon Tyne: Cambridge Scholars.

Lebovics, H. (1999) *'Mona Lisa's escort' André Malraux and the Reinvention of French Culture*. Ithaca, NY: Cornell University Press.

Liddicoat, A.J. (1996) The narrowing focus – Australia's changing language policy. *Babel* 31 (1), 1–6, 24.

Liddicoat, A.J. (2002) Language planning, linguistic diversity and democracy in Europe. In A.J. Liddicoat and K. Muller (eds) *Perspective on Europe: Language Issues and Language Planning in Europe* (pp. 21–39). Melbourne: Language Australia.

Liddicoat, A.J. (2005a) Corpus planning: Syllabus and materials development. In E. Hinkel (ed.) *Handbook of Research in Second Language Teaching and Learning* (pp. 993–1012). Mahwah, NJ: Lawrence Erlbaum.

Liddicoat, A.J. (2005b) Culture for language learning in Australian language-in-education policy. *Australian Review of Applied Linguistics* 28 (2), 1–28.

Liddicoat, A.J. (2007a) Discourses of the self and other: *Nihonjinron* and the intercultural in Japanese language-in-education policy. *Journal of Multicultural Discourses* 2 (1), 1–15.

Liddicoat, A.J. (2007b) Language planning for literacy: Issues and implications. In A.J. Liddicoat (ed.) *Language Planning and Policy: Issues in Language Planning and Literacy* (pp. 13–29). Clevedon: Multilingual Matters.

Liddicoat, A.J. (2009) Evolving ideologies of the intercultural in Australian multicultural and language education policy. *Journal of Multilingual and Multicultural Development* 30 (3), 189–203.

Liddicoat, A.J. (2012) Language planning as an element of religious practice. *Current Issues in Language Planning* 13 (2), 121–144.

Liddicoat, A.J. and Baldauf, R.B., Jr (2008) Language planning in local contexts: Agents, contexts and interactions. In A.J. Liddicoat and R.B. Baldauf, Jr (eds) *Language Planning in Local Contexts* (pp. 3–17). Clevedon: Multilingual Matters.

Liddicoat, A.J. and Curnow, T.J. (2007) Language-in-education policy in the context of language death: Policy and practice in Colombian ethnoeducation. In J. Siegel, J. Lynch and D. Eades (eds) *Language Description, History and Development: Linguistic Indulgence in Memory of Terry Crowley* (pp. 419–430). Amsterdam: John Benjamins.

Liddicoat, A.J. and Curnow, T.J. (2009) The place of languages in the school curriculum: Policy and practice in Australian schools. In A. Mahboob and C. Lipovsky (eds) *Studies in Applied Linguistics and Language Learning* (pp. 124–138). Cambridge: Cambridge Scholars.

Liddicoat, A.J. and Díaz, A. (2008) Engaging with diversity: The construction of intercultural education policy in Italy. *Journal of Intercultural Education* 19 (2), 137–150.

Littlewood, W. (1984) *Foreign and Second Language Learning*. Cambridge: Cambridge University Press.

Liu, S. (2007) Living with others: Mapping the routes to acculturation in a multicultural society. *International Journal of Intercultural Relations* 31, 761–778.

Lo Bianco, J. (1987) *National Policy on Languages*. Canberra: Australian Government Publishing Service.

Lo Bianco, J. (1988) Multiculturalism and the national policy on languages. *Journal of Intercultural Studies* 9 (1), 25–38.

Lo Bianco, J. (1999) The language of policy: What sort of policy making is the officialisation of English in the United States. In T. Huebner, K.A. Davis and J. Lo Bianco (eds) *Sociopolitical Perspectives on Language Policy and Planning in the USA* (pp. 39–65). Amsterdam: John Benjamins.

Lo Bianco, J. (2005) Including discourse in language planning theory. In P. Bruthiaux, D. Atkinson, W.G. Eggington, W. Grabe and V. Ramanathan (eds) *Directions in Applied Linguistics: Essays in Honor of Robert B. Kaplan* (pp. 255–264). Clevedon: Multilingual Matters.

Lo Bianco, J. (2008) Tense times and language planning. *Current Issues in Language Planning* 9 (2), 155–178.

Lo Bianco, J. and Gvozdenko, I. (2006) *Collaboration and Innovation in the Provision of Languages Other Than English in Australian Universities*. Retrieved 7 June 2008 from http://www.lcnau.org/pdfs/LO%20BIANCO%20GVOZDENKO%20LOTES%20 in%20Australian%20Universities.pdf.

Lockie, S. (2000) Crisis and conflict: Shifting discourses of rural and regional Australia. In B. Pritchard and P. McManus (eds) *Land of Discontent: The Dynamics of Change in Rural and Regional Australia* (pp. 14–32). Sydney: UNSW Press.

Lukács, G. (1988) *Geschichte und Klassenbewußtsein: Studien* über *marxistische Dialektik* [*History and Class Consciousness*]. Darmstadt: Luchterhand (original worked published 1923).

Luke, A. (1992) The body literate: Discourse and inscription in early literacy training. *Linguistics and Education* 4, 107–129.

Luke, A., Nakata, M., Singh, M.G. and Smith, R. (1993) Policy and politics of representation: Torres Strait Islanders and Aborigines at the margins. In J. Knight, B. Lingard and P. Porter (eds) *Schooling Reform in Hard Times* (pp. 139–152). London: Falmer Press.

Maeda, N. (2003) Influence of kotodamaism on Japanese journalism. *Media, Culture and Society* 25, 757–772.

Maher, J. and Yashiro, K. (1995) Multilingual Japan: An introduction. In J. Maher and K. Yashiro (eds) *Multilingual Japan* (pp. 1–17). Clevedon: Multilingual Matters.

Martin, S. (1998) The AMEP: A 50-year contribution to the development of a multicultural nation. *Prospect* 13 (3), 11–23.

Marx, K. and Engels, F. (2011) *Die deutsche Ideologie* [*The German Ideology*]. Berlin: Cotumax (original work written 1846, published 1932).

Masden, K. (1997) The impact of Ministry of Education policy on pluralism in Japanese education: An examination of recent issues. In D.Y.H. Wu, H. McQueen and Y. Yamanoto (eds) *Emerging Pluralism in Asia and the Pacific* (pp. 29–63). Hong Kong: Hong Kong Institute of Asia-Pacific Studies, Chinese University of Hong Kong.

MCEECDYA (Ministerial Council for Education, Early Childhood Development and Youth Affairs) (2011) *Aboriginal and Torres Strait Islander Education Action Plan (2010–2014)*. Carlton: MCEECDYA.

MCEETYA (Ministerial Council on Education, Employment, Training and Youth Affairs) (1998) *National Report on Australian Schooling – 1997*. Carlton: Curriculum Corporation.

MCEETYA (Ministerial Council on Education, Employment, Training and Youth Affairs) (2005) *National Statement for Languages Education in Australian Schools: National Plan for Languages Education in Australian Schools 2005–2008*. Adelaide: South Australian Department of Education and Children's Services.

McNamara, T. (2005) 21st century shibboleth: Language tests, identity and intergroup conflict. *Language Policy* 4 (4), 351–370.

MEN (Ministerio de Educación Nacional) (2005) *Colombia Bilingüe* [*Bilingual Colombia*]. Altablero No. 37. Retrieved 15 November 2011 from http://www.mineducacion.gov.co/1621/article-97495.html

MEN (Ministerio de Educación Nacional) (2009) *Programa Nacional de Bilingüismo* [*National Bilingualism Program*]. Retrieved 18 February 2010 from http://www.colombiaaprende.edu.co/html/productos/1685/article-158720.html

MEXT (Ministry of Education, Culture, Sports, Science and Technology) (2004a) *REX* プログラムでは次のような活動を行います [*Kinds of Activities Done Under the REX Program*]. Retrieved 9 September 2005 from http://www.mext.go.jp/a_menu/shotou/rex/002.htm.

MEXT (Ministry of Education, Culture, Sports, Science and Technology) (2004b) 事前研修. [*Advance Study*]. Retrieved 9 September 2005 from http://www.mext.go.jp/a_menu/shotou/rex/005.htm

MEXT (Ministry of Education, Culture, Sports, Science and Technology) (2008) 小学

校学習指導要領解説：外国語活動編 [*Explanation of the Elementary School Course of Study: Foreign Language Activities Book*]. Retrieved 14 July 2011 from http://www.fuku-c.ed.jp/center/contents/kaisetsu/gaikokugo.pdf

MIC (Ministry of Internal Affairs and Communications) (2006) 地域における多文化共生推進プランについて [*Concerning the Plan for Multicultural Coexistence in Local Areas*]. Retrieved 20 July 2011 from http://www.soumu.go.jp/kokusai/pdf/sonota_b6.pdf

Miller, R.A. (1982) *Japan's Modern Myth: The Language and Beyond*. New York: Weatherhill.

Miller, R.A. (1986) *Nihongo: In Defence of Japanese*. London: Athlone Press.

MIUR (Ministero dell'Istruzione dell'Università e della Ricerca) (2006) *Linee guida per l'accoglienza e l'integrazione degli alunni stranieri* [*Guidelines for the Reception and Integration of Foreign Students*]. Retrieved 8 November 2012 from http://www.didaweb.net/mediatori/articolo.php?id_vol=1580.

Monbusho (Ministry of Education and Culture) (2002a) *The Course of Study for Lower Secondary School: Foreign Languages*. Retrieved 12 August 2004 from http://www.mext.go.jp/english/shotou/030301.htm

Monbusho (Ministry of Education and Culture) (2002b) 学習指導要領、外国語 [*The Course of Study for Lower Secondary School: Foreign Languages*]. Retrieved 12 August 2004 from http://www.mext.go.jp/b_menu/shuppan/sonota/990301/03122602/010.htm

Monbusho (Ministry of Education and Culture) (2002c) 「英語が使える日本人」の育成のための戦略構想、英語力・国語力増進プラン [*Developing a Strategic Plan to Cultivate 'Japanese With English Abilities' to Improve English and Japanese Abilities*]. Retrieved 12 August 2004 from http://www.mext.go.jp/b_menu/shingi/chousa/shotou/020/sesaku/020702.htm

Moore, H. (1991) Enchantments and displacements: Multiculturalism, language policy and Dawkins-speak. *Melbourne Studies in Education* 32, 45–85.

Mori, H. (1997) *Immigration Policy and Foreign Workers in Japan*. Houndmills: Macmillan.

Morita, T. (1988) 臨教審と日本人・日本文化論 [*Education Reform and Studies of Japanese People and Culture*]. Tokyo: Shin Nihon Shuppansha.

Morris-Suzuki, T. (1998) *Reinventing Japan: Time, Space, Nation*. Armonk, NY: M.E. Sharpe.

Morris-Suzuki, T. (2002) Immigration and citizenship in contemporary Japan. In S.J. Maswood, J. Graham and H. Miyajima (eds) *Japan: Change and Continuity* (pp. 163–178). New York: Routledge Curzon.

Mouer, R. and Sugimoto, Y. (1986) *Images of Japanese Society: A Study on the Structure of Social Reality*. London: Kegan Paul International.

MPI (Ministero della Pubblica Istruzione) (1989) Circolare Ministeriale 8 settembre 1989, n. 301: Oggetto: Inserimento degli stranieri nella scuola dell'obbligo: promozione e coordinamento delle iniziative per l'esercizio del diritto allo studio [Ministerial Circular 8 September 1989, no. 301: Subject: Inclusion of foreigners in compulsory schooling: Promotion and coordination of initiatives for excercising the right to study]. Retrieved 28 May 2007 from http://www.edscuola.it/archivio/norme/circolari/cm301_89.html

MPI (Ministero della Pubblica Istruzione) (1990) Circolare Ministeriale 26 luglio 1990, n. 205: Oggetto: La scuola dell'obbligo e gli alunni stranieri. L'educazione interculturale. [Ministerial Circular 26 July 1990, no. 205: Subject: Compulsory schooling and foreign students. Intercultural education]. Retrieved 28 May 2007 from http://www.edscuola.it/archivio/norme/circolari/cm205_90.html

MPI (Ministero della Pubblica Istruzione) (1992) Circolare Ministeriale 28 aprile 1992, n. 122: Oggetto: Pronuncia del Consiglio nazionale della P.I. sulla educazione interculturale nella scuola. [Ministerial Circular 28 April 1992, no. 122: Subject:

Pronouncement of the National Council of the P.I. on intercultural education in schools]. Retrieved 28 May 2007 from http://www.edscuola.it/archivio/norme/circolari/cm122_92.html

MPI (Ministero della Pubblica Istruzione) (1994) Circolare Ministeriale 2 marzo 1994, n. 73; Oggetto: Dialogo interculturale e convivenza democratica: l'impegno progettuale della scuola. [Ministerial Circular 2 March 1994, no. 73: Subject: Intercultural dialogue and democratic coexistence: Schools' involvement in planning]. Retrieved 28 May 2007 from http://www.edscuola.it/archivio/norme/circolari/cm073_94.html

Muetzelfeldt, M. (1992) Introduction: The changing dynamic of society, state and politics. In M. Muetzelfeldt (ed.) *Society State and Politics in Australia* (pp. 1–22). Sydney: Pluto Press.

Mühlhäusler, P. (2000) Language planning and language ecology. *Current Issues in Language Planning* 1 (3), 306–367.

Mumby, D.K. (1997) The problem of hegemony: Rereading Gramsci for organisational communication studies. *Western Journal of Communication* 61(4), 343–375.

Murphy-Shigematsu, S. (1993) Multiethnic Japan and the monoethnic myth. *MELUS* 18 (4), 63–80.

Murphy-Shigematsu, S. (2000) Identities of multiethnic Japan. In M. Douglas and G.S. Roberts (eds) *Japan and Global Migration: Foreign Workers and the Advent of Multiculturalism* (pp. 63–80). London: Routledge.

Musumeci, D. (2009) History of language teaching. In M.H. Long and C.J. Doughty (eds) *The Handbook of Language Teaching* (pp. 42–62). Chichester: Blackwell.

Nagata, Y. (1995) The 'culture' of Japanese language teaching in Australia. *Japanese Studies* 15 (2), 1–15.

Nakamura, K. (2002) Cultivating global literacy through English as an international language (EIL) education in Japan: A new paradigm for global education. *International Education Journal* 3, 64–74.

Nesdale, D. and Mak, A.S. (2003) Ethnic identification, self-esteem and immigrant psychological health. *International Journal of Intercultural Relations* 27 (1), 23–40.

Neto, F. (2002) Acculturation strategies among adolescents from immigrant families in Portugal. *International Journal of Intercultural Relations* 26 (1), 17–38.

Nicolson, H. (1955) The British Council 1934–1955. In *Report on the Work of the British Council 1934–1955: Anniversary Report* (pp. 4–30). London: British Council.

Noiri, N. (2011) Schooling and identity in Okinawa: Okinawans and Amerasians in Okinawa. In R. Tsuneyoshi, K.H. Okano and S. Boocock (eds) *Minorities and Education in Multicultural Japan* (pp. 77–99). London: Routledge.

Nomoto, H. (2007) Brazilian migrant workers' children in Japan and the challenges for response to their educational needs: A case study of Paolo Freire Community School. 人文学報. 教育学 [*Journal of Social Sciences and Humanities: Education*] 42, 123–143.

Office for Multicultural Affairs and Australian Advisory Council on Multicultural Affairs (1989) *National Agenda for a Multicultural Australia*. Canberra: Australian Government Publishing Service.

Office for the Arts (2009) *Indigenous Languages – A National Approach: The Importance of Australia's Indigenous Languages*. Retrieved 20 July 2011 from http://arts.gov.au/indigenous/languages

Ogoura, K. (2004) 世界における日本語教育の重要性を訴える – 日本が国際社会において一層の力を発揮するために [*The Importance of Japanese-Language Education Around the World – Helping Japan Exert an Even Greater Influence in the Global Community*].

Tokyo: Japan Foundation. Retrieved 9 September 2005 from http://www.jpf.go.jp/j/japan_j/news/0412/12-01.html

Okano, K.H. (2009) The dialectic of globalisation, identity, and local activism: Multicultural education policies in Japan. In J. Zajda, H. Daun and L.J. Saha (eds) *Nation-Building, Identity and Citizenship Education: Cross-Cultural Perspectives* (pp. 99–116). Dordrecht: Springer.

Okinawa-ken Kyouikuiinkai (1995) *Military Government Activities Reports*. Naha: Okinawa-ken Kyouikuiinkai.

Olsen, L. (2000) Learning English and learning America: Immigrants in the center of a storm. *Theory into Practice* 39 (4), 196–202.

Ozolins, U. (1993) *The Politics of Language in Australia*. Cambridge: Cambridge University Press.

Parmenter, L. and Tomita, Y. (2000) なぜ英語教育を行なう行うのか Part 1: 生徒の発達のための英語教育. [Why do we teach English? Part 1: English language teaching for student development.] 英語教育 [*English Language Teaching*] 49 (2), 40–41.

Parton, B.T. (2011) Stability for development, development for stability: The relationship between regional organizations and social cohesion through the lens of the EU and MERCOSUR. *Peabody Journal of Education* 86 (2), 129–143.

Patten, A. (2001) Political theory and language policy. *Political Theory* 29 (5), 691–715.

Pennycook, A. (2000) Language, ideology, and hindsight. In T. Ricento (ed.) *Ideology, Politics and Language* (pp. 49–66). Amsterdam: John Benjamins.

Pennycook, A. (2002) Language policy and docile bodies: Hong Kong and governmentality. In J.W. Tollefson (ed.) *Language Policies in Education* (pp. 91– 110). Mahwah, NJ: Erlbaum.

Petras, J. (1994) Cultural imperialism in the late 20th century. *Economic and Political Weekly* 29 (32), 2070–2073.

Phillips, A. (2010) *Gender and Culture*. Cambridge: Polity.

Phillipson, R. (1992) *Linguistic Imperialism*. Oxford: Oxford University Press.

Phillipson, R. (1994) English language spread policy. *International Journal for the Sociology of Language* 107, 7–24.

Phillipson, R. (1996) Linguistic imperialism: African perspectives. *ELT Journal* 50 (2), 160–167.

Phillipson, R. (1997) Realities and myths of linguistic imperialism. *Journal of Multilingual and Multicultural Development* 18 (3), 238–248.

Phillipson, R. (2010) *Linguistic Imperialism Continued*. London: Routledge.

Presidente de la República Colombiana (1976) Decreto 088 de enero 22 de 1976 por el cual se reestructura el sistema educativo y se reorganiza el Ministerio de Educación Nacional. [Decree 088 of 22 January 1976 by which the education system is restructured and the Ministry of Education is reorganised]. Retrieved 1 March 2006 from http://www.mineducacion.gov.co/1621/article-102584.html

Presidente de la República Colombiana (1978) Decreto 1142 de junio 19 de 1978 por el cual se reglamenta el artículo 118 del Decreto – ley número 088 de 1976 sobre educación de las comunidades indígenas [Decree 1142 of 19 June 1978 by which rules for article 118 of the Decree – law number 088 of 1976 on the education of indigenous communities are established]. Retrieved 1 March 2006, from http://www.mineducacion.gov.co/1621/article-102752.html

Presidente de la República Colombiana (1995a) Decreto 0804 de mayo 18 de 1995 por medio del cual se reglamenta la atención educativa para grupos étnicos [Decree 0804 of 18 May 1995 by which rules for the special education for ethnic groups are established]. Retrieved 1 March 2006 from http://www.mineducacion.gov.co/1621/article-103494.html

Presidente de la República Colombiana (1995b) Decreto 2249 de diciembre 22 de 1995 por el cual se conforma la Comisión Pedagógica de Comunidades Negras de que trata el artículo 42 de la Ley 70 de 1993 [Decree 2249 of 22 December 1995 which confirms the Education Commission for Black Communities which is addressed by article 42 of Law 70 of 1993]. Retrieved 1 March 2006 from http://www.mineducacion.gov.co/1621/article-104263.html

Presidente de la República Colombiana (2002) Decreto 3020 de diciembre 10 de 2002 por el cual se establecen los criterios y procedimientos para organizar las plantas de personal docente y administrativo del servicio educativo estatal que prestan las entidades territoriales y se dictan otras disposiciones [Decree 3020 of 10 December 2002 by which criteria and procedures are established to organise the programme for teaching and administrative personnel of the state education service that serve territorial entities and to issue other provisions]. Retrieved 1 March 2006 from http://www.mineducacion.gov.co/1621/article-104848.html

Presidente de la República Colombiana (2007) Decreto 2406 de junio 26 de 2007 por el cual se crea la Comisión Nacional de Trabajo y Concertación de la Educación para los Pueblos Indígenas en desarrollo del artículo 13 del Decreto 1397 de 1996 [Decree 2406 of 26 June 2007 by which the National Commission for the Conduct and Coordination of Education for Indigenous People is established to develop article 13 of Decree 1996]. Retrieved 1 March 2006 from http://www.mineducacion.gov.co/1621/article-128038.html

Presidenza della Repubblica (1982) Decreto Presidente Repubblica 10 settembre 1982, n. 722: Attuazione della direttiva (CEE) n. 77/486 relativa alla formazione scolastica dei lavoratori migranti. [Presidential Decree 10 September 1982, no. 722: Attenuation of Directive (CEE) no. 77/486 relative to the school education of migrant workers]. Retrieved 28 May 2007 from http://www.edscuola.it/archivio/norme/decreti/dpr722_82.html

Presidenza della Repubblica (1999) Decreto del Presidente della Repubblica 31 agosto 1999, n. 394: Regolamento recante norme di attuazione del testo unico delle disposizioni concernenti la disciplina dell'immigrazione e norme sulla condizione dello straniero, a norma dell'articolo 1, comma 6, del decreto legislativo 25 luglio 1998, n. 286. [Presidential Decree 31 August 1999, no. 394: Regulations bringing rules for the attenuation of the unified code of provisions concerning the education of immigrants and rules on the condition of foreigners, into accordance with article 1, section 6, of Legislative Decree 25 July 1998, no. 286]. Retrieved 28 May 2007 from http://www.istruzione.it/alfresco/d/d/workspace/SpacesStore/1ebac8e2-3ed5-49cd-8427-926c4e705122/dpr394_1999.pdf

Rabson, S. (1999) Assimilation policy in Okinawa. In C. Johnson (ed.) *Okinawa: Cold War Island* (pp. 133–148). Cardiff, CA: Japan Policy Research Center.

Ramanathan, V. (2005) *The English–Vernacular Divide: Postcolonial Language Politics and Practice*. Clevedon: Multilingual Matters.

Rees, T.L. (1998) *Mainstreaming Equality in the European Union: Education, Training and Labour*. Abingdon: Routledge.

Repubblica italiana (1986) Legge 30 dicembre 1986, n. 943 Collocamento di lavoratori: Norme in materia di collocamento e di trattamento dei lavoratori extracomunitari immigrati e contro le immigrazioni clandestine. [Law 30 December 1986, no. 943 Placement of workers: Rules relating to the placement and treatment of immigrant extra-communitarian workers and against illegal immigration]. Retrieved 28 May 2007 from http://www.stranieriinitalia.it/briguglio/immigrazione-e-asilo/1992/luglio/legge-943-86.html

Repubblica italiana (1998) Decreto Legislativo 25 luglio 1998, n. 286 (Legge Turco-Napolitano): Testo unico delle disposizioni concernenti la disciplina dell'immigrazione e norme sulla condizione dello straniero. [Legislative Decree 25 July 1998, no. 286 (Turco-Napolitano Law): Unified code of the dispositions concerning the education of immigrants and rules on the conditions of foreigners]. Retrieved 8 November 2012 from http://www.governo.it/Presidenza/USRI/confessioni/norme/dlegislativo_286_1998.pdf

República de Colombia (1991) Constitución Política de Colombia [Constitution of Colombia]. Retrieved 1 March 2006 from http://www.secretariasenado.gov.co/senado/basedoc/cp/constitucion_politica_1991.html

República de Colombia (1994) Ley 0115 de Febrero 8 de 1994 por la cual se expide la ley general de educación [Law 0115 of 8 February 1994 by which the general law on education is issued]. Retrieved 1 March 2006 from http://www.mineducacion.gov.co/1621/article-85906.html

Rex, J. (1995) Ethnic identity and the nation state: The political sociology of multi-cultural societies. *Social Identities* 1 (1), 21–34.

Rhee, M.J. (1992) Language planning in Korea under the Japanese colonial administration, 1910–1945. *Language, Culture and Curriculum* 5 (2), 87–97.

Ricento, T. (2003) Historical and theoretical perspectives in language policy and planning. *Journal of Sociolinguistics* 4 (2), 196–213.

Ricento, T. (2006) Language policy: Theory and practice – An introduction. In T. Ricento (ed.) *An Introduction to Language Policy: Theory and Method* (pp. 10–23). Oxford: Blackwell.

Ricento, T.K. and Hornberger, N.H. (1996) Unpeeling the onion: Language planning and policy and the ELT professional. *TESOL Quarterly* 30 (3), 401–427.

Roberts, G. (1994) A glossary of key terms. In P. Morris (ed.) *The Bakhtin Reader: Selected Writings of Bakhtin, Medvedev, Voloshinov* (pp. 245–251). London: Arnold

Salon, A. (1981) L'action culturelle de la France dans le monde: Analyse critique [The cultural action of France in the world: Critical analysis]. Thèse d'Etat, Université de Paris 1 Panthéon-Sorbonne, Paris.

Salon, A. (1985) La diffusion du français hors des pays francophones et francisants [The spread of French outside Francophone and French-speaking countries]. In G. Antoine and R. Martin (eds) *Histoire de la langue française (1880–1914)* [*History of the French Language (1880–1914)*] (pp. 421–432). Paris: CNRS.

Sánchez, A. (1996) Los inicios de la enseñanza del español en América: ¿Por la lengua hacia el imperio o por la lengua hacia Dios? [The beginnings of Spanish teaching in America: Through language to empire or through language to God?] *ACTAS del I Congreso Internacional de AESLA: El Español, Lengua Internacional* [*Acts of the First International Congress of AESLA: Spanish, International Language*] (pp. 35–47). Murcia: Compobell.

Sánchez, A. and Dueñas, M. (2002) Language planning in the Spanish-speaking world. *Current Issues in Language Planning* 3 (3), 280–305.

Saville-Troike, M. (2006) *Introducing Second Language Acquisition*. Cambridge: Cambridge University Press.

Sayers, J. (1996) Accidental language policy: Creating an ESL/bilingual teacher endorsement program in Utah. *TESOL Quarterly* 30 (3), 611–615.

Scarino, A. and Papademetre, L. (2001) Ideologies, languages, policies: Australia's ambivalent relationship with learning to communicate with the other. In J. Lo Bianco and R. Wickert (eds) *Australian Policy Activism in Language and Literacy* (pp. 305–324). Melbourne: Language Australia.

Schiffman, H.F. (1996) *Linguistic Culture and Language Policy*. London: Routledge.

Schmidt, A. (1990) *The Loss of Australia's Aboriginal Language Heritage*. Canberra: Aboriginal Studies Press.

Sewell, W.H., Jr (1999) The concept(s) of culture. In V.E. Bonnell and L. Hunt (eds) *Beyond the Cultural Turn* (pp. 35–61). Berkeley, CA: University of California Press.

Shibasaki, A. (1999) 近代日本と国際文化交流: 国際文化振興会の創設と展開 [*International Cultural Relations and Modern Japan: History of Kokusai Bunka Shinkokai, 1934–45*]. Tokyo: Yūshindō.

Shohamy, E. (2007) *Language Policy: Hidden Agendas and New Approaches*. London: Routledge.

Shore, B. (1996) *Culture in the Mind*. Oxford: Oxford University Press.

Siddle, R. (1996) *Race, Resistance and the Ainu of Japan*. London: Routledge.

Siddle, R. (2002) An epoch-making event? The 1997 Ainu Cultural Promotion Act and its impact. *Japan Forum: The International Journal of Japanese Studies* 14 (3), 405–423.

Siddle, R. (2003) The limits to citizenship in Japan: Multiculturalism, indigenous rights and the Ainu. *Citizenship Studies* 7 (4), 447–462.

Sonntag, S.K. (2000) Ideology and policy in the politics of the English language in north India. In T. Ricento (ed.) *Ideology, Politics and Language* (pp. 133–150). Amsterdam: John Benjamins.

Spaëth, V. (2010) Mondialisation du français dans la seconde partie du XIXe siècle: L'Alliance Israélite Universelle et l'Alliance Française [Globalisation of French in the second half of the 19th century: The Alliance Israélite Universelle and the Alliance Française]. *Langue Française* 167, 49–72.

Spiegel, A., Watson, V. and Wilkinson, P. (1999) Speaking truth to power: Some problems using ethnographic methods to influence the formulation of housing policy in South Africa. In A.P. Cheater (ed.) *The Anthropology of Power: Empowerment and Disempowerment in Changing Structures* (pp. 175–190). London: Routledge.

Spolsky, B. (2004) *Language Policy*. Cambridge: Cambridge University Press.

Stanley, J., Ingram, D. and Chittick, G. (1990) *The Relationship Between International Trade and Linguistic Competence*. Canberra: Australian Government Publishing Service.

Stephan, W.G., Renfro, C.L., Esses, V.M., Stephan, C.W. and Martin, T. (2005) The effects of feeling threatened on attitudes toward immigrants. *International Journal of Intercultural Relations* 29 (1), 1–19.

Stern, H.H. (1983) *Fundamental Considerations in Language Teaching*. Oxford: Oxford University Press.

Sugimoto, Y. (1999) Making sense of *nihonjinron*. *Thesis Eleven* 57 (May), 81–96.

Sugino, T. (2008) *Nikkei Brazilians at a Brazilian School in Japan: Factors Affecting Language Decisions and Education*. Tokyo: Keio University Press.

Sussex, R. (1991) The Green Paper on language and literacy: An overview and an assessment. In A.J. Liddicoat (ed.) *Language Planning and Language Policy in Australia* (pp. 39–63). Melbourne: ALAA.

Suzuki, T. (1978) なぜ外国人に日本語を教えるのか [Why teach Japanese to foreigners?]. In 日本語教育国際会議 [*International Conference on Japanese Language Education*] (pp. 104–120). Tokyo: Kokusai Kouryuu Kikin.

Suzuki, T. (1995) 日本語は国際語になりうるか [*Can Japanese Become an International Language?*] Tokyo: Kōdansha.

Tai, E. (2007) Multicultural education in Japan. *Asia-Pacific Journal: Japan Focus*. Retrieved 6 September 2011 from http://japanfocus.org/-Eika-TAI/2618

Takahashi, R. (1998) 思想戦としての国際文化交流：戦前の国際文化振興会の活動を巡って [International cultural exchange as game of ideas: Focusing on the activity of the pre-World War II International Cultural Organization]. 社会科学研究科紀要別冊 [*Shakaikagaku Kenkyūka Kiyō Bessatsu*] 2, 95–115.

Taylor, S., Rizvi, F., Lingard, B. and Henry, M. (1997) *Educational Policy and the Politics of Change*. Abingdon: Routledge.

Tollefson, J.W. (1991) *Planning Language, Planning Inequality: Language Policy in the Community*. London: Longman.

Tollefson, J.W. (2002) Introduction: Critical issues in educational language policy. In J.W. Tollefson (ed.) *Language Policies in Education: Critical Issues* (pp. 3–15). Mahwah, NJ: Lawrence Erlbaum.

Tollefson, J.W. and Tsui, A.B.M. (eds) (2004) *Medium of Instruction Policies: Which Agenda? Whose Agenda?* Mahwah, NJ: Lawrence Erlbaum.

Torii, R. (1903) 千島アイヌ [*The Kurile Ainu*]. Tokyo: Yoshikawa Kobunkan.

Toyama, A. (2002) 「英語が使える日本人」の育成のための行動計画の策定について. [Regarding the Establishment of an Action Plan to Cultivate 'Japanese With English Abilities'.] Press release, retrieved 12 August 2004 from http://www.mext.go.jp/b_menu/houdou/15/03/030318a.htm

Toyota, T. (1988) 日本語教育における日本事情 [Japanese way of life in Japanese language education]. 日本語教育 [*Japanese Language Education*] 63, 16–29.

Tsuneyoshi, R. (2004) The 'new' foreigners and the social reconstruction of difference: The cultural diversification of Japanese education. *Comparative Education* 40 (1), 55–81.

United Nations Organization (2008) *United Nations Declaration on the Rights of Indigenous Peoples*. Retrieved 17 December 2011 from http://www.un.org/esa/socdev/unpfii/documents/DRIPS_en.pdf

van Dijk, T.A. (2000) *Ideology: An Interdisciplinary Approach*. London: Sage.

van Els, T. (2005) Status planning for learning and teaching. In E. Hinkel (ed.) *Handbook of Research in Second Language Teaching and Learning* (pp. 971–992). Mahwah, NJ: Lawrence Erlbaum.

van Oudenhoven, J.P., Ward, C. and Masgoret, A.-M. (2006) Patterns of relations between immigrants and host societies. *International Journal of Intercultural Relations* 30 (6), 637–651.

Verscheuren, J. (2008) Intercultural communication and the challenges of migration. *Language and Intercultural Communication* 8 (1), 21–35.

Verscheuren, J. (2012) *Ideology and Language Use*. Cambridge: Cambridge University Press.

Voloshinov, V.N. (1929) *Марксизм и философия языка* [*Marxism and the Philosophy of Language*]. Leningrad: Priboy.

Wada, K. (1999) 英語化における国際理解教育 [*Teaching International Understanding Through English*]. Tokyo: Taishukan Shoten.

Walsh, M. (2005) Will indigenous languages survive? *Annual Review of Anthropology* 34, 293–315.

Watts, R. (1993/94) Government and modernity: An essay on thinking governmentality. *Arena Journal* 2, 103–157.

Weir, L. (2008) The concept of truth regime. *Canadian Journal of Sociology* 33 (2), 367–390.

Welch, A.R. (1988) Aboriginal education as internal colonialism: The schooling of an indigenous minority in Australia. *Comparative Education* 24 (2), 203–215.

Widdowson, H.G. (1972) The teaching of English as communication. *ELT Journal* 27 (7), 15–19.

Williamson, J. and Hardman, F. (1997) Those terrible marks of the beast: Non-standard dialect and children's writing. *Language and Education* 11 (4), 287–299.

Wodak, R. (2006) Linguistic analyses in language policies. In T. Ricento (ed.) *An Introduction to Language Policy: Theory and Method* (pp. 170–193). Malden, MA: Blackwell.

Wroblenski, M. (2011) Uneven voices: Languages of interculturality in Amazonian Ecuador. In F. Dervin, A. Gajardo and A. Lavanchy (eds) *Politics of Interculturality* (pp. 47–69). Newcastle upon Tyne: Cambridge Scholars.

Wykes, O. (1958) The teaching of French in New South Wales and Victoria, 1850–1958. Unpublished MEd thesis, University of Melbourne.

Wykes, O. and King, M.G. (1968) *Teaching of Foreign Languages in Australia*. Hawthorn: Australian Council for Educational Research.

Wyndham, H.S. (1957) *Report of the Committee Appointed to Survey Education in New South Wales*. Sydney: Government Printer.

Yoshimi, S. and Buist, D. (2003) 'America' as desire and violence: Americanization in postwar Japan and Asia during the Cold War. *Inter-Asia Cultural Studies* 4 (3), 433–450.

Yoshino, K. (1992) *Cultural Nationalism in Contemporary Japan: A Sociological Enquiry*. London: Routledge.

Zarate, G., Gohard-Radenkovic, A., Lussier, D. and Penz, H. (2004) *Médiation culturelle et didactique des langues* [*Culture Mediation and Language Learning and Teaching*]. Kapfenberg: Council of Europe Publishing.

Index